The Fifth Vital

Mike Majlak

with Riley J. Ford

First and foremost, I would like to thank each and every individual portrayed in this book for being a part of my journey and allowing me to be part of theirs. I recognize that their memories of the events described in this book may be different than my own, but I highly doubt it. To be perfectly clear, this book is a memoir, creative nonfiction, and reflects my present recollections of experiences over time, and frankly, much of that time may or may not have been spent under the influence or fighting to reclaim my own mental health. To that end, and to protect myself and the innocent (and not so innocent), some names and characteristics have been changed to protect the privacy of the people involved, some events have been compressed, and some dialogue has been paraphrased. With that, you the reader have become part of the journey. For that I am truly grateful and excited to see where you take my humbling experiences and use them to improve your own.

—*Mike Majlak*

This book is for the millions of people worldwide who struggle with mental illness, addiction, and hopelessness. I pray my story offers you a little warmth in a cold world.

Don't let your light go out.

preface

In our lives, we all suffer. For some, the experience of pain—whether physical or psychological—is blessedly short-lived. For others, it can be an enduring life sentence of torture.

Pain is the physical or psychological suffering that reduces a person's quality of life. The opposite of suffering is happiness. If human beings are to live full, happy, productive lives, then pain must be addressed in all its origins, causes, significance, management, and remedies.

According to Viktor Frankl, a Holocaust survivor and philosopher, "Meaning is possible even in spite of suffering—provided that the suffering is unavoidable. If it *were* avoidable, however, the meaningful thing to do would be to remove its cause."

In the 1990s, pain was thought to be undertreated in the healthcare field, so American medical professionals began looking for ways to eliminate pain in patients. In 1995, Purdue Pharma released OxyContin, a powerful painkiller, to the public. Purdue Pharma actively and unethically marketed this opioid as an innocuous drug that could be safely used to treat pain in a wide variety of people and

conditions without the risk of addiction.

In 2001, pain was newly classified as the "fifth vital sign" by the Joint Commission, the country's leading accrediting body for hospitals that helps health-care systems improve performance. The four other vital signs—body temperature, blood pressure, breathing rate, and pulse rate—continue to be definitively measured in order to know the state of a person's essential body functions. With good intentions designed to ease suffering, the medical field tried to measure pain, by asking patients to rate it on a scale of smiley-faces and frowny faces from "none" to "severe." This has erroneously led to the idea that patients can become completely "pain free."

Unfortunately, pain and suffering cannot be objectively measured. They are subjective.

The promise of drugs—opioids in particular—was to release the American people from their pain and suffering. Instead, opioids have become a death sentence for countless human beings. Overdose deaths from opioids, including painkillers, heroin, and synthetics like fentanyl, have increased exponentially every year since the release of OxyContin. Opioids kill more than forty thousand Americans each year. They annually take the lives of more people than cars or guns.

When a plane goes down and kills three hundred people, it becomes headline news. The drug deaths of forty thousand people a year in today's current condemnatory climate is sadly nothing more than a passing sound bite. But the deaths of so many human beings can't be dismissed. It is an epidemic. It is a tragedy. Statistically, most opioid users are young people—our sons, daughters, sisters, and brothers. We are losing our future generations to opioid addiction and overdoses. In our societal and personal quest to eliminate pain, we have created a larger, deeper kind of endless suffering—the destruction of lives, the

demise of family structures, and the deaths of people we know and love.

In understanding and managing our human pain from physical ailments, broken hearts, mental illness, or human existence, I hope we will one day find effective ways to relieve our suffering. Part of that is accepting that the human condition invariably involves some degree of suffering. We can't eliminate it completely. It's how we manage the pain that is the question. As a recovering opioid addict who has successfully climbed out of the depths of agony and darkness, I can unequivocally say that *human connection* can be one of the most powerful antidotes to human suffering and pain.

In summarizing the opioid crisis that continues to take so many lives, I leave you with another quote from Viktor Frankl: "For what matters is to bear witness to the uniquely human potential at its best, which is to transform a personal tragedy into triumph, to turn one's predicament into a human achievement. When we are no longer able to change a situation…we are challenged to change ourselves."

I was just a child when the drug company Purdue Pharma unleashed a tidal wave of the powerful narcotic OxyContin into Milford, Connecticut, the small town where I lived. My community wasn't alone. Every city in the United States was affected by what would become the largest drug crisis in U.S. history.

By the time the government and the American population discovered the true danger of OxyContin, it was too late. When Purdue

Pharma was convicted in 2007 for misrepresenting the risk of OxyContin and forced to pay $600 million in fines, the majority of Oxy addicts had already switched to heroin and powerful synthetic narcotics such as fentanyl. By 2016, there were more than 289 million prescriptions written each year for opioids and over 2.1 million opioid addicts.

By 2017 at the peak of the epidemic, Purdue Pharma was still actively promoting OxyContin and misleading doctors. Opioid overdoses had become the leading cause of accidental death in the United States. Between 1999 and 2019, almost one million Americans had died from accidental overdoses, 450,000 from opioids alone. The death rates were so high that they depressed the average life expectancy in America for many years in a row.

My loving, middle-class childhood could never have prepared me for what was waiting around the corner for me, my friends, and my family as opioids began to find a foothold in our town. There was no way to foresee that my friends and I—just average teenagers—would unwittingly get caught up in a drug epidemic that would have far-reaching consequences on all our lives. Eventually, I would go from a normal, happy kid who played basketball, hung out with my friends, and got good grades in school to a full-fledged opioid addict and drug dealer. My teens and early twenties would come to resemble a wasteland—a horror story that took place right in my hometown.

Instead of college graduations, where my friends and I would shift our tassels from right to left and throw our caps in the air, there were multiple-count felony indictments and courtrooms.

Instead of climbing the corporate ladder or saving for my first home, I was pulled out of cars at gunpoint during robbery attempts and Major Crime Task Force investigations.

Instead of romantic white weddings or sweet baptisms, I attended the funerals of lifelong friends who'd wanted to shoot up just one more bag of heroin and instead choked to death on their own vomit before exiting this world in a zipped black bag.

Fast-forward a decade to 2019, and suddenly the opioid epidemic had become a national conversation. Strewn across Facebook were photos of unconscious overdosed parents, slumped over the steering wheel while their kids cried in the back seat. First responders told horrific stories of being unable to keep up with the thousands of people strung out on heroin who needed assistance. In some states, freezers lined hospital parking lots because the morgue couldn't keep up with the number of dead overdose victims. Thousands of children went to foster care every year after their parents died from opioid overdoses and left them orphaned.

The situation had reached a critical level, and the government took major legislative action under extreme pressure from parents, schools, and local law enforcement. With over 135,000 people dying annually from addiction—40,000-plus from opioids alone—and more than 100 million people directly or indirectly affected by the disease, it became a conversation that went as far as influencing campaign promises for the 2016 Trump vs. Clinton presidential battle.

Finally, something was being done.

But in the early 2000s, my close friends and I essentially lived in a silo. There was no press coverage. There were no organizations dedicated to changing legislation and making sure the conversation was center stage. There was no conversation. There was just us...a group of seventeen- and eighteen-year-old kids who thought it might be cool to try a new drug called OxyContin. Some, like me, had been prescribed the drug for a past injury and remembered what Oxy felt

like. Others just wanted to give it a try during a weekend party.

Before we knew it, we found ourselves strung out on heroin and methadone, clinging on for dear life. We were on our own, navigating the filthy waters of this great American opioid epidemic, without the faintest idea if we'd ever make it back to shore alive.

This wasn't my story alone. This was the story of hundreds of thousands of other addicts who had fallen victim to the same epidemic. All over America, there were people just like me who spent their days feeling sick, defeated, scared, and ready to give up.

There were fathers who'd gotten injured while teaching their sons to play basketball and wound up hooked on prescription OxyContin, only to turn to heroin when they ran low on cash. They lost their jobs, their houses, and custody of their children as they struggled to support their addictions.

There were beauty queens from high schools like mine who'd decided to act cool at a party and weeks later found themselves unable to break a dependency that developed like a fever and detained them like handcuffs. They would soon find themselves selling their bodies to older men in exchange for heroin and a dirty needle to take away the pain.

There were stories of all-star high-school basketball players who went to the same parties I did and tried the same pills, but instead of becoming addicted and having the chance to battle their addiction, they collapsed on bathroom floors or stopped breathing altogether in the back seats of cars after their very first time using Oxy.

Some of these people had been prescribed drugs. Others had made an unwise decision to experiment. None of them were bad people. None of them could have ever imagined the horrors that their decisions would lead to in their lives. None of them deserved to die.

But so many of them did. And they continue to…every day.

I was eventually admitted to Connecticut Valley Hospital for Addiction Services, but in the months before, my life had taken a turn for the absolute worst. My drug use had led me down an indescribably nightmarish road. I had progressed to smoking large amounts of crack cocaine, snorting entire grams of heroin, and drinking up to a liter of vodka a day. I was also abusing Xanax and other prescription drugs.

Before detox, I was going entire weeks without sleep. When I finally did sleep, my nights were filled with terrifying nightmares, massive tremors, and night sweats. Every bone and muscle in my body burned and twitched from withdrawal and lack of sleep.

The month before I walked through those hospital doors, I began to experience a new emotion—a feeling I hadn't experienced before in the context of my drug use. It wasn't the feeling of pain from withdrawal, or guilt for betraying my family and closest friends. It wasn't the desperate state of my life, or loneliness, or depression. It wasn't even anxiety over my probation officer filling out paperwork that recommended my imprisonment for the full five-year felony sentence I had narrowly avoided until then.

For the first time since I could remember, I felt only one prominent emotion: fear.

Pure, unadulterated fear.

I knew I was going to die. It was inevitable. It wasn't a matter of if, but *when*.

I was scared that I was going to leave behind a family who truly loved me and wanted nothing more than for me to come back to them and return to the person I once was. I was scared that all the dreams I'd once had for myself in life would go unfulfilled. I was scared that I would be remembered only as Mike Majlak, the drug

addict. The kid who threw his life in the garbage, traded it all away for a few lines of heroin or cocaine. Swapped his family, his friends, and his potential for a good high and an early coffin.

This new fear—this belief that the end was close and the thought that I might not see another sunrise—pushed me through that set of hospital doors on a hot July afternoon.

Through this fear, I found another feeling that was burning deep within me—the courage to change. With that courage, I would forge a new path that would allow me to reclaim my life and inspire other addicts and sufferers to continue fighting.

This new path would be perilous, filled with its own failures, setbacks, and heartache. In the end, my decision to change would give me an opportunity to experience the one thing I had dreamed of for so long: redemption.

Drug Overdose Death Rates, United States 1999-2016

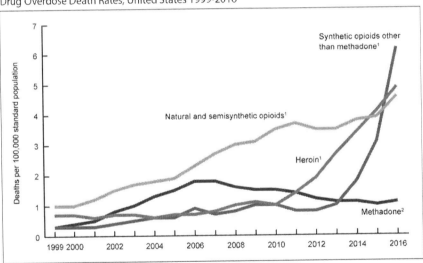

[1]Significant increasing trend from 1999 to 2016 with different rates of change over time, $p < 0.05$.
[2]Significant increasing trend from 1999 to 2006, then decreasing trend from 2006 to 2016, $p < 0.05$.
NOTES: Deaths are classified using the *International Classification of Diseases, Tenth Revision.* Drug-poisoning (overdose) deaths are identified using underlying cause-of-death codes X40–X44, X60–X64, X85, and Y10–Y14. Drug overdose deaths involving selected drug categories are identified by specific multiple-cause-of-death codes: heroin, T40.1; natural and semisynthetic opioids, T40.2; methadone, T40.3; and synthetic opioids other than methadone, T40.4. Deaths involving more than one opioid category (e.g., a death involving both methadone and a natural or semisynthetic opioid) are counted in both categories. The percentage of drug overdose deaths that identified the specific drugs involved varied by year, with ranges of 75%–79% from 1999 to 2013, and 81%–85% from 2014 to 2016. Access data table for Figure 4 at: https://www.cdc.gov/nchs/data/databriefs/db294_table.pdf#4.
SOURCE: NCHS, National Vital Statistics System, Mortality.

one

2005
U.S. opioid deaths: 14,918

"You better not be getting blood all over the place again!" Nicky smashed his fists against the locked bathroom door. "Last time, I couldn't get the blood off the fucking wall. Come out, you fucking *pendejo*!"

He beat the door so hard, I thought he was going to break it down.

Inside the bathroom, I huddled over the tiny porcelain sink. Blood poured down my face. I barely registered the sour taste on my tongue. In my hand, I held a rusty razor blade.

Outside, Nicky continued to pound on the door.

"Leave me alone," I shouted. "I'll be right out."

An hour earlier, I had sat with three others, bagging up hundreds of grams of powder cocaine and heroin. The basement was dimly lit and moist…so dank it sometimes made bagging the drugs nearly impossible. But still we persevered.

Sometimes I would sneak off, after hours of bagging up powder

and snorting line after line after line, and find solace in this cramped, dirty bathroom. It was my safe place…a place for me to be alone.

My nose was numb from twenty-four hours straight of sniffing, but I could still feel the scab tickling at my damaged septum. It clogged the passage of air. I couldn't breathe through my nose. My mouth was dry and parched. I wanted to clear the scab out. I *needed* to…I had to get rid of this nuisance.

So just like the night before, I dug at the scab with a razor. Blood dripped out of my nostrils and down my chin as I scraped the inside of my nasal canal with the rusty blade. The pain was a dull, throbbing background noise, numbed by the drugs and not nearly as important as my primary mission.

Finally, I severed the tissue. It gave way with a tug, releasing a gush of red liquid.

I pulled the rubbery tendon from my nose.

Satisfied, I gave one last hard blow into a tissue, filling it with blood, mucous, and cartilage. I turned the light off in the dank, dingy bathroom, leaving a streak of fresh red blood down the white switch.

When I came back into the room, Nicky was sitting at the bar in front of the digital scale and a mound of unbagged cocaine. He looked at me with revulsion. "I told you to stop with that shit," he said. "It's fucking disgusting."

I ignored him and took a seat at the bar. A loaded 9mm handgun lay next to me on the glass aquarium that doubled as a makeshift countertop. Two cameras equipped with cheap night-vision lenses gave us a full view of what was transpiring outside from monitors set up in the basement.

Nicky broke off a piece of scaly rock from the baseball-sized chunk sitting on the counter and crushed it under a Bic lighter. We'd

just scored a pound of this "fishscale" cocaine, so named because its holographic surface resembled the textured skin of a fish.

With my debit card, I scraped the yellowish white powder over to my side and lined up a massive rail. I rolled up a bill, scooted my stool closer, and sniffed the massive line into the same side of my nose I had just finished gouging out with a razor.

The fine powder tore through the raw flesh of my nostril like shards of glass. Ignoring the pain, I inhaled deeply, tasting the pungent mixture of cocaine and blood dripping down the back of my throat.

My entire face went numb. I closed my eyes, experiencing the familiar, filthy rush of energy that rushed through my brain and body.

My phone rang, jolting me back to reality. My customer was outside. I grabbed a $50 bag of coke that sat waiting next to the scale, quickly sniffed another line, swallowed one more big drip down my throat, then walked out the door into the crisp winter air.

It was time to work.

The year was 2005. I had graduated high school just two years earlier. Many of my classmates from my predominantly white Connecticut town had gone off to college. Instead, I'd skipped academics and had gone straight into a different kind of existence.

I'd had a good childhood. I'd had such a promising life.

Now, a decade later, I braved the most dangerous streets in the country to sell drugs so I could support my own insatiable addiction.

To support this addiction, I sold narcotics to others like me to keep from getting sick...to keep away the pain.

I often wondered, "How did I get here?"

But then I pushed away this distracting self-reflection and contin-

ued down the path I'd chosen for myself.

Except…I hadn't really chosen it.

In many ways, it had chosen me.

two

2018
U.S. opioid deaths: 46,802

"Mike, come on, man, what're you doing in there?" the producer yells through the door. "You can't just storm off like that."

I huddle over a large marble sink. I'm locked inside a bathroom on the first floor of an enormous Los Angeles mansion.

Beads of sweat roll down my face and into my mouth. I splash water on my face, fighting to catch my breath.

"I'll be right out, man," I say to the producer. "Just give me two minutes."

The year is 2018. At thirty-three years old, I've taken the social media world by storm. I've partnered with a world-famous multimillionaire social media celebrity and businessman named Logan Paul.

A few weeks ago, I'd moved into Logan's $7 million house just outside Hollywood. I'd relocated to the West Coast to assist in the rebranding of Logan's public image and his Maverick brand, which included a clothing line, a team of talent, vlogs, and other business

ventures. The move away from Connecticut has been therapeutic for me…a way to bookend a story of pain, grief, and regret that had rooted itself firmly in the town where I was born.

On this particular day, we're filming the pilot episode of a new Internet show and podcast, *Impaulsive*. We've been preparing for weeks leading up to this day. For our first episode, we'd booked a famous sex doctor. I'd mentally prepared for the show: what I was going to say, how I was going to act.

Everything was perfect.

Until it wasn't.

I was on set in the middle of filming when the waves of an anxiety attack started to take hold.

"So how did you get into this?" Logan was saying to Dr. Shannon Chavez, the sex expert. "Sex is kind of a taboo topic…"

It became harder to breathe. The stage lights felt as though they were 500 degrees. My chest tightened. Sweat gathered on my forehead. My stomach tied itself up in knots. It felt as though my whole life might suddenly crumble around me in an instant.

"I'm so sorry, guys, I need five minutes," I said. I stood up and rushed off set as the cast and crew glowered at me, not knowing why I was leaving.

"Did Mike just have a breakdown?" I heard Logan say jokingly behind me as laughter broke out from the panel. I raced toward the exit door of the studio. The sounds of the show faded to silence as I closed the door behind me, the giant spotlights replaced by darkness.

I ran into the bathroom and locked the door.

Now, here I am.

I splash more water on my face and take deep breaths.

I stare at my reflection in the mirror. My eyes look sad.

Why? Why is this happening? Will this ever go away?

My nerves are hard to control. Eight years after getting clean from drug addiction, the damage I caused is still there. It manifests itself in uncontrollable anxiety attacks and a revolving cycle of negative thoughts.

I ask myself, "Is this because I used drugs, or is this the reason I started using in the first place?" My brain is foggy, and sometimes I can't fully recall the horror—the visceral details—of being a drug addict.

It's not easy to remember exactly what it felt like to be thrown from a car and experience the flesh tearing off my body. It's difficult to remember seeing my friend get beaten in the face with a black 9mm pistol until blood coated the basement wall of a Bridgeport traphouse. I can't fully recall the agonizing details of waking up sick from heroin withdrawals and pulling old bags out of the garbage, trying to scrape enough residue together for a bump to make the pain go away.

I can't remember.

Maybe I don't want to remember.

In the eight years since I've gotten clean, the life I used to live has become an antiquated tale—something only a few of my current friends in L.A. even know about. My fans are aware of some of the skeletons from my past because of surface stories I've told in online content. But they don't really know much at all.

My closest friends, like Logan, know a little more from our late-night chats over lobster dinners in Beverly Hills or on first-class flights to the United Kingdom or Saudi Arabia. But even the dearest of my new friends don't know how deep the rabbit hole goes.

It really is quite astonishing, the trajectory of it all.

I've lived in L.A. for a short time but have already begun to leave a major mark. I've made a name for myself, building my own YouTube channel from nothing into millions of subscribers. I've received offers from MTV for a television show. I've had agents interested in selling the movie rights to the very book you're reading right now.

My life now plays out inside massive houses in the Hollywood Hills, partying with the elite. My roommates and I have a private chef who cooks us whatever our hearts desire. Life has quickly become something you might see on an episode of *Entourage.*

To be honest, I'm not exactly sure how I got to where I am today. It involved a lot of putting one foot in front of the other. Trying new things with confidence that I'd succeed. Looking to always be better than the day before.

At times, people ask me, "How the hell did you do it, man?" I don't always have the easiest answer for them. I usually say, "It's a mixture of God and working really fucking hard. Connecting with like-minded people. Staying positive when every sign says otherwise."

Whatever the formula, my career is on a meteoric rise. Week after week, I continue to blow past all expectations, including my own. I create and build incredible relationships for both myself and the Maverick brand. I get millions of views per week on videos I make for my YouTube channel on a range of topics, from interviews with Hollywood celebs to surreal poetry.

Around Los Angeles, I'm known as a positive, upbeat guy. Everyone from the hot new TikTok star to the door guy at Mastro's seems to love it when I come around. I get free food at Catch because the owner is a fan, and the valet guy brings my car up before anyone else's. I try my best to greet everyone I meet with a positive vibe. I take the time to hear people's issues and try to help them through their

problems. I want to brighten people's days, and I seem to do pretty well at it.

In public, I'm a regular comedian. I can make a joke out of just about anything and can make anyone laugh at any time. I make new friends everywhere I go, and women always have a girlfriend that I "just have to meet." I'm told I can hold a great conversation and really know how to work a room. People say I just know how to talk.

I wear a smile at all times, in all situations.

The people who watch my videos or see me at the club say, "Damn, man, you're killing it. I wish I could do that kinda shit!"

Through a grin, I say, "Yeah, I'm really blessed, man. It's a lot of fun."

When I get back to the house from an event or a dinner with studio executives, my jaw is tired from smiling. I kick off my shoes, put my feet up, and stare at the ceiling.

None of these people know shit...

The familiar dark thoughts start to cycle through my mind. Nobody knows a single fucking thing about what I've seen.

I have close friends now. Very close friends. Friends I've made over the last few years. We connect by way of the culture or the content we create. But they don't know what it's like to withdraw from heroin to the point where the thought of death is a welcome relief.

I have the opportunity for real romantic relationships now. When it comes time to let them in, though, I rarely do. Because of this, things hardly ever work out. Even after the girls get to "know" me, they know nothing about the shame of waiting outside a dealer's house on bleak days when money was tight and the only way I could stop the withdrawals was by my girlfriend sucking the drug connect's

dick in exchange for a couple bags of dope.

I have colleagues and costars now. I work next to them every single day. They don't know what it's like to hug your twenty-two-year-old best friend's mom at his funeral after he overdoses on heroin after trying desperately for years to get clean. There is no grief like wearing a shirt soaked with your own tears mixed with those of a mother who will never see her son again. And then doing it another two times, or four times, before the year ends.

One of the hardest things in the world is going through life with a secret. Out of sheer laziness or dedication to new business pursuits, I stopped going to Narcotics Anonymous meetings after about six months of sobriety. Even though NA was the only place I could freely talk about the horrors I'd witnessed, it became a chore that got in the way of my workouts, or my writing, or my social time.

So I wrote it off. I stopped going.

The people I grew up with, my best friends from childhood, are gone. People I called brothers my entire life have been annihilated, either dead or still lost in the cycle of despair and addiction—a world we once co-existed in together.

Not only are those people gone, but from time to time, my memories of them fade too. Occasionally, albeit rarely, I slip into a relaxed state of mind, and the pain of it all starts to leave my mind. But that's the thing about addiction and other traumas. No matter how old that wound is, it never heals completely. The pain manifests itself one way or another, whether we like to admit it or not.

"Mike, seriously, man!" the producer yells through the bathroom door. "What're you doing? Jerking off in there? Let's fucking go!"

I open the door. "My bad, man," I mutter under my breath. I wipe away the last few beads of sweat and walk back toward the set.

The producer marches beside me, his manner frustrated.

"First episode," I try to explain with feigned confidence. "I just got some heebie-jeebies there." We reach the set, and I settle back into my seat.

My anxiety, negative thoughts, and chaotic mind are my new addiction. Every single day, I deal with these evils. They have become part of my everyday life, at least for now.

Throughout life, everyone will be hit with obstacles. Many times, giving up seems like the most attractive option. We've all considered doing it.

Today, on the first day of the *Impaulsive* shoot, I could have adopted the popular "Hey, at least I tried" mentality. I could have given up today, right here and now. Thrown in the towel. Told Logan, "I'm sorry, the writing is on the wall. I can't do this."

But I didn't.

I could have said, "The anxiety and stress are too much to bear. They will break me."

But I didn't.

I've learned that the most important concept anyone will ever need to grasp in life is the notion to not give up, not ever.

I tell myself every day, "You will not give up in the face of adversity. You will look every obstacle, every hurdle, every demon in its face. You will lower your shoulders and drive through that motherfucker without hesitation or regret."

I believe that's what separates those who make it from those who don't. This is the mentality that got me through the most horrific, life-draining days of my addiction, and it is the same mentality that pushes me through every single moment I face today in my new career in this new L.A. world. I tell myself that if I'm able to let this

mentality seep into every cell of my body, I can never lose. And this goes for anyone and everyone...that I know for sure.

You will not give up. You will get through this. Just keep moving forward.

I take a deep breath, separate myself from my anxiety the best I can, and begin my first day on the first show of *Impaulsive*.

And I fucking kill it.

three

1993
U.S. opioid deaths: N/A

"Hold still, Gab, or I'm gonna mess it up," I said as I carefully chopped off another large chunk of my sister's hair.

"Mikey, are you sure this is a good idea?" Gabby said. "I don't think Mom is gonna be very happy." She stared wide-eyed at the locks of her curly hair falling like feathers to her feet. I gathered a big pile of the hair and threw it into the closet.

"Go look in the mirror, it's all done," I said. "You look great!"

She ran off to show our mom her newly short-cropped head.

My sister and I were six and eight years old respectively, just enjoying a normal day in our childhood. I'd always loved pretending to have different professions. On this day, I was a barber. I'd practiced on Gabby right before we were supposed to leave for a day at an amusement park with our family friends.

"My God, Gabby, what happened to your hair?" I heard my mother shriek from the kitchen.

"Mikey gave me a haircut," Gabby said with a blissful smile.

The punishment was immediate. For the rest of the day, I was forbidden to ride even a single ride at the amusement park. As a consequence of my bad behavior, I was forced to watch as my sisters rode the roller coasters, the waterslides, and the Ferris wheel without me.

From a young age, I knew about consequences because my parents had instilled a sense of right and wrong in me. I knew if I acted improperly, I would lose certain privileges. My parents wanted my sisters and me to become good citizens, so they parented with clear boundaries and moral concepts.

My sisters and I were born into an ordinary middle-class family where our existence was never a fight to survive. We didn't have to worry about where our next meal would come from, nor did we deal with neighborhood violence or dangerous schools. Instead, we had a family who loved us, childhood activities, sports, a nice home, healthy food, family vacations, Santa Claus, and the Easter Bunny—all the trappings of a comfortable, all-American homelife.

There was nothing about my childhood that would point to the bleak existence I would eventually lead. The safety of our small town afforded us the ability to learn by trial and error, and everyone knew each other and looked out for one another. Our lives were suffused with an innocence that once existed for the average American child, an innocence that, as of recently, seems lost forever.

My life began in the Connecticut beach town of Milford in January 1985. Milford was named one of the top beach places in the country, replete with Blue Ribbon schools, a beautiful downtown area, and a tight-knit community. Not far from New Haven, we had access to the best pizza in the world, and we were only a short train

ride from Manhattan.

I was born a healthy brown-eyed, brown-haired baby and was doted on from day one. Every birthday, every Christmas, every trip to the playground was recorded on 16mm film and treated like some sort of life-changing event.

As soon as I was old enough to swing a bat, I was registered in the Tee-Ball League and my entire family showed up to every game. My mother was a devoted PTA mom and always baked cupcakes for bake sales and sewed costumes for plays. She was there with a Band-Aid for every cut or scrape and cold medicine for every sniffle. The beds were always made, the house was always clean, and between my mom and my grandma, there was always a hot meal waiting for us.

My father was a hard-working marketing manager for a technology firm based in Rhode Island. He spoke fluent German and several other languages and traveled constantly out of the country for business.

He was a highly skilled negotiator and was well-versed in how to conduct himself in the corporate environment. He was also a stickler for good manners. He taught me to place a napkin in my lap at meals and how to properly sit and eat, and to stand whenever someone got up to leave the table. When I was ten years old, my dad gave me my first lessons on how to interact with a client at a business dinner.

I was blessed with two sisters, Lillian and Gabby. My older sister, Lillian, liked to tease me and rat me out to my parents when I did something wrong. She also had a gentle side where she pretended to be a teacher and hold classes for me and Gabby. Lillian would later go on to get her master's degree in education.

My younger sister, Gabby, was a much more jovial soul. Like me, she loved to clown around. We spent most of our childhood running

around with the neighborhood kids, playing cops and robbers and getting in trouble for walking through the house with wet feet from the pool.

When I was ten, I was chosen to be a part of Milford's enrichment program for gifted minds. My parents always knew I was quick to answer tough questions or spell tricky words. By the time I was in fourth grade, my teachers knew it too. Twice a week, I was bused to another school to undergo creative testing methods used to stimulate the mind for what the faculty considered to be gifted students. My mother and father couldn't be prouder of their "brainiac" child.

During that time, my teachers also started to notice my more problematic characteristics. I was constantly a distraction to other students in class. I made jokes and had outbursts that made it difficult for my classmates to learn. Teachers scolded me, saying that just because I grasped concepts easily didn't give me the right to distract others who needed to focus to learn. I didn't understand that, and it led to some prickly challenges at school.

My parents eventually took me to see a psychologist to try to figure out what was causing my disruptive behaviors. I would talk to him about things that were bothering me, and then my parents would wait for him to give some sort of diagnosis for my behavior. Each time, the diagnosis would eventually disprove itself. For example, when the psychologist suspected I had attention deficit disorder, the notion was quickly eliminated once he tested my ability to focus and then received my straight-A report cards. Focusing was never a problem for me; I just loved putting on a show.

Finally, my parents decided the answer might be to enroll me in a Catholic all-boys school for my freshman year of high school: Notre Dame of West Haven.

When it came to modern-day schooling, Notre Dame of West Haven was about as strict as it got. The students were forced to wear uniforms of white oxford button-downs, khaki pants, brown shoes, and neckties. Catholic brothers roamed the halls just waiting to witness an infraction. Some of them were cool; some...not so much.

None were harsher than the infamous "Brother Benjamin." He was about ninety years old and ruled the school with an iron fist. He didn't take shit from anyone, including the parents who paid the expensive fees for their sons to attend such an elite school. My parents figured this was exactly the kind of discipline I needed. In their view, they were willing to try anything to help me and give me a chance to better myself—a theme that would stay constant through the years.

From the outside, my family life appeared to be the perfect American story. Our house even had the proverbial white picket fence, so often referenced as an indicator of having achieved the "American dream."

In reality, every family has its problems. Marriages sour after years of miscommunication or misunderstanding. Spouses cheat on each other out of selfishness, spite, or lust. Houses are foreclosed, cars are repossessed, and financial burdens weigh down even the best of relationships. Unfortunately, those most likely to suffer from the fallout of such things are the children.

Our family, like others, had some of those problems. When my sisters and I were old enough to understand, our mother began to fill us in on some of the details that were causing the decay that would eventually crumble our seemingly perfect family life. Misconduct led to mistrust, which eventually broke down a marriage that had produced more than 23 wonderful years of good fortune and success.

By the time I entered Notre Dame, the relationship between my

mother and father had been stretched thin by mistrust, arguments, and indiscretions. It was eventually beyond repair. All the baby photos, the memories of better days, and the attempts to reconcile wouldn't be enough to postpone the inevitable any longer.

When I was fifteen, my mother sat me down at the kitchen table. "Mikey," she said, "your father and I aren't going to be together anymore."

The news hit me hard. I'd known the day was coming, but I still wasn't ready to hear the words. As a child, even as a young man, the thought of my parents not being together was one of the saddest things I could imagine. I struggled to make sense of the situation.

"I need you to know this isn't your fault," Mom said, gently rubbing my hair. "It's just how things go sometimes, kid. Everything is going to be just fine."

It seemed like the very next day, my dad was gone.

When he walked out the door, the strict rules he'd enforced for so many years left with him. All the discipline, the spankings, and my mom's threats of "I'm gonna tell your father" came to an end.

Together, my sisters and I carried on. We still got the chance to see our dad sometimes, which helped. He continued to coach my intramural basketball team and took me on ski trips where we bonded as father and son. But his absence at home was deeply felt.

One day at the end of ninth grade, he sat me down for a talk. "Mike, do you like Notre Dame?"

"I don't know, Dad," I said. "I mean, it's okay." I was unsure what he was asking. I didn't care much where I went to school. I figured "school was school" and I had to go either way, so it didn't really matter where.

"Listen," my father said, "now that your mother and I have split,

it's going to be really tough for me to continue to pay for Notre Dame." He explained that there was a lot of financial stress on the family, especially with my older sister on her way to UConn for college and my little sister in need of braces. "Your mom and I have agreed that it's best if we move you over to Foran next year."

Foran was one of two nearby public schools. It was considered a rough school compared to the sheltered, privileged environment of Notre Dame, but in the general community, Foran's reputation was simply that of a party school.

So, at fifteen years of age, I was abruptly pulled from my private Catholic high school in order to lessen the financial pressure on my parents during their divorce. Everything that Notre Dame stood for—the required necktie, the uniform, and most of all, the discipline—went out the window the day I made the switch to public school.

My life had changed again. From then on, everything was different.

It wasn't long before I began to act out.

four

2000

U.S. opioid deaths: 8,407

"Hit me, I'm open!" I yelled as Jeff dribbled the ball at the top of the key.

He was a short fellow with reddish-brown hair, only about five-foot-four, but he was quick on his feet and aggressive as a hornet. He faked the pass to me and instead drove to the basket himself for an easy layup.

"Come on, man. You're a fucking hog," I said as he dribbled back to the top of the key to inbound the ball again.

We were both fifteen and had been friends since elementary school. We'd lost touch for a while when I'd gone to private school, but we were quick to reconnect once I transferred to Foran High.

Jeff was originally from White Plains, New York, but had moved to Connecticut after his parents' divorce. His family struggles were something I could relate to, and this was one of our main bonds. We just got each other. Like many other kids, we knew what it was like to go through the splitting up of a family.

Jeff's mom, Caddie, was like a second mom to me. She cooked for me and her son, drove us to basketball practice, and was always around to bail us out if we got into trouble. Caddie had remarried a man named Danny Foster, who was abusive. He frequently hit Jeff, and I'd seen him treat Caddie violently in my presence. I was too young to know what to do about the situation. I felt a lot of empathy for Jeff and Caddie, and the whole situation unnerved me. As much as I bonded with Jeff over our homelife problems, his situation was clearly much worse than mine. That would become even more apparent over time.

One of the things we shared was an insatiable appetite and undying love for basketball. We loved playing basketball on his driveway, watched every basketball game we could on TV, went to Knicks games, took trips to the Hall of Fame, and played together for years in the town leagues. We lived for the sport, as did many of our closest friends.

On this particular day, Jeff and I had joined a large group of buddies to play a quick pickup game of basketball at a friend's house. The makeshift court was one we were used to playing on—a driveway with a portable hoop filled with sand.

It became a fairly aggressive game, and players were shoving and tripping. At the top of the court, I maneuvered to get open so Jeff could pass me the ball.

"Jeff, I'm open!" I shouted.

He snapped the ball to me, and I dribbled for a moment as I assessed my next move. I then took a quick step and drove hard toward the basket. As I leaped off the ground, one of the players guarding me stuck out his foot.

In a quick motion, my foot clipped under his leg. I smashed full

force onto the blacktop. I lay motionless for a long moment, facedown, unable to move. My vision was blurred and my ears were ringing. Finally, I rolled slowly over onto my back. I couldn't breathe. Intense pain radiated through my abdomen.

Jeff hovered over me. "Holy shit, dude, are you okay?" He offered a hand to help me up.

"I'm fine, I'm fine," I muttered. At that age I would have rather died than show any kind of pain or weakness.

I slowly picked myself up off the ground and began to walk around. I felt winded and could barely breathe. The pain in my abdomen was getting worse, radiating throughout my body. I'd experienced the feeling of the wind being completely knocked out of me after a hard fall during my BMX days, but this was different. The pain wasn't dissipating or lessening as it should.

I turned to Jeff and whispered with all my remaining strength, "I'm going inside to lie down for a bit. I'll be back out."

He nodded, not knowing how much pain I was in, and continued with the game.

Inside my friend's house, it was quiet. No one was home. A soft April breeze blew in through the open window, gently rippling the curtains. A large grandfather clock ticked methodically in the living room.

I found my way to my buddy's bedroom and lay down on his bed. Despite the excruciating pain, I was somehow able to drift into a nap. As I slipped away into my snooze, I was welcomed by an unusually profound feeling of peace and serenity.

I didn't know how much time had passed. When I came to, my friends were standing at the end of the bed with concerned expressions on their faces.

"Hey, man, you don't look so good," one buddy said.

"Your face is fucking blue, bro, you need to go to the hospital," Jeff said.

Something had to be seriously wrong. I called my father to pick me up. He arrived within minutes, and soon we were on our way to Milford Hospital.

I was immediately admitted to the emergency room, where I told the doctors I had fallen playing basketball. The doctors seemed puzzled by my symptoms and decided to run further tests. I was required to drink an entire gallon of dye-infused water and endure numerous CT scans before the doctors figured out what had happened.

During my powerful fall to the ground, something, possibly an elbow or the basketball itself, had penetrated beneath my ribcage and completely obliterated my spleen. The rupture had caused severe internal bleeding that was now filling my stomach. It was a serious emergency that needed to be acted on immediately.

What happened next still sneaks its way into my nightmares from time to time.

"Honey, we're going to have to pump your stomach," one of the nurses said. "Unfortunately, though, we won't be able to put you to sleep first. We need to feed a tube into your nose and snake it down your throat to your stomach in order to remove the blood."

I began to shake. "No. No. I can't do this."

The nurses tried to calm me down, to no avail. The doctor approached my bed with a long, clear plastic hose. A nurse wearing latex gloves rubbed a lubricant on the cylindrical tip of the hose.

By now my mother and my little sister had arrived. They huddled together in the corner of the room, looking on helplessly with tears in

their eyes as the nurses forcibly restrained me and began the barbaric procedure. The medical staff forced the long tube up my nose, then around a tight turn in my throat—causing me to gurgle and whimper in pain—and down into my stomach. A suction machine spun on. Dark brown blood and bile slowly snaked up the tube, through my nose, and out into a giant collection tank. Every five minutes or so, the nurses would replace the tank with a fresh one and the process would start again.

Take a breath. You will get through this.

All I could do was hold on and endure until it was over. In the end, I lost almost a third of my blood as a result of the basketball accident. Luckily, Milford had a large community of blood donors that literally saved my life.

After an hour of draining blood, tests, and assessment, the doctors then informed my distressed family that I would have to undergo life-saving surgery to remove my spleen.

I couldn't believe this was happening to me. Everything was a blur, coming at me in surreal slow motion. I was in a daze…but the pain was very, very real.

I was rushed to a pre-op room and prepped for surgery.

"Count back from ten…nine…eight…," the anesthesiologist whispered to me. That would be the first time I heard those words, but it wouldn't be the last.

I woke up several hours later in the recovery room. The surgery had been a success, and the doctors expected a full recovery. However, I was still in excruciating pain.

My family was overcome with joy and rushed in to hug me and provide me with encouragement. I was moved to another room, where I would stay for the next two weeks.

Within an hour of being moved to my recovery room, a nurse came in with a clipboard. She checked my four vital signs: body temperature, pulse, breathing rate, and blood pressure. She must have known I was suffering deeply because she looked at me with a kind, compassionate expression and asked, "Are you in pain, honey?"

Those words…

Yes, God, yes, I'm in pain.

I struggled to respond, but my suffering was too acute to speak. Instead, I nodded.

"Okay, sweetie," the nurse said. "Can you tell me how much pain you're experiencing, on a scale from one to ten?"

"A lot," I blurted, my voice hoarse. "Ten."

"Aw, don't worry, sweetie. We'll take care of that." She gave me a comforting smile.

She turned and screwed a vial of liquid into my IV line. I watched as a small clear bubble began to mix into the line, soon to push into my veins through the tiny needle attached to my arm.

After a few moments, the nurse checked on me again. "You shouldn't be feeling any pain now."

She was right. A warm feeling of euphoria had begun to envelop my senses. My body and mind relaxed as a calm blanket of peace descended upon me. All the pain drained away, replaced by a powerful, radiant sense of well-being.

Later that day, a doctor came into my room with a larger pouch of the same substance, which turned out to be liquid morphine. The medical staff attached the pouch to my IV line, and I was given a button so I could self-administer pain meds every half hour as needed.

Every half hour, I did just that. I pushed the button and all the physical suffering went away…and along with it, all the worries, bad

thoughts, stress, and anxieties.

Gone.

That release, that instant gratification foreshadowed things to come.

One day, after my extended time in the recovery room, a nurse rolled me out of the hospital in a wheelchair into the bright spring sunshine.

A few weeks ago, I'd been an otherwise unremarkable fifteen-year-old kid. Now, I bore the results of a horrible accident: traumatic emotional memories from my surgery, hospital experience, and pain; and a massive abdominal scar as the physical reminder of what I'd been through.

For the first week after I got out of the hospital, everyone did the best they could to act like a family. My father spent some time at the house with all of us, and my sisters and my mom worked hard to take care of me.

The fresh scar on my stomach required constant cleaning, and I managed my pain with prescribed Percocet. I got into the habit of taking the pills at even the faintest sense of pain. I figured, "Why be in pain when these pills could make it all go away?"

Since I was mostly bedridden, I spent much of the first two weeks at home watching TV and listening to music. It was already April, and school was almost out, so I figured I would just leisurely recover and then spend my summer hanging out with my friends.

One night, three weeks after the surgery, I awoke screaming in pain. My abdomen felt as if it were on fire. Stabbing pain pulsed through my stomach like an unrelenting drill. My mother called my father, and he rushed over with a shopping bag full of antacid tablets and milk of magnesia. But the pain was nothing that Pepto-Bismol

could alleviate.

I sat on the toilet for an hour, writhing in agony. Something was terribly wrong. I knew I had to go back to the hospital.

The doctors ran tests and discovered I'd had a "post-surgical relapse." As a result of the surgery to remove my spleen, my intestines had become entangled in a knot and were blocking the digestion and passing of food through my body.

There I was, right back in the same Milford Hospital operating room I'd left just a few weeks before, and with the same surgeon who'd done my original procedure. As I thrashed in excruciating pain, the team went back in, cut me open, untangled my small intestine, and sewed the incision up for a second time. I was lucid for the operation, enduring a torturous, unmedicated agony that seemed like it would never end.

Pain, pain, pain was all my mind could chatter until it was over.

Family members later said that the doctor told them that my first incision was still so fresh that he was able to open it back up with his thumb, with no need for a scalpel or scissors.

When I came out of surgery, I was dismayed to learn that the thin, straight scar from the first procedure had now manifested into a wide, oblong eternal keepsake of trauma.

After my second surgery came another two weeks of inpatient recovery, more gray hair for my distraught mother, and of course, another two weeks of intravenous morphine drip. The door in my life that had been cracked open for future drug addiction had just been propped open a little bit wider…

five

"Fuck you, Koch!" someone yelled as they hid under a chair. Someone else in the audience threw a rolled-up wad of paper.

It was the first day of my sophomore year at Foran High School. I had been directed to the school's auditorium for what was supposed to be a welcome-back ceremony and orientation.

Within minutes of taking our seats, the audience grew restless. That's when the shit-talking started, and the shit-throwing as well. The assistant principal ducked and dodged projectiles. The crowd got more and more rowdy until finally the orientation was cancelled. This was a reoccurring theme at Foran—a student body that didn't respect authority and hurtled toward bigger problems in the future.

Foran had a reputation in Milford as the wilder of the town's two public schools—lenient in its policy on parties, skipping class, and alcohol and drug use. Even during my time at Notre Dame, I'd heard stories about Foran escapades. Like other high schools, there was cigarette smoking in the bathrooms, students ditching school early, and fights in the lunchroom, but Foran was known for taking it to another level. There were even stories of seniors having keg parties on

campus during school hours.

With all that I'd heard about the school, nothing could prepare me for the things I actually witnessed and experienced while attending Foran High.

During the first week of my freshman year, I'd gotten shoved up against a wall because I failed to call out "straight" when I walked into the bathroom. That was how people doing drugs in the stalls knew that it wasn't security coming in. A week later, on my way up the stairs after gym class, I'd stumbled upon a girl from a lower grade giving head to a senior right there in the stairwell.

"Nothing to see here, man!" the senior had said, chortling as I passed by. I couldn't help but snicker a bit myself. Foran was something else.

Without a strong headmaster to crack the whip, I was reinstated as class clown. Creating disturbances in class, playing daily pranks—those became the fastest ways for me to make new friends…with all the wrong people.

One of my favorite acts was to run down the hallways between classes with my arms full of books, pretending to be clumsy and inept. The halls were always loaded with students, which made it a great opportunity for a show.

As I ran down the corridor, my friends would all take notice, most already knowing what was about to happen.

"Look out, look out," I would yell. "I've got to get to class!" Then I would pretend to trip over something and throw books and papers everywhere. Everyone would burst out laughing. What made it even funnier was that, without fail, a teacher would always rush to me in shock, assuming it was a terrible accident and that I must be hurt.

I enjoyed the attention. I always wanted to go bigger than anyone

else, most of the time to cause a spectacle, but often for the feeling of acceptance I got from people's reactions. In some ways, this type of activity was a precursor to some of my darker behaviors down the road.

But before the drugs, it was only pranks.

"I'm fucking crying, man," my buddy Kenny said to me as we walked away from another time where I'd just fallen with all my books. "That shit gets me every time!" Other kids passed by with tears rolling down their cheeks from laughing so hard.

"I actually hurt my elbow on that one bro, not gonna lie," I said, clutching my arm.

Before moving to Foran High, I'd been introduced to Kenny Howe in middle school. He was a tall, muscular Irish kid who was another product of a broken family from when he was young. He was shy and reserved at first, but once we got to know each other better, I learned of a deep-seated anger in Kenny that became an uncontrollable rage when unleashed. He always had my back and was one of my closest friends.

"We're all going to Kenny's house today after school to get high," Jeff said to me one day in class. "Wanna come?"

I'd never smoked weed before but knew I wanted to try it. It seemed like every sixteen-year-old I knew had already tried it by that point. Kenny had started smoking weed with his older brother long before I met him. Jeff often went over to Kenny's house after school, and they would smoke out on his brother's bong or from poorly rolled joints of mid-grade marijuana.

After my basketball injury, I knew from direct experience the numbing escape that drugs could provide. A curiosity had been incited in me, and I wanted to see what weed was all about.

"Yeah, that's cool with me," I said to Jeff. "Let's do it."

As the school day drew to a close, I tried to get in the right frame of mind to get high for the first time. I'd heard stories about how some people had a rough time getting into the vibe and flow with their first experience with marijuana.

Kenny's room was in the attic of his parents' home. He had sloppily decorated it with black lights, lava lamps, psychedelic posters of mushroom people smoking bongs, and old Pink Floyd memorabilia. There were holes in the walls from roughhousing, and the carpet reeked of spilled bong water. There was resin on the end table and cigarette burns on the carpet. He'd turned his room into his own little haven to smoke and forget all the problems of teenage life.

I sat on Kenny's mattress, which hung halfway off the edge of a hand-me-down metal frame. The fitted sheet had slipped off the top corner, exposing a stained, ripped mattress. I watched as he lit a white paper joint and took a hit. He coughed several times and then passed it to Jeff, who did the same. Fitting tunes wafted through the room—Sublime's *Second-Hand Smoke* album.

"Here ya go, man," Jeff said with purpose as he handed me the spliff.

I grabbed the joint with my thumb and index finger, put it to my lips, and inhaled. I held the hit in my lungs for ten seconds, like I'd seen my buddies do, and then slowly let it out. I then hit it again. The thick smoke filled my lungs, and I began to choke uncontrollably. I passed the joint back to Kenny and grabbed a bottle of Gatorade that was next to the bed. Trying not to cough as I drank, I chugged the red liquid straight down.

Soon, I began to feel weightless…and very uneasy. I felt as though I couldn't control my body, which triggered terrible anxiety in me.

This would be the first of many times that I realized weed just wasn't my drug. It spiked my anxiety and forced me to wade through thoughts I usually kept locked away in the back of my mind.

I sat on the edge of Kenny's bed, paralyzed with racing thoughts, paranoia, and anxiety. Jeff decided to choose that moment to be funny. He grabbed Kenny's authentic-looking BB gun and pointed it at me.

"We brought you here today to kill you," he said ominously. Kenny nodded slowly as he looked me dead in the eyes.

"Sorry it has to be like this, man," Jeff whispered. He lifted the gun and pointed it at my head.

This was my first time high, paired with what I thought was a real pistol pointed at my head. It was too much. I took off running and almost fell down the back stairs. I turned back to see Jeff and Kenny rolling on the ground in laughter.

Those types of things always took place at the Howe house. Kenny's single mom worked long hours to support her family, and we were young and ignorant enough to take full advantage of this freedom.

As the year went on, Jeff, Kenny, and I began to spend more time at Kenny's house. Our friend Alex soon joined us, and we became a posse of four.

Many days, we ditched school halfway through instead of waiting for it to end. We would put up the hoods on our sweatshirts and make a run for it, dashing out of school while avoiding the cameras and security guards.

We were filled with naive excitement and the hubris of youth. Everything seemed fun and exciting. We were entering a time of experimentation, drawn to the allure of the unknown that is often

typical of teenagers.

We listened to Eminem's first albums on repeat as he made his rise to superstardom. He rapped about a broken home and being misunderstood—something we all related to. His music also spoke about sex, drug abuse, and violence. He did it in a way that seemed cool, and his stories just amplified our curiosity for new things.

Slowly but surely, my appetite for marijuana grew, along with that of my friends. We started out buying a couple grams of weed for 30 bucks, and it would last a whole day and night. It came from random dealers who sold us pot on the school bus or outside the lunchroom. Soon, we started buying eighths (3.5 grams) and smoking it all in one sitting.

As my friends and I began buying more weed, the transactions started to take place outside of school, which meant interacting with strangers from different walks of life. Random people stopped by Kenny's room day or night to drop off the weed. We didn't know much about these people, who they were or where they came from.

I started to develop an interest in the prices, weight, and money associated with the dealing side of weed. While everyone else was concerned with getting the weed and immediately putting it in a pipe or bong, I liked weighing it on the digital scale and observing the THC crystals of the bud. I was interested in discussing the strains and what made the OG Haze a better buy than the Jack Herer, for example.

The business aspect of dealing attracted me because of the power the dealer had over his buyers. He set the prices. He determined where meets happened. He made all the rules. Imagining having that kind of control lit a fire in my soul. It made up for all the other places in my life that were out of control.

From the second I witnessed that lifestyle, I fucking *wanted it.*

six

"Yo, bitch, let's go to my house after school and hit the bong," Alex said as he playfully shoved me. "We can get Chicken Basket and watch *Family Guy*."

"Yeah, your fat ass *would* be thinking about Chicken Basket at 9 a.m.," I said, shoving him back.

Alex Finnegan, or "Finn," as we called him, was a tall, porky guy with a jolly attitude. Even as a sophomore in high school, the kid was probably six-foot-four, 250 pounds. He played on the football team, and his father owned an architectural firm that we would all eventually work for at one point or another. Alex was a massive ball of energy and a force to be reckoned with both on and off the field.

Out of the four of us, Alex was the only one who still had married parents and an intact family. He had two sisters and a large extended Greek family who were probably the loudest people I'd ever met in my life. Throughout high school, Alex and I shared a strong bond and knew every intimate detail of each other's lives.

As our sophomore year inched on, Alex, Jeff, Kenny, and I became inseparable. We had each other's backs unconditionally, and it was known that if you messed with one of us, then you were buying a

fight with all four. We were brothers. We had a bond that couldn't be broken.

It wasn't long before our small group of friends started being known as a group who liked to party, smoke weed, and get "fucked up." Other groups like ours started to take notice.

One day after school, we were all at Alex's house, ripping on a bong. A guy named Jared stopped by. I'd met him a few times before at Kenny's house.

Jared was one of the main weed suppliers in the area, and much of it trickled down to the students at Foran. He picked up pounds and sold mostly ounces. The people who bought off him would then break down $20 bags and eighths and sell to kids who had extra money from doing chores or saving up unused lunch money.

During Jared's visits to Kenny's house, he'd observed my curiosity for the business side of weed and was more than willing to help me make a jump into dealing. He was only a year older than me, and although I'd never sold anything in my life, he saw potential in me. He also saw a lucrative opportunity for himself by adding another dealer below him.

"Mike, right?" he said as he sat down next to me on Alex's shitty old couch in the smoke chamber he called a bedroom.

I nodded.

Jared appraised me. "Hey, let's go out on the porch and chop it up for a few minutes."

We walked down the creaky old steps of the 1940s raised ranch and out onto the wooden deck. It slanted so hard I'd almost toppled off it during many a drunken night.

"Hey, man," he said, "if I start giving you some weed, you think you can off it to your friends for me? You'll have whatever you want

to smoke and even some scratch on the side if you do good."

"When can I start?" I said without a moment of hesitation. Secretly, I'd been hoping for this since the moment I'd bought my first bag of weed.

Five minutes later, we were driving in Jared's Acura to his house, where he introduced me to the game that would change my life forever.

Over the next few months, he taught me everything a kid needed to know about selling drugs. He taught me how to balance a digital scale, how to bag up, where to meet people, and, most importantly, how to behave around customers and connects.

I didn't understand the leap I was taking. I looked at it as an opportunity to meet a couple friends, sell them a little weed, and in the end, get a bit of free weed for myself along with a few bucks in my pocket. I couldn't begin to comprehend the road I was embarking on.

The first bag of weed I ever sold was to a freshman from Foran. I met him at a park around the corner from school after class let out.

"Let me just get a twenty," he said, meaning as much weed he could buy for $20.

"That's fine. I have eighths too," I said, trying to upsell him. "I'll do one for you for $50 today. They're normally $60."

"Fifty is all I have until Friday, man," he said reluctantly. "I gotta eat lunch and shit."

I sat on a wooden bench and just looked at him. I said nothing.

He hesitated, and then said, "Yeah, okay, you know what? Fuck it. I'll figure it out. Give me the eighth."

He placed two crumpled twenties and a ten in my hand.

I'd just sold my first eighth of weed. After that, I used upsell tactics on everyone I met, no matter how close a friend they were. The

more I moved, the lower my price. It benefited me to sell a bit lower to move quantity, and there was always more weed to replace what was sold. I never waited more than a night for a "re-up," or to replenish my supplies.

Within a very short time, I began to sell larger amounts. Profit of hundreds became profit of thousands. At first, I would get a quarter pound from my supplier and then bag up eighths and twenties. I took calls from kids who'd raked their parents' lawn or washed a car to earn $20 and wanted to get high.

I met students from Foran in parking lots or in their parents' homes, after school and on weekends. I became highly efficient and good at marketing myself, upselling customers way above their original orders.

I was also effective at bagging the weed up and making sure there was just enough in the bag to register a gram up on a digital scale. I saved a half gram on almost every 1/8 bag I sold, which added up and allowed me to pocket even more profit.

It all came so naturally to me. I wondered if that was due to the marketing lessons I'd gotten from my dad, along with his endless teachings on the art of the sale.

As I started to sell more weed, so did my connect. Jared quickly rose through the ranks in our small town to become one of its biggest suppliers.

"I got ten pounds coming in from Canada this week," he said to me one day during a "blunt ride." Since it was difficult to find places to smoke, we would often ride around town in his car with the windows slightly cracked. We'd burn while listening to Jay-Z, Nas, and The Lox.

"Ten pounds?" I replied, taken aback by the quantity. "I've been

moving QPs, but I guess I can take a half pound at a time…"

"I was thinking you should just start taking whole pounds, man," he said. "Make it work. You're like me, man. You were built for this shit." It was clear he was confident in my ability to step up my game—which I did.

At just sixteen years old, I was now the youngest kid in that town making that volume of moves. Over time, I'd built up an impressive customer base within Milford and the surrounding cities. I'd even started giving ounces to kids younger than me at a premium to sell to their own friends.

As I continued to move up the chain, I made fewer sales of larger quantities. When I showed up to house parties, everyone would clear the room so I could weigh out ounces on the digital scale.

In school, I was still the same strong student I'd been my whole life. I'd always been able to balance my extracurricular activities with my studies—but this new hustle wasn't exactly intramural basketball. I'd found my niche and was getting attention from everyone around school.

For many teenagers trying weed for the first time, the kid selling was placed on a pedestal. Girls who had never even noticed me before started asking me to hang out or come to a house party because their parents had gone to the Caymans for the weekend.

One night, I went to a party with more than four hundred people in attendance. It was at the home of a girl who went to our town's all-girls Catholic high school. It was a Cape Cod style house on a one-way street with a huge backyard surrounded by woods.

The music was blaring, and people were getting blackout drunk from kegs and an endless supply of jungle juice, a concoction of grain alcohol and fruit punch that had probably killed a few people in its

time. Everyone was smoking weed, and some of the older kids were doing coke and other drugs.

I'd spent most of my night in the bathroom, weighing out bags for people, making and taking phone calls, and counting money. I'd run through a quarter pound of weed and was finally taking a break to smoke a joint on the pool deck with some friends. It was a cool, crisp autumn night and everyone was filled with a youthful, upbeat lust for life.

"Hey, man, you see that airplane?" a buddy said to me, pointing at the sky. "One of the guys on that plane right now is trying to talk to me, but I can't understand what he's saying."

People would say all kinds of shit like that to me when they were high, but even this seemed a little out there.

"Are you good, man?" I asked.

"I just did two bumps of ecstasy," he said. "I'm rolling my fucking face off."

It turned out he'd taken a pure form of ecstasy called molly. Long before it made its own rise to drug superstardom, kids in my hometown were mixing molly with mushrooms and LSD for extremely intense trips. It would be another year or so before I would have my first experience with ecstasy or any other major psychedelic drug.

My friend and I both started laughing hysterically at his hallucination. I then shrugged my shoulders and passed him a joint, and we carried on as if nothing strange had happened.

A bunch of dogs began barking in the front yard. I thought little of it and went on chatting and smoking with my buddy. The barking grew louder, so I peeked around the corner to locate the source of the sound.

Twenty or more police officers were charging the yard with four large baying German shepherds!

Shit.

"Milford Police; nobody move!" the lead cop shouted through a megaphone.

The cops showing up at a party filled with drugs meant only one thing: Run for your life. We did just that. People bolted in all directions, dropping plastic keg cups and other things they shouldn't have had in their possession. Hundreds of kids scurried into the dark woods behind the house chased by cops and K-9 units…a typical end to many Foran parties.

That was how I spent my sophomore year of high school: selling drugs and attending parties. I began to have less time to complete homework or focus on my studies. Slowly but surely, my grades began to plummet.

My GPA dropped from 3.3 to 2.0. I began getting into more trouble at school and often spent Saturdays in my school's extended detention period for troublemakers. I was always in good company. Alex was basically rewriting the record on suspension and detention. He probably spent more time in the principal's office than in class. Jeff and Kenny weren't too far behind.

All four of us had come from decent enough homes, but within a short run in high school, we'd built a reputation for trouble and disobedience. We'd become the "bad kids," and it was no secret. The parents, administrators, and cops all knew who we were. I, especially, was in the crosshairs for my associations with potheads, users, and dealers.

Unfortunately, all this unwanted attention and punishment did little to deter me from the path I was on.

seven

As much harmful activity as my friends and I were involved in, we still found a way to stay engaged in some positive pursuits. Alex and Kenny started for the Foran Lions football team, and all of us maintained a strong passion for basketball. We participated in a rec-league team that my father coached.

We liked to tease my dad because he wore a suit to games and carried a clipboard like Pat Riley of the New York Knicks. He did his best to discipline us at practice and teach us about hard work and leadership, but we were becoming unreachable. We went to most of our practices high on weed or too drunk to stand. Some of the kids in the league took an over-the-counter drug called Coricidin, which, when taken at very high doses, would mimic the effects of acid.

Outside of basketball, Kenny and I also shared a common interest the rest of the group didn't—a love for skiing. During cold months, we often drove from Connecticut to Vermont to ski the fresh snowfall at Killington or Mount Snow.

Kenny would bring weed, and we'd smoke in the woods with all our ski gear on. We explored the whole mountain, taking in the beautiful views offered from a mountain peak in the upper Northeast.

We would stand there and look out over the open land, breathing it all in. It was a natural escape for me, and I felt as though I was a million miles away from my problems back home.

Even with all the partying and dealing, I tried to stay connected to the things I loved from my childhood. When I was a kid and my family was still intact, we used to take trips together to Vermont to ski. As I got older, going to those same places was a way for me to hold on to pieces of my childhood that I remembered fondly.

In mid-December of 2000, my friends and I boarded a bus to Killington, Vermont, for a day trip run by a local ski shop. The bus left Milford early in the morning and was supposed to return that evening. My mom was worried and told me to be careful.

It was extremely cold on the ski lift going up the mountain. The anticipation of fresh snow was the only thing keeping me warm.

As the chair approached the top of the mountain, I was filled with excitement. Kenny and I disembarked and started our run. Without hesitation, I led him toward the terrain park filled with big jumps. With the popularity of the X Games, the jumps had been getting bigger every year.

I spotted a massive jump in the middle of the trail. It was my first run of the day, and I'd entered an expert-level terrain park. As a teenager, the last thing on my mind was to heed my mother's advice to "be careful."

"Yo," I shouted to Kenny as adrenaline pumped through my veins. "Come hit this big one with me."

Usually, skiers will "spot" a jump before going off it, meaning they will go past the hit and get a visual idea of what to expect. In my youthful ignorance, though, I decided not to take this precaution.

Instead, I pointed my tips downhill and charged full speed at the

enormous wall of snow that stood before me. I rolled off the transition and felt my skis leave the snow.

I knew I was in trouble as soon as I lifted off. The steep angle of the takeoff awkwardly threw my legs out from under me. I was completely helpless, flying through the air twenty feet from the ground. I flailed wildly. I felt airborne for eternity.

I crashed to the icy surface with a shattering thud. The rest is only a hazy memory. From what I heard from others after the accident, I lay on the ground motionless for many minutes. When I regained consciousness and slowly opened my eyes, I could barely make out the group of people—silhouettes against the sky—surrounding me.

I blinked a few times. I wiggled my fingers. The ground was cold against my back. The sharp wind burned my face. I looked to my right, trying to get my bearings. When I glanced to my left, a bolt of sheer panic hit my heart. My left foot with its ski boot was twisted into view, no more than an inch from my face.

It was the last thing I saw before I passed out.

I later learned that I'd hit the ground so hard that my femur—the largest bone in my body—had snapped like a piece of dry kindling at a force of fifteen times my body weight. I'd also severely fractured my skull. Passersby spoke afterward about a large pool of dark crimson blood where my head had made contact with the ice, followed by a slick forty-foot trail of red that led to my limp body.

Shortly after the accident, a Killington ski patrol came across the horrific scene. They hastily radioed a medic who came to my aid on the hill. I was placed on a cloth sled and hooked to the back of a snowmobile.

I came to as I slid along the frozen snow on the way down the massive mountain. I felt helpless, bundled like a cocoon in a flimsy

sled as I hurtled over the bumpy ice behind the roaring snowmobile. Trees and skiers passed in a surreal blur.

"We've got a severe trauma incident here," the patrolman said into his radio as we sped down the hill. "You'd better call University Medical and have them prep an ICU bed."

It felt like it took forever to reach the base of the mountain. I was loaded into an ambulance and rushed to the University of Vermont Medical Center.

As we drove, bursts of light blasted through my closed eyelids. Thoughts rolled through my head:

How could this have happened?

Why did this happen to me?

I want to see my parents.

Where is my family?

Take a breath. You will get through this.

But unlike other accidents I'd been in, I couldn't expect to see my family anytime soon. I was four hours away from home. Although I'd taken a bus to the mountain with friends, they'd had to catch the bus home without me.

I was alone.

When I arrived at the hospital, I was given the option to call my parents.

I pondered this. Although I needed them, I knew how my mother was going to react. She was going to be terrified. I didn't want to put her through this.

But I had no choice.

With the phone up to my ear, I strained to get the words out of my mouth. "Mom…"

I didn't know that the doctors had already told her about the

accident.

"Mom, I fell skiing," I whispered. "My leg is broken."

My mom began to sob.

Everything went black. With my traumatic head injury, the consciousness came and went in waves.

To this day, I only remember slivers of the snowmobile pulling me down the mountain, the whirring of the ambulance siren, and bits and pieces of the emergency room.

One thing I will *never* forget, though, was the fear in my mother's voice during that phone call. There was nothing I could say to relieve her terror or worry from her son being admitted to the intensive care unit hours away from his family.

When I faded back in, I tried to reassure her. "Don't worry, Mom, everything is going to be okay," I said. "Please don't cry. I love you." And then I fell back into unconsciousness again.

My stay at the hospital was cloudy, with only slivers of memory. I remember being slid into the cold, confined MRI machine. I remember the sheer and unrelenting pain of waking up in traction with my leg hanging down from the ceiling. But most of all, I distinctly remember being handed a small, round pink pill.

Just moments before, a short nurse with curly brown hair came in to check my vitals. She read my temperature and pulse and checked on my respiration and blood pressure.

Then she asked, "Honey, are you feeling any pain right now?"

I'd been here before. "Yes!" I was writhing in anguish.

"How much pain, on a scale of one to ten?"

"Ten!" I screamed in agony. "Please help me. Please!"

Five minutes later she was back with the doctor. She handed me a small plastic cup with a pill in it—a 20mg dose of OxyContin.

I gulped it down as if it were the first thing I'd eaten in years.

All the pain faded away…

I woke up hours later in a recovery room. My father sat in a chair beside me. He had traveled all night to get to the hospital. While I'd been asleep, the doctors had performed an emergency surgery to repair my leg. They had made two small incisions, one on my hip and one near my knee, and inserted a titanium rod inside my femoral bone. The rod was then secured with two screws. The bleeding in my brain and the swelling had subsided.

I lay there and looked at my dad. He looked back at me. There was nothing to say.

I was alive.

"Hey, buddy," he finally said. He reached over and put his hand on my shoulder.

I started to cry. I couldn't tell if it was from the pain or from my dad's comforting touch during my time of need.

My head ached and my leg burned in agony. Due to my overwhelming pain, the doctors again opted to put me on a self-managed morphine drip. Any time I felt the slightest discomfort, pain, or anxiety, I would push the button.

Drip. Drip. Drip.

And the pain would go away.

eight

2001
U.S. opioid deaths: 9,496

I spent a week at the hospital in Vermont before I was able to come home. When I arrived back, I entered an intensive rehabilitation program. There was no cast, but I had to use crutches to get around. Just like with my basketball accident, I missed weeks of school to recover at home. I was unable to walk on my left leg for months. As serious as the injury was, it did little to change my partying ways.

In January 2001, I celebrated my sixteenth birthday. I was finally moving around well enough to go back to school. Another traumatic event had tested me and my family. The stress was tangible. But with hard work and dedication, we got through it. It wasn't long before my social life recovered, as did the pot dealing and poor decisions that came along with it. By now, I was taking full advantage of the fact that my parents were divorced and my dad wasn't home. My mother was losing the ability to control her growing son. I was starting to make my own choices, many of them foolish.

My junior year of high school wasn't much different than the year before. There were parties every weekend. Everyone I knew was smoking weed and drinking.

My drug sales continued to grow at a rapid pace. My desire to hang out with friends and party on the weekends paled in comparison to my fervor for selling. While everyone else partied, I kept to myself, bagging up, meeting other dealers, counting money.

Many drug dealers were infamous for their big heads and cocky attitudes, and I was no exception. While everyone else partied, got fucked up, and spent money on drugs, I was the guy who made out. I made the money. I had the girls. I had the power.

My ego became a gift and a curse. It gave me confidence in business transactions and social situations. It also gave me a feeling of invincibility during moments of conflict or indecision, which could be dangerous.

As months passed, my reputation for being a successful dealer continued to flourish.

One day, Jared's connect, John, approached me. We bantered for a bit. Then he leaned in and lowered his voice. "I just want you to know that you don't gotta go through Jared no more. Just call me. I got whatever you need, bro."

John had been Jared's connect since Jared got his initial start. John was one of the big shots in Milford. He brought in hundreds of pounds annually through connects in Canada and upstate New York. I'd heard stories of the beefs he'd had with other dealers, and the resulting violence. He'd dropped out of college intentionally. He wasn't selling weed to make a few bucks to supplement a job. Selling weed *was* his job, and he did it very well.

I accepted John's offer. Just like that, I'd jumped a rung on the

ladder.

As many teens are, I was easily impressed with the marks of success. John, my new connect, had accumulated a lot of wealth through dealing. While others got picked up by their parents after school or drove beat-up cars, John would come get me in his brand-new Acura 3.2 TL with enormous chrome rims and an upgraded stereo system bumping "Ether" by Nas or the new Jay-Z album.

Rap music had a huge effect on me. My parents and the media seemed to think the music was going to negatively influence the kids of my generation. Adults did everything they could to shut down the rap industry, going all the way back to when Snoop Dogg released *Doggystyle*. I'd grown up sneaking a listen to Biggie or 2Pac while my parents tried their best to shelter me from the music. But as soon as my dad left, rap became a core influence in my life.

The attempts to censor the music always seemed a waste to me. I believed people would make choices based on all different kinds of motives, not solely because of the music they listened to. In hindsight, maybe the lyrics—especially the parts that glorified drugs—influenced me more than I knew.

It was the most exhilarating feeling to drive around Milford selling drugs while listening to Jay-Z's "Can't Knock the Hustle" or "Ten Crack Commandments" as popularized by Tony Montana in *Scarface* and then ironicized for eternity with Biggie's song. While I couldn't relate to much of the dark content in the songs yet, the parts about drug dealing made me feel as though I was part of a culture. As a somewhat sheltered middle-class white kid, it was exhilarating and new. Anytime one of the songs referenced smoking weed, selling drugs, or partying, it gave me goosebumps. Slowly but surely, my lifestyle was beginning to mirror the lyrics in my favorite music.

Throughout my junior year, I continued to prolifically sell marijuana. At seventeen, I lived at home with my mom and my little sister, since my older sister was still attending college at UConn. Half my battle was trying to hide the smell of the weed from my mom. I was moving pounds at a time, and the stench was unbearable.

Privacy had always been a rare commodity at my home. As teens, we weren't allowed to have locks on our bedroom doors, and my mother would randomly come in from time to time to snoop around.

This presented a problem due to my expanding dealing business. Through my ability to talk and build relationships, I'd grown my massive customer list to the point that it now stretched across multiple cities. With this expanded customer base came expanded opportunities on the supply side.

Because of my youth and inability to put up the $3,200 necessary to purchase a pound of weed to sell, the higher-ups had started "fronting" me the product—or giving it to me on credit—until I could off-load it and pay them back. They took the risk because they knew I was beneficial to their bottom line due to the volume of sales I was capable of making.

In the middle of my junior year, my connects received a major shipment from Canada of some of the smelliest, most pungent "BC Bud," named after the area where the weed was grown, in British Columbia. We wrapped the stuff in Ziploc after Ziploc, but it was no use. There was no masking the skunky aroma no matter how hard we tried to disguise it.

One morning in my room before school, I split a pound of the BC Bud into two separate bags and double- and triple-wrapped them. I hid both bags in the back of my closet inside my ski boots. I figured there was no chance my mom would look inside those boots.

When I arrived home from school that day, my mom was in my room, waiting for me. She held up the two giant bags of marijuana.

"What is this?" she screamed. "You're selling drugs, aren't you?"

"How did you get that?" I said, my voice rising. Anger surged through me. "What are you fucking doing in my room?" My questions deflected the fact that I'd just been caught hiding a felony-sized stash of weed in my room.

Up until then, my mom had only a vague notion that I was up to no good. She'd found stashes of money in my room, and she knew I was buying lots of new clothes. I often left at random times, sometimes during dinner, for no apparent reason. I'd rush out with a pound of weed, just as the meatloaf came out of the oven, and then return with $4,000 in my pocket right when dessert was served. My mom suspected something was going on, but she'd had no idea of the extent of my activities.

Now there was no avoiding the truth. For the first time, my mom realized the seriousness of the situation. Her son was selling drugs.

With her discovery came an ultimatum.

"I can either flush it," she said, "and you can stay. Or you can have it back and leave the house today."

I chose to leave.

As much as I wanted to stay, I owed a lot of money for the product. The consequences for non-payment would be harsher than a few weeks on the street.

In a rage tinged with a sinking feeling of sadness, I stuffed what I could of my belongings into my L.L. Bean backpack. I grabbed my pillow and headed down the stairs, knowing that leaving home at seventeen was a momentous decision.

My mom stood at the door and watched me with tears rolling

down her cheeks. She was putting her foot down, but I could see she also didn't want me to leave. Her face was etched in despair, and I could see in her expression that she hoped I would change my mind and turn around.

But I was resolute. I stuffed my belongings into the back seat of my 1999 Volkswagen Jetta and drove off as my little sister Gabby watched, sobbing, through the pane glass of the front door.

As I drove away from my family and the life I knew, waves of dark despair rolled over me. I knew I was making bad choices, but I felt unable to change the course of my life. I felt swept away on a tide I couldn't control.

I stayed at a friend's house for a week, until my mom called and told me I could come back home, as long as I stopped selling.

I came home with the intention to do right by my family and myself. I informed my dealers that I was done selling. I told my friends I wouldn't get high anymore. But soon, those sentiments went out the window and I was right back to using and selling again.

After my mom went to sleep at 9 p.m., I would sneak out and make sales. I slid the screen door open and tiptoed out the back door to meet buyers under the streetlights.

The silence of the night was calm but eerie. There was the uneasy feeling that someone might be watching me or that at any minute, a cop might roll up on me and find enough drugs to lock me up.

I was getting away with something, living on the edge. It was exhilarating...an adrenaline rush. I was addicted to this high more than anything else.

And so the cycle began, the pattern of being kicked out of my home, then being let back in, being trusted again and subsequently betraying that trust—a struggle that would consume my life for the

next ten years.

It was quite literally a fight between good and evil. The drugs and money had an inexplicable power to pull me back in, time and again.

They were forces to be reckoned with, all-consuming and without equal.

nine

I spent the rest of my junior year caught up in my chosen lifestyle. The parties were endless, and every weekend they seemed to get bigger. There were kegs and bottles, and people smoking weed, and none of our actions seemed to garner serious consequences.

We drove blackout drunk every weekend, sometimes bashing through fences and ending up in people's yards. If the car was still running, we'd simply drive it away.

We got in massive brawls with our crosstown-rival high school that resulted in people going to the hospital with broken noses and concussions, and then we laughed about it until we did it all over again the next weekend.

We had rampant, unprotected sex. It wasn't unusual at a party to see people having intercourse on the lawn in front of everyone, or to stumble upon a girl giving a guy head in the bathroom. At sixteen, I was already out of control sexually, something that would lead to an addiction problem of its own later in my life.

My friends and I lived hedonistically, did exactly what we wanted, and never worried about the results. School took a back seat to the

partying, and my grades continued to nosedive.

Later in our junior year, my friends and I took what we considered the next logical step in our experimentation with drugs. We started experimenting with psychoactive drugs like mushrooms, LSD, and ecstasy. Jeff, Kenny, Alex, and I got into music by Pink Floyd, The Doors, and Led Zeppelin. I grew my hair out, started wearing tie-dyed shirts, and began looking at life through the lens of a psychedelic mindset, seeing things in new ways.

One night, the four of us decided to go to a Dave Matthews concert in Hartford. Practically everyone we knew was going to be there. We didn't really care about seeing Dave Matthews perform. We were mostly going for the tailgate party before the concert. It was sure to be a drinking-and-drug-fest, as in years gone by.

A few years earlier, in 1999, my older sister had attended a Dave Matthews show and witnessed firsthand rioting partiers as they overturned cars and set them on fire. The police used mace and rubber bullets to break up thousands of fans who were drunk and drugged out of their minds after extended tailgating and boozing inside the arena.

From then on, whenever Dave Matthews performed in Hartford, there was a massive police presence and riot squads to keep order.

On this particular evening, my buddies and I decided to head to the stadium early to begin our tailgate party. As we approached the arena, we saw large mobile response units parked around the perimeter of the concert venue. Police officers carrying riot shields patrolled the parking lot on horseback.

We parked in the enormous gravel parking lot and took in the scene. People of all ages were getting drunk and taking every drug under the sun. Weed smoke filled the air. Music blasted from cars as

people laughed, bantered, and partied.

My friends and I walked around the lot from car to car with a bottle of Smirnoff vodka, passing it to each other and taking swigs.

I was mid-laugh about something when Kenny got my attention.

"Mike," he said, his Irish face beet-red from the booze, "Jeff's sister's boyfriend is here. He has those white ecstasy pills we keep hearing about."

I put the bottle down and followed Kenny deeper into the gravel parking lot that was alive with debauchery. The sun was setting, and the crowd was beginning to get rambunctious.

It was about 7 p.m. when we ran into the guy who had "triple-stack Rolls Royce pills"—referring to the size and stamp on the ecstasy. He was surrounded by other buyers. I pulled a $20 bill from the wad of cash in my pocket and placed it on top of the crumpled bills that each of the other boys had put forward.

Kenny and I were soon back at the car, pills in hand. I was wasted drunk at that point. Kenny, Jeff, Alex, and I looked at each other, shrugged, and all made the same "fuck it" face. Down the hatch. We washed our pills down with a shot of shitty vodka.

We resumed walking around.

Within half an hour, we were all gripped tightly by the effects of the drug. My jaw clenched shut, and I began to grind my teeth. My brain flooded with serotonin and dopamine. A warm, fuzzy sensation enveloped my body and moved down to my penis. Everything felt good to the touch.

The four of us hung out in the parking lot with all the other fans, waiting for the stadium doors to open. We planned on leaving as soon as the crowds went in.

The sky grew dark and the crowd began to move restlessly toward

the arena doors. It had only been two hours since I'd taken the ecstasy, and I wasn't in good shape to drive. We stood next to the car, contemplating what to do next. The parking lot was almost empty, and we still didn't have a plan.

I was consumed with worry about the situation.

Jeff was ruminating about a weed transaction he'd just made. "I bought a bag off this black guy, and it's skimpy as fuck," Jeff said. "I'm going to find him and get my money back." He turned and walked off.

Since we weren't driving anytime soon, we followed him. In our confusion, we didn't notice that we'd crossed the tracks into a dangerous part of North Hartford until it was too late.

"C'mon, Jeff, let's go," I said. "You're not getting your money back. How much was it? Ten dollars? I'll just give it to you." My voice rose to a yell. "And why did you even buy weed, anyway? I have an ounce with me!"

Jeff's face darkened. He didn't like being lectured. He took off running. We took off after him.

That was the thing about Jeff—it wasn't that he didn't *show* fear, he didn't *have* fear. No matter how big or scary the opponent, Jeff never stepped back from a fight. For as long as I'd known him, he embodied a Napoleon complex where he believed nothing was too big for him to overcome. That never changed, even after several ass-beatings from people twice his size.

The three of us looked at each other, unsure of what to do. Alex moved first, and then we were off and running after Jeff—straight into an urban war zone. Before we could reach him, a car of six Hispanic guys pulled up next to us.

"Take off your fucking shoes," they shouted. "Empty your pock-

ets. *Now!*"

I didn't stop or react. Instead, I ran in the opposite direction.

While the other guys stood around in shock, I'd made a run for it. My leg still hurt from the ski accident, but I moved as fast as I could and didn't look back.

As I reached the concert arena parking lot, I saw a bigger problem. The riot squads were sweeping non-concertgoers off the property. They'd lined up in a battle formation and were marching through the parking lot toward my car. They moved in a long single line, beating their shields with their batons.

I'd never seen anything like it. As the massive line of police moved closer to my car, I saw some drunk kids shit-talking at the cops. Others refused to leave. Within seconds, the police sprayed those individuals with mace, beat them, and dragged them away in handcuffs. The cops were taking no chances this year.

I sprinted to my car, hopped in the driver's seat, and prayed that the rest of my group had lived through the robbery situation. I hoped they would return to the car before the troops got to it.

The looming riot squad marched closer. There were now only two cars between me and them.

Suddenly, my car doors flew open and my three friends jumped in.

"Go," Alex screamed as the cops closed in. "Fucking *go*, man!"

We sped off with no time to spare.

As I drove, my heart thumped wildly in my chest. My vision was blurred from the drugs. I was overwhelmed with fear, anxiety, and the effects of MDMA. Still, I was able to drive, for the most part. The events of the evening had sobered me up just enough to get us all home in one piece.

Those kinds of suspenseful, razor's edge experiences were becoming more commonplace for me. Run-ins with cops, driving under the influence of psychoactive drugs, and life-threatening situations were a mainstay in the lives of me and my friends. We'd settled into a pattern of terrible decision-making, rampant drug abuse, and most of all, ignorance about the well-being of ourselves and others.

We saw our use of psychedelic drugs as something that expanded our minds and allowed us to experience things that we normally would not. With that being said, we didn't use as much of these drugs as other people at our school did. There were kids who dropped acid and ecstasy three or four times a week and thought nothing of it. In the few times that I did these psychedelic drugs, I noticed a profound change in who I was. In the days after a trip or an ecstasy roll, my attitude and outlook on life were completely different. Some of the effects I noticed were anxiety, depression, memory loss, impaired mental capabilities, and disorganized thinking.

In the years after my friends and I took those drugs, I noticed more of the long-term effects on our brains, and moreover, on the brains of the heavier users. Many of the kids I knew who frequently used ecstasy and acid did irreparable damage to themselves and would never be the same again. I still sometimes wonder about the permanent harm that those few hits of psychedelic drugs did to my psyche.

Along with the new risks I was taking and the growth in my partying, there was growth in my dealing as well. I had customers all over New Haven and Fairfield County and even up Route 8 into the valley. I drove out to houses in cities I'd never even heard of to sell weed to people I'd never met.

Pounds would come and go, and it became a tedious task just to count the money. Many times, I would just hand a brick of cash over

to a friend and ask him to count it. Dealing had become my full-time profession, and I would operate from the minute I woke up to the minute I went to bed.

On weekends, I would drive around with my scale and sell weight to anyone who wanted it. During the week, I would take pre-bagged eighths to school with me and do deals in the cafeteria bathrooms before and after lunch.

I took pride in my reputation. There was always a healthy competition between dealers in and around the city. Some claimed to have bigger bags and others claimed to have better product. The customers and dealers would argue about who was pushing the most weight.

I reveled in the competition.

Through all the dealing, I'd started to make friends with people at Foran who led an even riskier lifestyle than I did. Most of them were deep into much harder drugs. While in class, I often saw those kids sniff pills or coke right off their desks or books. I naturally gravitated toward them as I instinctively sensed I was headed in the same direction.

Little did I know that this path would soon take an even sharper and more destructive turn. A new drug was in my future, more powerful than anything I had ever tried before…

ten

As teenagers in a time of rapid experimentation, my friends and I smoked weed, drank, and tried Percocet or Vicodin at parties. We didn't think anything of it. In our estimation, this type of activity wasn't any different than previous generations who'd experimented with LSD, quaaludes, or prescription narcotics. When a new and exciting pill hit our streets, it was inevitable that the young people of Milford wanted to experiment with that, too.

OxyContin was different from other drugs. It was a pain pill manufactured with a time-release seal so that after taken orally, the effects of the drug would be released slowly into the bloodstream over a delayed period of time. This was Oxy's claim to fame for cancer sufferers who had to take multiple pills to relieve their pain. Now the patient could take one pill in the morning and the powerful opioid would be slowly rationed into the blood, allowing pain to be managed for hours or even entire days from just one dose.

This time-release seal allowed Purdue Pharma to pack a highly concentrated amount of opioid painkiller into a single pill. This was the major way OxyContin differed from Percocet or Vicodin. By some

estimates, one 80mg OxyContin tablet could pack as much as 30 extra-strength Percocet pills into a neat package to be swallowed by a terminally ill or chronically affected patient. The toxicity of these pills would normally be lethal to most users but, when placed behind a time release seal, the flow to the blood was controlled, and the toxicity was therefore also controlled.

For a short time, the pills did exactly what they were meant to do. But it wasn't long before people found a way to remove the proprietary time-release seal off the pill. By putting the pill in the mouth, a person could suck away at the seal until it faded away completely. Whatever was left of the seal could then be wiped away with a paper towel or T-shirt. The result: an incredibly powerful dose of pure oxycodone.

Once the seal had been removed, people would crush the pills and sniff them for instantaneous delivery. Initially, it appeared that Purdue Pharma had created and extensively marketed a powerful new painkiller effective against the pain suffered by terminally ill or seriously injured patients. In fact, it was a legal form of heroin for the general public.

Years later, investigations into America's opioid epidemic shone a light onto the dark secret that Purdue Pharma clearly knew all along what was going on and had deliberately misrepresented the addictive potential of OxyContin to both doctors and the public in order to protect their profits.

As seventeen-year-olds in our safe little town of Milford, none of us knew the true nature of these new pills or what was happening behind the scenes at Purdue Pharma during the company's unethical quest for profit at our expense.

We were just kids. We were curious, like all teenagers. On one

level, we knew that our recreational drug use was wrong. We were harming our bodies and doing things that weren't safe, but we didn't fully realize the implications. None of us could begin to prepare, or even imagine, the horrors that lay ahead on the path we were about to embark on, and what that path would do to our lives.

We decided to dip our feet in a river of curiosity and intrigue. Before it was over, many of us would lose sight of the shore. Some of us would wade in so deep that we would never return home. And the most unfortunate of us would drown completely.

In the beginning, our experimentation with OxyContin was innocent. There was something new on the market, and we were more than willing to try it out.

I'd already had my first tastes of both morphine and OxyContin pills in the hospital after my injuries, so the idea of trying Oxy recreationally appealed to me.

It was the spring semester of my junior year at Foran. The weather was picture-perfect. The sun shone down, and the air was balmy. There wasn't a cloud in the sky.

A group of us left school together. I jumped in a car with a friend named Brian who'd recently been driving me home from school every day. The windows were cracked slightly open, and sweet spring air filled the car.

As we left the parking lot, Brian pulled a crumpled cellophane wrapper from his pocket and held it up to show me its contents.

"Yo, have you tried one of these yet?" he asked. Nestled inside the cellophane was a small green pill—an 80mg OxyContin.

"Nah," I said, "but I hear they're amazing."

Although I'd already experienced Oxy in a medical setting, I had yet to try it recreationally. I'd been hearing stories about kids sniffing

Oxy at parties. The thought of it frightened me a little, but I was also intrigued by the new fad. Everyone described a euphoric experience. I remembered the sensation of pain-relieving drugs, how good they'd felt, and how they'd taken all my cares away. I had the teen mentality of trying new things, rebelling against the rules, and disregarding the consequences of my actions. I felt invincible. What would it hurt to sniff Oxy as part of another fun experiment?

Brian pulled over in a condo parking lot. We were going to do this.

A surge of adrenaline hit my veins. There was a palpable rush inside me; it was as if my body knew I was about to take a huge, significant leap.

I watched Brian take the green pill out of the cellophane wrapper. One side of the pill was marked "OC" and the other side "80." This stamp and the pill it designated—the 80mg OxyContin—would become known as the holy grail for prescription drugs.

Brian placed the pill in his mouth and allowed his spit to break down the time-release seal. After a minute, he removed the pill from his mouth and used his T-shirt to wipe the green coating away, leaving behind the Oxy 80 logo in a vibrant green circle on the white cloth. This imprint was something I'd already seen many times before at school. Numerous kids walked around campus sporting white T-shirts bearing the familiar green emblems—evidence of their active Oxy use.

Brian pulled a razor from his center console and chopped the pill in half. He wrapped one half of the pill back up to save, then placed the other half inside a $20 bill and smashed down on it with a Bic lighter. He poured the finely ground powder onto a Bone Thugs-N-Harmony *E. 1999 Eternal* CD case and split the powder into two

minuscule lines.

"How is that gonna get us high?" I said jokingly. "Those tiny-ass lines?"

Ignoring me, he rolled the same $20 bill he'd used to smash the pill into a tight tube and placed it inside his right nostril. I watched him lift the CD case to his face. He moved the bill swiftly down the case, sniffing up one of the small lines. His eyes glazed over, and his body went limp. A serene smile radiated across his face.

Then he slid the CD case in my direction.

Until that moment, I'd never sniffed anything in my life, nor had I planned to when I left home that morning. I looked down at the case and thought, "Well, what the hell is that tiny line gonna do to me, anyway?"

Brian didn't urge me or force me. He just held the CD case in front of me. Truthfully, it was just another "fuck it, I'll try it once" kind of moment for me. Just like my ski accident at Killington, I didn't check things out before I hit the jump. I just pointed my tips downhill and let myself fly.

Sitting in that parking lot not a hundred yards from my high school, I took a deep breath, placed the rolled-up bill in my nose, and sniffed my very first 20mg of OxyContin.

The high was instantaneous.

I asked Brian if I had died and gone to heaven.

All pain in my body was instantly erased. Any depression, worries, or anxiety were removed in their entirety. My whole life, I had suffered from an anxious mind and a feeling of not completely fitting in with the people around me. It oftentimes felt as though people were naturally against me, opposed to my views and overall being. But all that weight lifted off my shoulders when I swallowed that

chalky powder drip and felt it travel from my nasal cavity down into my throat.

The high felt like a living version of The Beatles' "Here Comes the Sun." The bright April day was made that much brighter. All my troubles seemed a thousand miles away.

Brian and I drove around for hours. I just stared out the window and let the feeling of intense sunshine pour all over and through my body. The music thumping from Brian's stereo was all around me, infusing my body with its sound. My bones, muscles, and mind were in complete harmony and relaxation.

I wasn't the only one having that experience. Everywhere I looked, people were giving OxyContin a try. At weekend parties, the bathrooms were filled with high-school kids experimenting with the drug. After school on weekdays, teens were trying it out at friends' houses. Soon there were even kids sniffing OxyContin off the back of toilets at lunch or at desks during study hall.

No one understood the risks. I doubt that even Purdue was aware of the outcome that mass-marketing this drug would produce within society. Like us, the company was experimenting with this new drug too. They just happened to be using the residents of towns like mine as human guinea pigs.

The new drug epidemic hit hard and fast. Society was already familiar with the heroin epidemic of the 1970s and the inner-city problem with crack cocaine in the 1980s. However, both of those epidemics were centered in predominantly black, low-income areas.

This new epidemic, however, had a much different face. There were no sleazy crime lords importing the drug, and no boarded-up buildings filled with addicts lining the streets. There were no dirty needles in the gutters—not yet, at least—and no drug-related murders

flashing across the news each night.

This new drug, OxyContin, was especially dangerous because it was all around us. It was in our medicine cabinets at home. Our aging grandparents took it to relieve severe pain related to cancer or chronic illness. The pharmacies were loaded with it—a result of Purdue's aggressive rollout—and doctors were more than willing to prescribe the drug to anyone who wanted it. This saturation and overall ease of access were what allowed the residents of cities like Milford to so effortlessly experiment with the drug.

The overabundance of Oxy, a lack of knowledge about its side effects, and a completely underprepared school system created the perfect storm. In a short time, what started out as a drug that people tried on a whim turned into a full-blown epidemic of dependence and addiction. A drug wave like no one had ever seen washed up in communities all over America.

Slowly but surely, the use of all other drugs ground to a halt. People who'd only smoked weed before now transitioned into the use of OxyContin. The dealers started to recognize where the demand was headed and adjusted their supply accordingly.

John, my supplier, was ready to move into the Oxy market as well, and he wanted me to come with him.

"The whole town has switched over," he said to me as he slid a small mirror of white-powder lines toward me. "I've never seen anything like it."

We were sitting in his parents' home. They both worked full-time, so we basically ran the shop from there.

"I don't know," I said. "This all seems really sketchy." I leaned over and sniffed a line. I leaned back in my chair and waited for the chemical taste to drip into the back of my throat.

"The package is smaller than weed," John said. "The dogs can't smell it, and the profit is unlimited." He paused and fixed his eyes on me. "But hey, if you want to keep selling ounces to the freshmen, I can find somebody else…"

"Whoa," I said, putting my hand up. The familiar blood rush of adrenaline pumped through my veins. "Okay, man, let's do it."

John handed me a cellophane with twenty OxyContin 80s. "I'm giving you these for $40 apiece. Sell them for $60. Make a quick $400. Come back and get more."

That's all it took. I was now in the business of selling prescription pills.

Throughout my entire sales career of Oxy, or of any addictive substance thereafter, I maintained one golden rule: Never turn anyone on to the drug. I can say to this day that I was never responsible for directly giving someone their first OxyContin. Every drug dealer had a code. Although that may seem like a tiny consolation to people looking in from the outside, I had my own personal ethics that I lived by. Some things were just off-limits. I never wanted to be responsible for someone else's descent into addiction. It offered me a small amount of solace.

Even though I knew what I was doing was wrong, the deep feelings of guilt and regret wouldn't come until later, when I looked back on the totality of the destruction left behind. At seventeen, though, selling Oxy just seemed like an easy way to make money, and I used every excuse in the book to justify my selling.

The sales patterns of this new drug were mind-blowing to me. It was hard to fathom that high-school kids were buying something so expensive and in such large quantities. The street price was lower in the beginning, but soon $60 a pill was the widely accepted price.

At first, I was selling around twenty pills a day. Some days I would sell fifty. It soon became clear why selling Oxy was so alluring to me and other young dealers. I was one of only a few kids in the city's high schools selling Oxy, and my business grew exponentially because of it. With profit of $400 a day, the potential was limitless.

With that kind of margin, I should have been enjoying lavish vacations, luxury car purchases and fine dining. However, I was already breaking the most important rule of dealing drugs as popularized by Biggie's "Ten Crack Commandments"—never get high on your own supply.

As my dealing of Oxy picked up, so did my use. For every twenty pills I sold, I sniffed three or four. A few people would come by with $55 total to spend and would ask me to spot them the difference. Of course, they never paid me back. At the end of the day, after all the bullshit, the gas in the car, and what went up my nose, there was never much profit.

Even as our sales and usage spiked, my friends and I were still unaware of the long-term effects of OxyContin. The drug was becoming a centerpiece at most parties, and some of us coined the term "weekend warrior" for our ability to use the drug and still pass classes and partake in day-to-day life. We thought we could just pick and choose when to use it, like weed, with no ill effects.

As our junior year went on, however, the drug became more prevalent in our lives. Crazy weekend nights when everyone used Oxy recreationally together gave way to people using the drug all alone in their rooms after school.

By the end of the school year, larger numbers of kids were coming to school high on Oxy. There were tell-tale signs for people high on the drug—clues we displayed ourselves. Early morning homeroom

classes were filled with kids with tiny "pinned" pupils and itchy noses. Many kids nodded off or slept through classes altogether.

As our junior year came to a close, the problem stayed off the radar of most teachers, parents, and administrators.

It was the last year that any of us still possessed a tiny shred of childish, adolescent innocence.

Everything was about to change.

eleven

2002

U.S. opioid deaths: 11,920

My time as a class clown had made me quite the comedian, and everyone was still laughing along with me during high school. As teens, we still found humor in the smallest of pranks and practical jokes.

At Foran High School, a favorite tradition was Senior Prank Day. The pranks were always on the edge of acceptability, never warranting real consequences.

For example, the senior girls might play jokes on classmates or write derogatory messages in shaving cream on each other's cars. One time, my friend Danny mowed the shape of a giant penis into the grass outside the student parking lot. It was only visible from an airplane and soon went viral online.

Such things were usually harmless jokes, but times were changing and the students at Foran were starting to become increasingly brazen.

When Senior Prank Day rolled around at the end of my junior

year, I was, as usual, willing to put on a show. The seniors always knew to call on me if they needed a distraction or someone to make a crowd burst into laughter.

"Hey, Mike," one of the senior boys said to me that day. "We need you do something crazy at lunch today, just to get everyone's attention for a few minutes. Can you think of something?"

"Sure," I said. "I'll be ready. I've got a plan."

As the lunch period rolled on, the senior boy gave me the signal.

I walked across the lunchroom carrying a tray of food. Then, at the right moment, I tripped over a chair and fell to the ground, launching my lunch tray across the room.

The lunchroom erupted into laughter and loud cheers. I didn't know why the seniors had asked me to distract the room, but it didn't matter. It was the laugh I wanted.

As I got up off the ground with everyone chanting and cheering, the principal, administrators, and teachers rushed over to quiet the room.

Just then, a male ran into the lunchroom wearing a black ski mask.

Without warning, the masked attacker ambushed the school officials with water balloons and shaving cream.

The lunchroom burst into complete anarchy.

Food flew through the air, people threw chairs at each other, and teachers tried in vain to control the scene. Within minutes, the Milford Police arrived to stop the debacle.

Once the dust had settled and everyone had left the lunchroom to go back to class, the administrators looked for the culprit, the person to blame. The masked man who'd thrown the water balloons had run away and was never apprehended. So who would take the fall for

what had happened? Of course, the most visible person in the room, the one who'd initiated the chaos. Me.

Without knowing what I was getting into, I'd unwittingly triggered the tipping point for a senior prank gone too far.

I was dragged into the principal's office, where I faced both law enforcement and school administrators. They'd found their scapegoat.

The cops showed me no mercy. Due to my past problems in school, neither did the principal.

"You're being charged with inciting a riot," said a Milford police officer. "It's only a misdemeanor, but you'll have to go to court."

The principal looked at me disapprovingly. "You will also be suspended for the final days of the year, Mike. We're all very disappointed in you."

I wasn't cuffed or searched or brought to the station, but the summons to court was considered an arrest.

That was how my junior year at high school came to a close.

The summer between my junior and senior years brought more partying and drinking, which paved the way for a continued descent into the world of OxyContin. People around me were starting to use more frequently and in higher doses. I continued to sell drugs around town as the only way to support my own Oxy habit.

When my senior year came, my mother asked if I could start driving Gabby and her friend Brittany to school. I agreed, but my behavior didn't change. I still smoked weed on the way to school regardless of who was in the car.

One day, I picked up Kenny and we fired up a joint as we drove.

I caught Gabby's eye in the back seat as Kenny passed me the blunt. Our windows were cracked to let the marijuana smoke escape. I inhaled deeply and passed the joint back to my friend.

Gabby watched silently from the back seat. She was only fifteen

and knew nothing about weed or the drug culture. She'd heard about drugs in her D.A.R.E. class, as all kids did, but that hadn't prepared her for her brother's own usage.

After school that day, I smoked again as I drove my sister home.

Gabby stared at me with a worried expression. "Hey, Mikey, are you sure you should be doing that stuff? Isn't it dangerous?"

"Don't worry about it," I said abruptly, brushing her off.

Gabby was still close with my parents. My dad drove her to tennis practice and helped her with her homework. My mom ate dinner with her and picked her up from her friends' houses after sleepovers.

I, on the other hand, couldn't be bothered with my parents. They only served as an obstacle and an annoyance.

Meanwhile, my friends and I were experiencing the first symptoms of addiction. In school, we'd been taught that "drugs were bad" and told "never do drugs," but no one had ever taught us what would happen if we actually did the drugs. No one had taught us what it would feel like to desperately need a drug with no hope of stopping.

There was no one to offer help or advice, no one to monitor our mental well-being, no one to look for warning signs in us. We battled in complete silence without any idea of how to reach out or find help for ourselves or each other.

Those of us who sniffed Oxys operated as a small group within the school. We knew the other kids who were using, and we would talk among ourselves.

A typical conversation went like this:

"Yo, Ryan is getting really bad, man, did you see him today? He can barely fucking stand."

"What a moron. He's gonna get caught. He doesn't have shit on him, does he?"

I started to notice the occurrence of something unusual due to my drug use. After binge-using for a few straight days, I couldn't abstain without feeling sick.

After twenty-four hours of not using, I began to sweat. My muscles tightened and ached. I became even more anxious, withdrawn, and depressed.

I didn't understand what was happening. But it was starting to happen to my friends Jeff, Kenny, and Alex as well. It was also happening to other kids who were using Oxy.

We told ourselves, "This just must be how it feels when the drug wears off." We were so young, so naive in many ways. It didn't take long, though, before we realized what was really happening.

One day during English class, I started to feel terribly sick to my stomach. Sweat poured off my skin, and my muscles were tinged with feverish pain.

I raised my hand. "Can I go to the nurse's office? I don't feel well." My teacher took one look at me and sent me to the office.

When I arrived, the nurse walked over to meet me at the door. "What's wrong, Mike?" she asked.

I responded, gripping my abdomen. "My stomach feels awful." Sweat dotted my brows. My joints burned. "I need to use your bathroom."

"Sure, go ahead," she said.

Inside the bathroom, I locked the door. The nurse's bathroom felt luxurious compared to the regular school bathroom. I was going to take full advantage of it.

I took a yellow 40mg Oxy (my friends and I called them "peaches") and a bill out of my pocket. While the nurse waited outside, I smashed the Oxy on the back of the toilet. Then I rolled up the bill and sniffed the chunky line right up my nostril.

Within minutes, I felt like a million bucks. I'd walked into the nurse's office feeling horribly ill. I'd been one step away from having my temperature taken and being sent home.

Now, with one simple sniff, I had been turned into Superman. All the pain dissipated. The sweat stopped. The flu-like feeling subsided. My body felt incredible.

I sauntered out to the office and threw my hall pass on the counter. "I feel much better now," I said, smirking at the nurse's look of surprise. "I'm gonna head back to class."

My body had become dependent on the drug. The sickness that my friends and I felt after not using was the classic onset of withdrawal symptoms.

We were seventeen years old, and we were addicted to narcotics.

All the days of "optional use" and "getting high" were now behind us. In just a few short months of use, my friends and I had to use every single day just to avoid feeling sick.

When my buddies and I had first started using Oxy, we'd made a fun ritual out of crushing the pill and rolling up the bill. There was an excitement to it all that we collectively shared. But by my senior year, I awoke to pre-made lines that I'd carefully constructed the night before, placed atop CD cases hidden in my sock drawer. I would shower, get dressed, and eat breakfast with Gabby. And then, just as I was about to walk out the door to drive us both to school, I would sniff an Oxy.

That was the start of a new ritual called "getting by," which also described my senior year of high school.

On most days, I had a pill each morning to keep me from suffering withdrawal. Some days, though, there was nothing available, and the town was completely dry. Then we all got sick.

The nurse's office became overrun with my friends complaining

76

of flu-like symptoms, trying to get permission to leave school for the day. Unfortunately, we started leaving so often that the nurse began denying us permission. But this never stopped us. If the nurse told us we had to stay in class, we would make a run for it.

Nothing was going to keep us in class while we experienced those kinds of withdrawals.

Needless to say, my grades plummeted. There was no time for statistics homework or studying for biology exams. There was no time for after-school activities or applying to colleges. There was no way to balance a high-school workload and an addiction to opioids.

In an instant, an entire lifetime of hard work at school slipped away. All the homework assignments, all the dioramas, the late nights studying for exams—none of it mattered anymore. I had found new meaning in life…using drugs.

This might have been the time for someone to "save" me, for a teacher or my parents to notice the drop in my grades and the change in my attitude, and to acknowledge that something was seriously wrong. It would have been the time for someone to force me to buckle down and alter my ways.

My mom and dad tried to help. They realized early on that I was heading in a troubling direction. But like everyone else, they were unprepared for the Oxy epidemic. This new addiction was thrust upon the communities before a radical change happened in substance abuse policies. My parents were caught off-guard as much as the schools and the rest of society were.

My addiction to OxyContin grew. By the time I was eighteen, in the fall semester of my senior year, I had to use multiple times a day to keep from experiencing withdrawal symptoms. I woke up in the mornings writhing in agony. I needed to immediately sniff a line just to start the day.

While everyone else around me was preparing to graduate high school or start college, I was stuck in a personal hell of addiction.

Within my small group, I wasn't the only person suffering. Jeff was addicted. Kenny was addicted. Alex was addicted. The only difference was that they didn't sell drugs to support their habits as I did. Instead, they began looking for other means to get money. Most weren't legal.

School life was getting more out of control as well. The other addicts were taking on more risks. There were increasing incidents of lockers being robbed and cars broken into. People were starting to do whatever it took to support their addictions, at whatever cost.

My friends and I had now joined the other addicts sniffing pills in bathroom stalls or snorting pills off our desks when the teacher left the room. OxyContin had a tight grip around our necks and had absolutely no plan to let go.

My younger sister was front and center, watching all this happen.

One morning before school, she came to my bedroom door.

"Mikey, are you ready to go?" she said.

As she spoke, I quickly brushed the CD case and rolled-up bill into my dresser drawer and then swiftly closed it.

"What was that?" Gabby asked.

"Nothing," I said. "I was just rolling up some weed. I'll be ready soon." At her scared expression, annoyance flared up in me. My voice rose to a yell. "Get the *fuck* out of my room!"

Gabby lowered her head and ducked out of my room, closing the door behind her. Her expression said it all. She knew I was no longer just smoking weed. She knew I had progressed into doing something much worse. She knew my life was heading downhill and that she was powerless to stop it.

As my life continued to get more reckless, Gabby bore the brunt

of my actions. She watched as my mom and I had fight after fight over my behavior, some resulting in physical violence, when my mother and I actually pushed or shoved each other. I continued to get caught in lies about using drugs or selling them. This continued the cycle of being kicked out of the house time and time again. I'd camp out on my friends' couches or at my grandmother's house before being allowed back home again. I saw Gabby's heart grew heavy with the knowledge that her older brother was throwing his life away.

At a time when my little sister needed me the most, I was not present in her life. While she sat home coping with our father's absence and wondering if things were going to be okay, I was out getting high. She watched me transact drug deals in my mother's kitchen, sniff pills off my CD cases and dresser, and in the end, almost give my life in the pursuit of a high. All along, she expressed her concerns and fears to my parents and to me, but it didn't change a thing.

Gabby was one of the first of many people in my life who would feel the destructive effects of my dependence. As the years progressed, she would continue to be hard-hit by my addiction to drugs and alcohol. Her story, like the stories of so many other relatives affected by a loved one's addiction, is one of collateral damage. It's a story that is not part of the everyday narrative on drugs.

But it's painful, and it's real.

As Gabby grew older and went to her prom and started school at a prestigious university in Rhode Island, I continued to be absent from her life. That absence is now just another sadness that I carry from a long list of regrets about the wrongs I committed as an addict.

At the time, though, I felt none of that. I was graduating high school and embarking on new endeavors.

Life seemed exciting. And it was…but in all the wrong ways.

twelve

As my senior year progressed, I continued to take risks. I regularly brought weed and pills to school to make sales. One day, a kid approached me in the lunchroom as I slid my food tray down the line.

"Yo, can you do a twenty-bag right now?" he whispered.

It was a small order, but I was never one to turn down a sale.

"I gotta run to the bathroom to get it ready," I said. "Give me the money, and I'll be right back."

I never bagged up my weed anymore. I carried all my marijuana in a plastic cylinder because it masked some of the scent. From my early days in the drug game, I'd been taught that possessing more than one bag meant "intent to sell," which was a whole new ball-game. Plus, I was hardly selling weed anymore because everyone was spending all their money on Oxy.

I went to the bathroom nearest the lunchroom and entered one of the stalls. I pulled some weed out of the container, separating what I intended to sell for $20. High on Oxy and not caring, I'd foolishly left the stall door open.

Since the recent shootings at Columbine High School, my school

now had dedicated security guards patrolling the halls. While I was in the process of separating the marijuana, the bathroom door burst open and a security guard named Jim entered.

At the time, the security guards and school administrators had been starting to pick up on who was using and dealing drugs around campus.

When Jim came through the door, he was on a mission.

As I heard his footsteps stalking purposefully toward my open bathroom stall, I reacted quickly by stuffing the container of weed in one pocket of my cargo shorts and the loose weed I was bagging for sale in another. Still another of my pockets was taken up by a half-eaten bag of Cheetos.

I must have looked panicked and jumpy. Jim, a former police detective, was quick to notice.

"What do you got there, Mike?" he said, motioning toward my pocket.

"Nothing, Jim." I tried to sound as calm as possible, but it was easy to hear the fear in my voice.

"Let me see," he said, reaching for my pocket.

I moved away from him. "You're not searching me, man," I said in a smart-ass way. "You have no cause. I'm going back to lunch."

"You're coming with me to the office," he said sternly, "or the cops can come take you in front of everyone."

His words ignited the fight-or-flight response in me. My brain whirled with options.

What should I do? Run? Plead with him to let me walk away? Give up altogether and admit my guilt?

I was eighteen years old and scared shitless.

In the end, I didn't run, I didn't admit to anything...but I didn't

give up either. I followed Jim down to the principal's office, then sat and waited for the police to arrive and search me. As I waited, fear knotted my stomach, but I was resolute. My inner soldier kicked in, telling me, "You will get through this. There has to be a solution. Somehow, some way. Just remain calm and focus."

The rest of the security staff came in to monitor me and the situation. The office receptionists continued to answer the phones, glancing at me uneasily while they worked.

I didn't have many options at that point.

Then I remembered the bag of cheese puffs in my pocket. Jim disappeared into the principal's office to confer on the situation. A relaxed guard named Steve was assigned to watch over me in lieu of Jim.

Maybe this is my chance.

I casually pulled the Cheetos bag from my pocket and then stealthily slipped in the loose weed. "Steve, I'm done with this bag," I said. "Can I throw it away?" My voice was calm, belying the desperate panic I felt inside.

"Okay, that's fine," Steve said.

I stood up and threw the "empty" bag into the trash can next to the receptionists' desk.

I had just literally thrown away an "intent to sell" charge.

Unfortunately, there was very little I could do about the cylinder container that held the majority of the weed. This was long before I learned to seriously argue my Fourth Amendment right to legal search and seizure.

The principal approached me. He was a tall, slender man with graying hair. He'd always taken an interest in me and would talk to me from time to time about seeing my potential and wanting more

for my life.

"Mike," he said, "we're going to need to see everything that's in your pockets."

"Come on, Mr. Koch, why are you doing this?" I pleaded. Fear laced my voice.

"Mike," he said firmly. "Everything. On the table now."

I reluctantly complied. As I placed everything from my pockets on the table, two Milford police officers arrived.

Mr. Koch met my eyes. "What's in the plastic case, Mike?"

Terror rushed through my veins, paralyzing me.

"It's…my film from photography class." I sounded like a scared child lying about breaking something by mistake.

A police officer stepped forward and opened the container while Mr. Koch watched.

When the skunky marijuana was exposed, my principal shook his head. His face was etched in anger and disappointment.

I put my head down on the table and began to weep. I knew I was in big trouble. The worst part, though, was seeing Mr. Koch's disappointment in me and knowing it was going to be a thousand times worse with my parents.

I was allowed to call one parent, so I dialed my father. I couldn't call my mother because I knew how she would react.

My dad said he would drive over to see what he could do to help me, but we both knew it would be fruitless.

"Turn around and put your hands behind your back," a police officer said.

As he handcuffed me, I became aware of an audience in the office and outside the windows. Teachers, staff, and peers stared at me. A deep sense of shame crawled through me at seeing myself through

their eyes.

A police officer searched the rest of my pockets. "Do you have anything sharp that's going to stick me?" he asked.

I shook my head.

After searching me, the cops walked me out to the police cruiser with my hands cuffed behind my back. Passing students gaped at me, whispering.

My father arrived at school just in time to see the officers pressing my head down so I could enter the back seat of the police car. Through the window of the cruiser, I met my father's eyes as we drove away. The look on his face filled my own eyes with tears.

It was the first time in my life that my father couldn't help me.

He was helpless, and so was I.

I was driven to the Milford police headquarters and charged with possession of marijuana.

I was fingerprinted.

I had a mug shot taken.

I sat in a holding cell for hours.

Finally, I was released on a written promise to appear in court, and my father drove me back to my mom's house. She wasn't home yet.

I went to my room and lay on my bed in silence, waiting for my mother to get home. My mind spiraled out of control. I thought about the repercussions I would face at school, the challenges of finding work with a criminal record, and the stigma that I would face when the public would read of my drug arrest.

Just when I thought things couldn't get any worse, my bedroom door burst open. My mother and older sister entered like rabid wolves.

"You piece of shit!" my sister screamed. "How could you do this to Mom?"

"Michael, you disgust me," my mom yelled at the top of her lungs, her face dark with anger and disappointment. "You should be completely ashamed of yourself!"

They tore me from my bed and unleashed a family-style assault on me like I'd never experienced before. I didn't even try to fight back. In my attempt to get away from them, I fell backward onto my right wrist, which I'd broken years earlier on my BMX bike. It refractured, and later I had to go to the hospital. I wore a cast for six weeks after being arrested—an outward symbol of the pain I'd caused everyone, including myself.

My mother was outraged. She cried for days and called me every name in the book. She told me that I had wasted everything I'd worked for and had embarrassed the family.

Things got worse when I was brought in front of the school board. As angry as my mother was at me, she still sat right beside me as the town administrators revealed my fate.

"Our hands are tied on this, Michael," they said. "The possession of drugs in school means a mandatory expulsion for a minimum of one full semester."

I was immediately kicked out of school. I was a quarter of the way through my senior year of high school, and I could not return.

The thought of not being able to graduate with my class was shattering. I was scared and confused. I also had to face criminal charges for possession of marijuana in the Superior Court. I was addicted to OxyContin. The deck was starting to stack against me, and I had no idea where to turn for help.

Take a breath. You will get through this.

This was not the first time in my life that I'd been dealt more than I could bear. Through the injuries and the divorce, I'd always pushed forward. But this was different. This time I'd created the problem myself. I was the only one to blame. But I was still unwilling to accept responsibility for my actions. I made every excuse I could for what I'd done.

I blamed my parents for divorcing. I blamed Jeff, Kenny, and Alex for dragging me into a life of drugs and crime. I blamed my connects for supplying me with the weed that led to my arrest. I even blamed the security guard for barging in on me while I was trying to bag it up.

Fuck, I blamed whoever I could just so I didn't have to take responsibility for what I was doing to myself.

After I completed 120 hours of community service and drug education classes, the criminal charges were removed from my record. With a month left in my senior year, I returned to school. I was given a tutor for my classes at Foran, with whom I met daily at the local library. She worked hard to help me pass the classes I needed to graduate.

There were still people who saw the good in me, even after all my drug abuse, dealing, and rebellion. One of my teachers, a man named Michael Dzubaty, had always taken a special interest in me and saw my untapped potential.

He taught astronomy, a subject I'd taken an interest in during my time at Foran High, which also happened to have its own planetarium. He was a round, jolly man in his early sixties who played Pink Floyd and The Doors during class while explaining how to spot Orion's Belt or Mars in the summer skies. He had an off-the-beaten-path teaching style, as well as a reputation for being rebellious. He

once got downright violent when the school threatened to shut down the planetarium.

Unlike other teachers, Mr. Dzubaty seemed genuinely concerned about the troubled students. Instead of sending us to the office at the simplest disruption, he met with us after class.

"Talk to me, Mike?" he'd ask me in a gentle tone. "Is something going on you want to talk to me about?"

It was obvious that he truly cared. During my expulsion, Mr. Dzubaty met with me twice a week at Dunkin' Donuts to make sure I would pass his classes. In a time that could make or break the rest of my life, Mr. Dzubaty personally made it his mission to encourage me to stay positive and on track. He also met with my mom and grandmother and told them, "Michael is one of the brightest minds I've ever had in my class." This offered them solace as well.

Miraculously, I passed all the classes required for graduation. Mr. Dzubaty had been instrumental in getting me there.

But despite his help and all that I'd been through—all the shame, pain, school worries, and family distress—in the end, nothing much changed.

Soon, it was business as usual again…

Except this time, it wasn't.

thirteen

2003-2005
U.S. opioid deaths: 12,940-14,918

In the spring of 2003 I was allowed to walk with my graduating class. My family had forgiven me for my arrest, and I was taking steps to fix my name the best I could.

In the eyes of the people around me, I'd made an error in judgment and was trying to right my wrongs. I'd rejoined my friends at school and appeared to be back on track. But very few knew what was really happening behind closed doors. For all the time I'd spent working to fix one problem, I was diving headfirst into a much bigger one.

The day I graduated high school was a bright, hot day. My family and friends gathered in the bleachers of the Foran football field. My relatives were filled with excitement to see their son, brother, and grandson graduate with his class. They knew I'd been in trouble but still had high hopes for me. They were confident I'd use my wits and intelligence to rebound.

The sun shone down in a way that made the day feel even more

important. I saw the excitement in the eyes of my classmates. We were young, and we were about to be free of what we thought were the horrible, restrictive constraints of high-school life.

On that day, all our cares were behind us. We were eager young souls, ready to take on the world. The boys had gotten fresh haircuts, and the girls wore new dresses under their long graduation gowns. With all the preparation, the graduating class of 2003 looked magnificent, and we felt even better.

Sadly, some of us had prepared in a much more sinister way. Prior to walking onstage to receive our diplomas, my group of friends and I had each sniffed an entire 80mg OxyContin off a dusty CD case just a few hundred yards away from where our families and friends gathered to celebrate a bright moment in our young lives.

That was the thing about drug addiction—it didn't have a pause button. Once a user got to a certain point, as we had, it was impossible to say, "I have something important to do today; the drugs will have to wait until tomorrow."

Drugs never waited.

On the day my friends and I graduated high school, we were full-blown addicts. There was no way we could walk onstage to receive our diplomas without being high. There was no way we could shake the principal's hand in front of the large crowd without being high.

So that was what we did.

We got high.

I carried myself proudly down the aisle in front of the people of my town. My family looked on proudly as my name was called and I was handed my diploma. After receiving my tied scroll of paper, I performed a full 360-degree spin onstage in my usual class clown persona. The bottom of my gown breezed over the ground as I spun.

Everyone laughed and cheered on the performance of a young, carefree teenager excited for his future. What they didn't see was the fear and desperation behind my bright smile, the desperation of a scared boy living out the last days of his youthful innocence.

High school had been a place that offered me the only real direction I'd had in life.

Once it was over, I drifted, and so did my friends. While many of our peers started college, we continued down our road of self-destruction.

Although there was a huge population of drug users in Milford, Alex, Jeff, Kenny, and I stayed close. It was still just the four of us against the world. The bond we had as young addicts was strong—or so we thought. It wouldn't be long before that house of cards would collapse around us, too.

After our peers moved away to pursue their future endeavors, most of those left behind were the kids addicted to OxyContin. The culture in my small town was showing signs of serious decay.

Stories began to circulate about robberies at pharmacies in Milford. A graduate of Foran, a guy I knew, was apprehended after holding up a drugstore at gunpoint less than a mile from our school. There were reports of health-care workers being investigated for stealing Oxys from their jobs. As one of the main narcotics dealer in town, these stories scared me. Every time a person was arrested, I didn't know what he or she might say to the cops about me.

At that time, I was unaware that OxyContin abuse had also started to gain national attention. The number of overdoses nationwide had begun ascending, and the government wanted answers. This would be the beginning of a full-blown drug epidemic that would leave more than half a million Americans, more than all of the World War II and

Vietnam casualties combined, dead in the first decade.

In the drug business world, all our moves were planned. We never talked about drugs on cell phones. Any information sent by text message regarding the sale of drugs was in code. We called Oxy 80s "green beans" and Oxy 40s "peaches." We drove with as little product on us as possible, and we used false-bottomed soda cans to stash drugs. Sales were conducted at high speed. Sometimes we used public areas and sometimes we went to homes.

More often, however, we did sales window to window on Milford back roads. A customer would call me for two beans, and I would make sure they were waiting, parked on a residential street, before I even got there. By the time I rolled up, they had the money in hand and their window down. I would pull up, my open driver's side window right next to theirs, and we'd exchange goods for currency in seconds, then drive away as if nothing had happened.

I never stopped to count the money. Clients were loyal to dealers because their ability to get high depended on us. If someone burned a dealer, who then told the other dealers in town, that client would likely not get his fix the next day. The result was an unspoken code between addicts and dealers.

The process of dealing drugs was an art form to us. Pills came in by the hundreds and quickly turned into cash in the tens of thousands. My friends and I sold all day long, got high all night, and partied and had sex with girls who liked drugs. We did this until the sun came up and then started all over again. Even with all the heat and drama, we were still living it up...or so we thought.

It wasn't long until the whole operation began to deteriorate. A federal investigation by the Drug Enforcement Agency resulted in the arrest of one of our suppliers, a married man with kids. He was brought in on charges of stealing and forging prescriptions in order to

obtain Oxy from local pharmacies.

A month earlier, a friend had explained the elaborate plan to me.

"Brandon is having this doctor write him fake scripts," he said. "It costs him like $1,000 a pop, but then he'll get ninety beans for it."

"Are you serious?" I replied. "That's incredible. What's he selling 'em for? I'll take all ninety."

"He doesn't sell them in bulk," he said. "He legit sits on them and then sells them at $60 apiece. He doesn't need the money at this point. He keeps most of them for girls who are hurting, and they'll usually suck him off for an 80 or some shit."

My friend knew all this because he would drive Brandon to the pharmacies in neighboring towns to pick up the prescriptions. Brandon would walk in with a cane, pretending to have a serious leg injury. No one ever questioned him, not even once.

At first, Brandon was only doing a few prescriptions a month. But as that number grew, the DEA caught wind of the operation.

Although Brandon was mostly selling and using OxyContin, he also fell into a ferocious cocaine addiction. While under DEA investigation, he was drugged out of his mind and not sleeping for weeks at a time. He grew so paranoid that he started carrying a microscope with him and asking us to look at his boogers, shit, and blood under the lens to see if bugs were swimming in them. One day, we heard he'd had a full-blown psychotic attack where he thought bugs had infested his entire body. His wife and kids watched as he collected his own fecal specimens from the toilet while ranting about insects.

Eventually, the DEA arrested Brandon and hauled him away. We heard he eventually ended up in a psych ward.

Just like that, someone close to our circle and one of the biggest suppliers in the city was gone.

For our group of suburban kids, the stakes had suddenly gotten much higher. Something we'd originally started off doing for fun was now producing some extremely chilling consequences. As time went on, those consequences began to hit closer to home.

Jeff had been my closest friend since elementary school. We grew up in the same neighborhood and walked to the local park every day after school to play basketball. I was his confidant when his first girlfriend broke his heart. We went through a lot of the awkward days of adolescence together.

After high school, Jeff became the first of us to experience the dark demons of addiction. As he fell deeper into his dependency on OxyContin, it became increasingly difficult for him to fund his habit. He began to run out of options. He couldn't hold down a job because of his struggle with drugs. His parents had cut him off. With no options left to pay for his addiction and an unwillingness to seek help and change his life, Jeff resorted to robbing houses.

A year after graduating high school, Jeff was charged with several counts of larceny and breaking and entering. He was nineteen years old.

Although the courts gave him numerous chances, he didn't show up for scheduled appearances and repeatedly failed drug tests.

At first, he was able to avoid jail time by participating in a lengthy probation and drug education program. But time and again he failed to meet the requirements of the program. The court finally had enough, and Jeff was sentenced to three years in jail. He served six months before being released.

Watching my childhood friend get taken away to prison did little to dampen my fervor for drugs. While I was sad about what had happened, I'd already begun to drift away from him. Dealing was my life now, and Jeff had become a liability. My friends and I were all

now independently fighting to survive.

Our previous ritual of using drugs for fun was now gone. There was no more intrigue or appeal left. The excitement of experimentation had long ago worn off, replaced with a sheer desperation to fill a need. But still I kept using. Dependency had taken over my life. Not a second went by when I wasn't thinking about where I could get my next high. Fear consumed my life. Would I have something for the next day? Would I be sick? Would I be arrested for possession or for selling?

A drug addict lives in a perpetual world of not knowing.

Days would go by when I'd question whether tomorrow would even come. And if tomorrow did come, would it be worth seeing?

On my nineteenth birthday in January 2004, I was living back home again with my mom after having been repeatedly kicked out for my drug use. Gabby was still going to Foran High, and Lillian had graduated college and was making a life for herself in New York City as a high-end nanny for celebrities and wealth managers.

Every day my mom would go off to work in the morning before I woke up. My eyes would peel open around 10 a.m., with my body twitching and burning from withdrawals. I'd lie in bed and stare at the ceiling. My brain was filled with fear, sadness, and regret. The worst was the haunting depression that never left my side. I'd pull myself up and head over to my wooden dresser. I'd open the drawer and pull out the familiar cracked CD case. Then my daily ritual would begin: Smash a pill, sniff it, taste the drip, feel better…for now.

My involvement in the sale of narcotics had sharply increased, but every dollar I made went up my nose. With no classes to attend and very little guidance in my life, I was free to drive around all day selling pills. The amount of money that went through my hands was surreal. Thousands and thousands of dollars came and went on a day-

to-day basis, but all the profits I made simply funded my addiction.

One day I took a ride with John to see his supplier in the next town over. I'd always heard Brett's name but had never met him. He was the main man, though; I knew that much. If something was moving in Milford or any of the surrounding towns, chances were it came from him.

Brett took John and me for a ride in his new Lexus. I sat in the back while John rode in the front passenger seat. We pulled into a gas station, and Brett told John to go inside and get him some cigarettes. When John left the car, Brett turned around to face me.

"Listen," he said, "I know you're moving all the Oxys, and I know John is making all the money. Fuck that. Call me directly from now on." He handed me a matchbook with his cell phone number scribbled on it.

From then on, I called Brett directly. I'd moved up another rung on the ladder. This time, it was a big one.

I never saw my friend and supplier John again. All the time we'd spent together just faded away into the noise of the past. The next time I saw him was years later, in December 2016. He was lying in a casket as his grief-stricken parents sobbed by his lifeless body. Before his death, John had been clean of drugs for a year but had slipped back into heroin after a breakup with his girlfriend. His first bag of heroin had contained enough fentanyl to put him into a coma before ultimately robbing him of his life. The peace I saw on his face in death was in sharp contrast to the hell we'd endured together.

My new supplier, Brett, effortlessly replaced John in my dealing life. The first time I went to his house to pick up drugs, he pulled a Ziploc bag out of his freezer filled with more than five hundred 80mg OxyContin pills. That bag of pills had a street value of over $30,000.

"How many of these can you move?" Brett asked.

"Well, I mean…all of them," I replied, a bit reluctantly. These were major quantities. I was now moving into the territory of federal drug trafficking.

But move them I did. About two weeks later, I'd sold five hundred Oxy 80s at street value. Within the first two weeks of running with Brett, I proved myself and expanded on my already ironclad street cred.

The only thing I was doing more than selling was sniffing. In a short time, I'd gone from using an Oxy 20mg on the weekend to sniffing more than five Oxy 80s a day. Most of the time, I'd be short paying back my connect because my friends and I had used more of the product than I'd sold. This massive new influx of product for sale added exponentially to our level of abuse.

While some people would work all day to scrounge up the $60 needed to buy an Oxy at street level, I would have a hundred of them in my possession at all times. I always kept track of exactly how many pills I needed to sell and how many I could take for myself so that I could pay back my dealer. But the drugs began to overtake all my common sense. Even when I knew that my volume of sniffing pills would push me below the needed payback number, I used anyway.

In 2005, just two years after finishing high school, everything around us was quickly and dramatically changing. With thousands of reports of overdoses rolling in, along with the chilling tales of addiction and dependency on OxyContin, Purdue Pharma began to make its first attempts to pull back its aggressive marketing campaign of the drug. The company even went so far as releasing a new, crush-proof Oxy tablet. The tablet contained a gel coating which, when broken, corrupted the pill so it couldn't be crushed into powder. Purdue, as well as law enforcement and government officials, identified this change as a major step in curbing the growing

epidemic.

Unfortunately, the damage had already been done. The first waves of the incredibly powerful narcotic had pulled me, my peers, and millions of kids like us into a web of addiction that many would never escape.

Around the same time Purdue began to pull Oxy off the streets, the parents, local administrators, and teachers of Milford began to come to terms with the devastating impact the drug was having on the town. Many of my classmates and lifelong friends were now full-on drug addicts. Middle-class kids who came from strong local families were resorting to violence and crime to support their addictions to drugs.

In the past, there'd always been a few fringe problem kids who'd gotten mixed up with the wrong crowd and turned to a life of crime and drugs—but never like this. The most frightening part about what was happening in Milford and surrounding towns was the sheer number of young addicts. Hundreds of kids were caught up in active addiction to prescription pills. Once the stories came to light about what was happening to our community, shock turned to worry over what could be done to fix the problem.

As the town began to wake up to the destruction around us, my parents began to see the more serious signs of my own addiction to Oxy.

My mother had already gone back and forth on allowing me to live in her home. She and my sister Lillian had repeatedly caught me selling drugs from the house, but they didn't know I was dealing to support my own dependency or how far gone I was in my addiction.

One night, I snuck outside around 2 a.m. to put a couple of Oxys in our mailbox so a buyer could pick them up and leave the money. Lillian was staying for the weekend and heard me go outside. She

came downstairs to investigate.

When she looked out the window and saw a car driving down the street with its headlights off, she went outside to take a closer look. When the buyer saw her, he got spooked and drove off, leaving the pills in the mailbox for my sister to easily discover.

She woke up my mom, and together they angrily flushed the product down the toilet in front of me. I'd never seen Lillian so angry and disappointed.

"Selling fucking pills out of our mother's house!" she screamed at me with tears filling her eyes. "I fucking hate you, Mike. I fucking *hate* you, you piece of shit!"

Her words seared into me. I stood there, dazed and high on Oxy, watching my mother and sister cry as they embraced each other, their shoulders shaking in sobs.

I think it had finally become clear to my family by my actions and behavior that I was not only dealing Oxy but addicted as well.

My younger sister was still just a junior in high school, and my mother worried for her safety. I'd had beefs with other dealers around town, which had led to such incidents as my car windows getting broken or our mailbox being smashed with baseball bats.

It was becoming impossible for my mother to allow me to stay in my childhood home without jeopardizing the safety of everyone in the house. Now that she was aware of the level of my addiction and dealing, she was torn between showing tough love by kicking me out onto the streets or nurturing me as she'd always done.

My mother was already overwhelmed by stress and worry from her recent divorce, along with my traumatic accidents and surgeries. The addition of my drug addiction was enough to push her to a place of mental breakdown.

I started noticing a change in her. She became withdrawn, de-

pressed, and anxious. At times, she seemed confused as how to move forward at all. She was a single mother with her plate filled with more than she could handle.

I should have been there to assist and comfort my mother in her pain and struggles, but instead I did the exact opposite by adding another all-consuming stressor in her life. I am still haunted in adulthood by the guilt of driving my mother to daily tears during those years.

But this is the way of addiction. Everyone becomes a casualty.

Unfortunately, at age nineteen, I still wasn't ready for change. Not even seeing my mother's and sisters' palpable pain was enough to wake me up.

For the next few years, I would continue to sell and abuse drugs daily. My mother continued to kick me out of her house in her attempts to gain control of the situation. Sometimes I would go to a friend's house and crash on a basement sofa or floor. Other times, I would seek refuge at my grandmother's apartment in senior housing.

The relationship between me and my grandmother Jane was a complex one. When my mother was young, Jane had walked out of her life, leaving behind her husband and two kids. For whatever reason, Jane decided not to be a part of the lives of her children and her husband for many years. Down the road, my mother and Jane would eventually make peace, and my grandma became an integral part of my childhood.

My sisters and I called my grandmother "Gammy," eventually shortening it to "Gag." From as far back as I could remember, Gag was a major part of my life. She helped my mother around the house, cooked meals, and took care of us kids when my mother traveled with my father on business. Gag took me and Gabby to the arcade to play video games or to the mall to go clothes shopping. When I needed

new parts for my bicycle, I called Gag. When I wanted new skis, I called Gag. If there was one thing to be said about my grandmother, the word "no" was not a part of her vocabulary.

As I began to age into a young adult and, more importantly, as I began to abuse drugs and break the law, my grandmother continued giving me whatever I wanted. Now, instead of buying me skis or clothes, she bought me my first car. When I acted stupidly and crashed my first car, she bought me my second car. Gag paid for my cell phone, and she continued to give me cash for clothes and food. She spoiled me as many grandparents spoil their favorite grandkids. Her love for me was unwavering and unconditional.

From the outside, this may look like a beautiful thing—a grandmother giving her grandson everything he could ever want and need. And for the longest time, it was. But as my problems in school worsened and turned into problems with the law, my grandmother never stepped back to look at the bigger picture. Whenever my mother decided she'd had enough of the dealing and lying and addiction, she kicked me out onto the street. This was her way of cutting me off with "tough love" in the hopes that I would suffer the consequences of what I was doing.

As hard as it was for my mom, she did this with the wish that it would wake me up and bring me back. But every time my mother kicked me out, my grandmother would take me in. Gag did what she did out of love. She couldn't understand that she was playing the role of an enabler.

This began to strain the relationship between her and my mother, and eventually the bond they'd worked so hard to rebuild was once again broken… another casualty of my addiction.

fourteen

2006
U.S. opioid deaths: 17,545

As another year passed and 2005 rolled into 2006, a radical and disturbing change began to occur in Milford. Since Purdue Pharma was aggressively pulling OxyContin off the shelves of local pharmacies, the kids in town were searching for a substitute. Unfortunately, there was nothing close to the potency of Oxy.

Pills like Roxycodone (also called Roxies, 30s, or simply "blues") and other substitutes began to hit the scene, but none came close to the nefarious level of the original OC 80. That version of Oxy held a disgusting and deadly throne in the narcotic hierarchy. For the original addicts in this epidemic, every pill that came after was an unworthy alternate, and weaker pills such as Vicodin or Percocet were certainly not strong enough to calm the withdrawals of our opioid addiction.

One day, while I was at a friend's house discussing ways to score Oxy, someone told me that another drug was starting to find its way

into town…heroin.

To understand the drug trade in Milford and how it ties into the East Coast narcotics underbelly, one must understand where the town sits geographically. Although Milford is a middle-class beach community, it's close to two of the poorest and most dangerous cities in the country—Bridgeport and New Haven. Almost 100 percent of the illegal drugs that enter Milford come from one of those two places. The majority of cocaine and heroin that comes into Bridgeport and New Haven arrives via New York City boatyards, no more than an hour and half drive from Milford.

Since OxyContin was a doctor-prescribed substance, it was a drug that bucked that trend. Oxy users in Milford had nothing to do with our inner-city neighbors, but once the opioid was no longer accessible in Milford, the drug trade between Bridgeport, New Haven, and Milford was given new life.

As in most inner-city environments in America, there was a small trade revolving around designer drugs, pills, and marijuana. But as any law enforcement agent or dealer from Bridgeport will tell you, the big players are the powder, rock cocaine, and heroin from the inner cities.

On the particular day that I first heard about heroin making its rounds, I was out of Oxy. I called all my connects, but they were completely dry too. Then I began calling my buyers.

"Hey, Brian, any greens around?" I asked my buddy who'd given me my very first Oxy pill.

"Nothing, man," he said. "But I have a couple of bags of D if you want 'em."

"D? What do you mean?" I asked.

"Dope, man. I got dope from Bridgeport. I needed something and

it was all I could find," he replied.

Dope. Heroin.

I couldn't believe what I was hearing. How could anyone in a middle-class, suburban community fall anywhere near the grip of such a dangerous and destructive drug as heroin?

The answer to that question went right back to the pill that got it all started in the first place—OxyContin. Whereas most kids who smoked marijuana could never imagine sniffing or shooting up heroin, a massive valley was bridged by the powerful opioid. OxyContin was so potent and created such dependency that it made the transition to heroin extremely plausible.

Just like that, I watched heroin sneak its ugly fucking face into the homes of many of my closest friends.

Since there was a new drug in town plus dwindling supplies of Oxy, my friends and I saw a business opportunity. Alex told me about someone in his extended family who sold small quantities of cocaine in a rough part of Bridgeport. He wanted me to go down there to talk to his relative about getting us drugs at a good price to sell in Milford.

At the time, with such a limited supply of Oxy in Milford and no other connects in the area for drugs, I agreed to meet with a man who would become infamous in my life: "Uncle Nicky." The far-reaching effects of this meeting were something I could never have foreseen in my worst nightmares.

"You guys want a line?" Uncle Nicky asked Alex and me, shortly after we arrived.

It was 2 o'clock on a Tuesday afternoon. We'd stopped by Nicky's house to ask if he knew anyone with Oxys in Bridgeport.

"Sure, why the fuck not," Alex said. I watched him lean over the glass counter and stick a $20 bill in his nose, then suck up the fine

white powder.

"Nicky, did you talk to any of your boys out here?" I asked. "We have a situation in Milford. We can't get shit, man."

Uncle Nicky was a short, pudgy Puerto Rican man. He was about forty years old and five-foot-seven, with a big protruding tummy and a sometimes-playful attitude. He lived on a one-way street in one of Bridgeport's toughest neighborhoods, called The Hollow.

The thought of even walking down that street would induce fear in most. The Hollow was the bottom of the bottom. Gunshots rang out there daily, and the street served as many a police pursuit's final destination. For a sheltered white kid from suburban Milford, this was a place where I would never have expected to find myself. My life was so reckless and out of control, though, that it didn't bother me. In fact, it made me feel as though I was finally part of the urban culture I'd chased so hard in my earlier years.

"I asked around," said Uncle Nicky in a thick accent as he hunched over to do another line. "I can't find any Oxys out here either, homie."

Nicky, like me, was a businessman. Alex had told Nicky about my client base and how I had more customers than anyone else around. There seemed to be a possible business partnership in store for both of us. We just had to see how it would pan out.

In the beginning, my visits with Uncle Nicky were more of a social thing. It was also a chance for us to get to know each other and feel each other out. I didn't push too much and just waited to see what would unfold.

Eventually, I began to spend more time in the inner city. It was a place of urban despair, vastly different than the environment I'd grown up in. Junk was strewn across the sidewalks. Used needles and

condoms littered the streets. An odor of filth and poverty lingered in the air. People screamed and fought outside their run-down houses. There was a perpetual feeling of hopelessness, unrest, and insecurity that never went away. It was a far cry from anything a suburban kid from Connecticut had ever seen.

Finally, after the fifth time I met with Nicky, all the bullshit back-and-forth stopped. I walked in the door one day to see a short Puerto Rican man standing next to Uncle Nicky. Whereas Nicky was a jolly, joking kind of fellow, it was quickly apparent that this other man was not.

Nicky introduced me to Loki, his connect. Loki was a stocky, muscular bulldog with a close-cropped haircut. He emitted a vibe of pure cartel. During the entire time I spent around him, he never once smiled.

"Mike," Nicky said, "Loki can't get you Oxys, but he can get you as much heroin as you want, and cheap."

During that meeting, Nicky and Loki proposed what would become a new operation. They would supply the mid-sized quantity of heroin that I would take back to Milford to sell to all the people who could no longer find Oxy.

It seemed like a perfect plan. The cost for me, being so high up on the dealing food chain, was low. It allowed for a ton of profit.

Before the meeting ended, however, Nicky and Loki wanted one more thing from me. They told me I should sample the product. As an addict, it didn't seem like much of a stretch for me—just a different-colored line.

Nicky chopped up the brown powdered dope into a line and motioned to me.

Without hesitating, I tried my first line of heroin.

That was how things went for an addict. When I first started to experiment with drugs, I had all sorts of preset conceptions and rules. I told myself things like "I would never try this" and "I would never do that." I thought I was just doing drugs because they were happening around me and were fun.

But for those who take it too far and form a dependence on drugs, all those rules are forgotten with the onset of true desperation. All the pride that exists within people, the self-respect that might stop them from ever messing with dope, is nonexistent when faced with the pain of dependence and withdrawal.

I didn't view trying heroin for the first time as some sort of horrible decision. I was an addict, and I'd a found a new way to get high. Simple as that.

For the next few months, my town got familiar with their new drug of choice. At first, I was driving heroin from Bridgeport to Milford and selling it there. But after another falling-out with my mother, I was forced to leave my home yet again. My relationship with Nicky had grown on both the business and personal level, so when he asked if I wanted to move to Bridgeport and live in his house, it made sense.

At the age of twenty-one, I now called the North End of Bridgeport my home. I now walked the same streets that I once would never have set foot on in broad daylight. It didn't faze me to walk to the corner bodega at 3 a.m. with the sounds of a late-night horror show all around me.

Fear and a sense of self-preservation barely existed in me anymore. As opposed to running heroin to Milford, I turned Nicky's house into a one-stop drug market. White kids would pull up at all hours of the day and night to buy cocaine and heroin. Of course, we knew traffic

like that brought unwanted attention to the house and to us, but we didn't much care. For months, we operated as we pleased.

Nicky was a genius with machines and motors, so he installed two night-vision cameras on the porch. He rigged them up with motors from remote-controlled toy cars so he could pan the cameras up and down the street.

He installed a large metal bar over the back door to hold a battering ram in place. There were secret compartments all over the house, and even a secret exit through one of the back rooms. The place was like a fortress.

After we set up shop in Bridgeport, I continued to see the faces of many of my peers from high school. Kids I remembered as National Honors students, all-star point guards, and local Boy and Girl Scouts…one by one, they came to Nicky's house to buy drugs to feed their addictions.

The physical toll showed on their wan faces. The distress and lack of sleep sank their eyeballs. Their speech was fuzzy and sloppy from the opioid's effects on their brains. They wore torn-up clothes and shoes. But for all the effects of addiction that I saw in everyone else, I failed to notice the effect it was having on me.

Within a few months of starting in Bridgeport, my friends and I had turned Nicky's house into a cash cow. I'd never seen this kind of money in all my life. The quantity of cocaine and heroin sold from the house was beyond anything I'd ever imagined. As a dealer in Milford, I'd seen a few thousand dollars pile up over the course of a week. But now several thousand dollars came in with each sale.

People traveled from all over the area to buy large quantities of narcotics from us. With all that money came a certain amount of power—a power that we abused whenever we could.

There was never a shortage of girls willing to exchange their "company" for drugs. As much as our connects capitalized on this, my core group of friends and I were naive enough to think these girls actually liked us or wanted something more from us than drugs…at least in the beginning. Many times, fights broke out upon discovering that someone's girl from our camp had fucked another dealer after our drug-well had temporarily run dry. In our circles, taking another man's woman in this manner was considered the highest form of disrespect, and such behavior undoubtedly contributed to the body count in urban America.

In the end, many of us were left brokenhearted after discovering the true intentions of these female addicts who were slaves to their own addictions.

Even with the amount of money that came in, little ended up becoming cash profit for me. There was always a party at Nicky's house and always someone who wanted to do a few lines. The only thing that outweighed the quantity being sold was the quantity that we were using. Every day we sold thousands of dollars' worth of drugs, and every night we snorted thousands of dollars' worth of lines.

For a while, the business ran smoothly at Nicky's. But over time, things eventually began to disintegrate. Although the money was pouring in, it was just never enough. My friends and I had no idea that when we brought customers to Nicky's house he was going behind our backs and getting their numbers. He would tell us that he had to run out to the store, but he was actually making sales directly to our customers. Because Nicky was undercutting my prices, my customers were more than willing to go to him instead.

One day, I got a call from a kid who had started buying larger

quantities of cocaine.

"Hey, man, can you do two right now?"

"Two what, man? Two grams?" I asked in an annoyed tone. "You don't have to call. Just come down, man."

"No, dude, I need two ounces," he replied.

Two ounces of cocaine was a pretty chunky order. I told him to come to the house with $2,200 and I would take care of it. I waited for a couple hours and ended up getting off-task handling other sales.

Eventually, I remembered and called the buyer to ask where he was.

"Ah, man, sorry, dude, I actually don't need it anymore," he said. His voice sounded anxious.

"What the fuck do you mean, you don't need it?" I shouted. "I've been holding two O's for you all fucking day!"

He hemmed and hawed, acted shady, and said he didn't have the money anymore. I immediately knew something was fishy. Just then, I noticed Nicky returning back home "from the store."

In an instant, I knew what had happened.

Within weeks, most of my buyers were purchasing large quantities of cocaine and heroin directly from Nicky.

In my unstable life as a user and dealer, things had changed again.

fifteen

Along with the shady dealings, my drug use hit an all-time high. My friends and I sniffed and sniffed until we couldn't sniff anymore. We snorted in creative ways such as pouring cocaine on a girl's tits or making art designs on the table before sniffing it up. Days passed. I spent every waking moment of my time bagging up product and snorting lines.

I began to notice the physical effects of such rampant drug use on the inside of my nose. After weeks of endless abuse, the inside of my nostrils entered a cycle of bleeding and scabbing. I became hyper-aware of this during my insane highs on coke. The inside of my nostrils would burn and tickle from the constant bleeding and scabbing, so I took to standing in front of a mirror in the bathroom and digging into my nasal cavity with a razor blade.

That was what my life had become. That was what the drugs had done to me.

As bad as my suffering was, my easy access to drugs saved me in some ways. I didn't have to resort to the low things many others were forced to do in order to keep their highs and prevent withdrawals.

A shocking example of such a low occurred with a close friend of

mine named Alyssa, who'd been my classmate since elementary school. She had a bright smile and was intelligent and witty. She played varsity softball all through high school and maintained strong grades. Unfortunately, like the rest of us, Alyssa had initially experimented casually with drugs for fun, then fell hard into the use of OxyContin…which then led to heroin.

The first time I used heroin with Alyssa was memorable. While I sniffed the soft brown powder off a friend's kitchen counter, Alyssa poured a bag of dope into a spoon and topped it with some water. She lit a lighter below the spoon until the water started to boil, then pulled a needle, syringe, and cotton ball out of her pocket. She put the cotton ball on the spoon to strain the liquid and weed out chunks of impurities that hadn't melted. She used the needle and syringe to extract the liquid through the cotton filter. Then she tied off her arm with a leather belt and jammed the needle point into her skin.

I watched as Alyssa pulled blood from a large vein in her arm. Her eyes lit up with anticipation as her crimson blood mixed with the heroin-brown water in the syringe barrel. She slowly pushed the plunger of the syringe until the bloody brown water filled her vein.

She pulled the belt loose, and it dropped to the ground. Her eyes rolled back into her head in ecstasy.

That was the first time I saw a friend shoot heroin.

It wouldn't be the last.

Of all the spectacles I'd seen in the drug world, nothing was more visceral than watching a heroin addict like Alyssa tap a vein. There was a certain intimacy that existed between the intravenous user and his/her craft that was unlike anything I'd ever witnessed.

In her quest for drugs, Alyssa often traveled to the rough inner-city neighborhood of Bridgeport. She began to meet older Puerto

Rican men who were interested in young white girls from middle-class Milford. As Alyssa's addiction to opioids grew, those men began offering her drugs in exchange for sex.

At first, she fought off the urge to score easy drugs. But as her dependence grew, she gave up fighting the battle. In her case, as in many others, self-respect would take a back seat to drugs. Before my run in Bridgeport came to an end, Alyssa was regularly selling her body to men in exchange for heroin.

One day, she called me, crying.

"Can I come see you?" she asked. "Please, Mike?" I could hear the snot sniffling in her nose and the desperation in her voice as she held back tears.

"What do you want?" I asked. Before she could answer, I said, "Listen, I'm not fronting you shit, Alyssa. If you don't have cash, don't come."

"But I need it," she said, sobbing. "How about if I suck your dick? Then can you give me a bundle?" She said the last words quickly, almost as if she wished she could take them back.

I'd always liked Alyssa growing up. She'd been one of the most stunning girls in our school. Before any of us had gotten into drugs, I'd asked her out on a date a few times. She'd always turned me down.

I was reluctant to take her up on her offer...but what the hell? I'd always been attracted to her, and she sounded so needy. I knew what it felt like to be desperate for drugs. Who was I to judge?

"Please, Mike," she begged.

"Fine," I said. "Just come here. We can figure something out."

I instantly felt sick to my stomach that I'd accepted her offer. In my heart, I didn't want to follow through. Even with all the terrible things I'd done and continued to do, this would be a new low for me.

But when beautiful Alyssa walked in the door and came straight up to me, my morals quickly took a vacation. She caressed my penis, pulled it out, and then put it in her mouth.

Afterward, she got her drugs…and I got another dose of shame and regret after being faced with my disgusting actions.

This was not the first or last time I'd go against my inner compass in the name of addiction. "Giving up" was a common theme for drug addicts. Whenever we attempted to rid ourselves of the drugs and get clean, something else reared up to block our progress. It always happened that way.

Something always drove us back to the destruction, whether it was desperate need, the physical pain of withdrawal, the shame cast on us by old friends or family members, or the guilt of watching our lives slip away. It was easier to do drugs than to deal with the pain.

As addicts, we lived a life of instant gratification. Family members begged us to stop, telling us we could have a nice life down the road. We remembered the good lives we'd had before and saw the contrast with the misery we were now living. But that wasn't enough to tear us away from the drugs.

I continued to sell at Nicky's house and in his neighborhood. One night while leaving his house, I looked in my rearview mirror and saw what appeared to be an unmarked police car following closely behind me.

This was not an unfamiliar sight, but since I'd been sniffing coke all day, I didn't know if my mind was playing tricks on me.

If it was undercover cops, I knew they wouldn't blow their cover, so I decided to try to lose them. When I approached a yellow light, I pushed the gas pedal to the floor and barreled as fast as I could through the intersection. I raced through the back roads of neighbor-

ing small towns, my car picking up speed. I didn't care how fast I was going. I was determined to shake off the unmarked cop car that may or may not have been a product of my imagination. Little did I know that a traffic cop was sitting in a parking lot along the way as I flew by going 80 miles an hour in a 35 mph zone.

With sirens wailing, the officer pulled out and gave chase. Since I had two grams of heroin on me, there was no way I was going to pull over. I took a left in my Jeep Liberty and charged up a hill into an area of winding curves and sloping hills.

As I raced dangerously fast up the dark, tree-lined roads, I was able to keep a good distance between myself and the traffic cop. Since it was a few weeks into winter, the leaves had fallen off the trees and were scattered across the road. As I wound up higher into the hills, I could see down to the streets below. More officers had joined the chase behind me, lights flashing and sirens blaring.

It struck me that since I could see their lights, they could see mine as well. I turned them off. I reached the top of the hill, turned, and headed back down a different street. Now I was flying down a treacherously winding road at breakneck speed with no lights on in order to not be spotted. If anyone had backed out of their driveway at that moment, both of us would have been dead.

Twenty minutes later, I made a few quick turns and got out of the area. I found my way back to the highway and returned to Nicky's house, unscathed and un-caught.

Normally, when a situation like this resolved, I felt calm and relieved. Not today. The panic I'd felt during the chase was hard to shake. I was jittery with nerves. I knew that at any moment the cops could show up at the house.

Luckily for me, they never did. They hadn't gotten close enough

to get my license plate number. Nevertheless, I dumped my car a few streets over from the house and waited a few days before I ran over to get it.

Those were the kind of sketchy decisions I was making in my life—anything to stay out of jail and survive one more night on the streets.

My day-to-day life continued on as before. I was still doing business with Nicky despite his betrayal. He was my main connect, so I'd let it go. Losing a percentage of the business to him was the price I had to pay in exchange for his product and a place to stay.

However, I was in the dark about some other things that were going on at his house. Unbeknownst to me, Nicky had racked up $10,000 in debt over the course of six months. His supplier, Loki, was tired of waiting for payment.

One day, while I sat in Nicky's bedroom, weighing and bagging coke, I glanced up at the camera monitor and saw a man running through the front gate. He was wearing black pants, a black hoodie, boots, and a black hat.

I realized it was Loki.

I'd seen Loki angry before, but this time I could tell it was different by the way he was moving.

We usually kept the back door locked with the metal bar, but today it had been left unsecured due to someone's error. (Kenny was later blamed for it, but no one ever knew who actually left the door unlocked.)

There were three of us in the house that day, including Nicky. We stood frozen in place as Loki crashed through the back door. He approached Nicky purposefully, his face twisted in rage, then whipped out a black 9mm handgun. He pressed it against Nicky's

head.

"Where the fuck is my money?" Loki shouted.

"I'm gonna have it, man," Nicky said, stuttering. "Just give me a—"

Loki pistol-whipped Nicky across the eye, causing it to burst open. He punched Nicky repeatedly in unleashed fury. Blood splattered across the living room floor. Nicky was no match for Loki, and soon his beaten body slumped to the ground.

Even though Nicky was unconscious, Loki continued to pummel him. I knew I was going to see a man die before my eyes. I rushed over and begged Loki to stop.

"Please, man, we'll get the money today," I said. "We have five people coming down for shit."

Loki spun around and instantly shoved the gun against my forehead.

I looked into his dark, blank, soulless eyes and saw a sociopath who didn't give a shit about what happened that day. There was nothing to stop him from pulling the trigger. He was capable of killing all of us if he felt like it, without a second thought or a blip of remorse.

I backed away slowly, my heart pounding and blood rushing in my ears. I sat down on the bed with my hands held up in a praying formation.

Loki turned and went back to Nicky's body, which lay motionless and bleeding on the floor.

"You got one week, *pendejo*," he snarled. "Don't fuck around." He spit on Nicky and walked out.

After that, Nicky took product from various connects and used the money from those sales to pay back a large portion of his debt to Loki. He spent the next few months trying to get the rest. He would

never be fully caught up, though, so we had to look over our shoulders more than ever.

After that, business in Bridgeport deteriorated rapidly. There were repeated problems at the house and an increase in violent crime directed toward dealers and innocent bystanders in the neighborhood. Finally, I made the decision to leave Bridgeport for good.

I packed up the few belongings I had and moved into a friend's house back in Milford. My instincts were right. The violence in Bridgeport had gotten completely out of control. A week after I left, a hardworking bodega owner I'd befriended, a father of three, was shot during an attempted robbery and left paralyzed from the waist down.

Alex also had a falling-out with Nicky and stopped going to the house. The only person who stayed behind was Kenny.

Two months after I left Nicky's house, I got a call from Kenny. He'd just been released from the DEA Regional Headquarters in Bridgeport. He'd been nabbed in a federal raid that had hit Nicky's house along with the house of one of his main suppliers. Loki wasn't part of the raid, but another of Nicky's main connects was taken down.

Kenny explained the details of how it all went down. At around 6 o'clock one morning, just as the sun was coming up, Nicky and Kenny had glanced at the camera monitor saw a van pulling up in front of the house. While most people were sleeping at that hour, Nicky and Kenny were still awake from the night before, bagging and sniffing cocaine. By the time they were able to make sense of what was happening, it was already too late.

A team of ten to fifteen federal DEA agents stormed the house in full bulletproof vests and ski masks. They carried M16 rifles and smashed through the smash-proof back door with ease. With no time

to act or escape, both Kenny and Nicky were taken into custody.

Although Kenny was taken to DEA headquarters and questioned, he was later released without being charged. Nicky would not be so lucky. The raid was a result of a federal grand jury indictment aimed at Nicky and his associates in the Bridgeport area.

Little did we know that over the past few months, the DEA had employed numerous agents for surveillance of Nicky's operation. They'd even used full helicopter surveillance for the two weeks leading up to the raid. The operation was aimed only at distribution-level characters, and for this reason, all the "smaller" fish, such as Kenny and me, were not charged.

When Nicky appeared in court, I was shocked to hear the charges against him.

The results of the investigation were charges of conspiracy to distribute more than 1,000 grams of heroin and conspiracy to distribute more than 1,000 grams of cocaine, along with other drug-related charges.

The biggest blow to Nicky came from the so-called Kingpin Act, which targeted those who possessed large quantities of narcotics and firearms. He was charged with possession of a firearm in connection with a drug trafficking offense, a charge that alone carried a sentence of twenty-five years in jail.

He was locked up for nine years in a federal penitentiary, and we never heard from him again. Years later, I learned he'd been released, turned his life around, and became a devout Christian.

After Nicky's arrest, my family hoped this would be the beginning of change in my life. My friends' families hoped the same for them.

Unfortunately, nothing dampened our appetite for drugs, not even the thought of federal surveillance or prison or the violence we'd

seen…not even knowing it could happen to us next.

As my family experienced more heartache at my refusal to change, they gave up on me a little more. I'd felt them slipping away for years, fighting for me less as time went by. They had no choice but to let me go. I had no intention of seeing the light, and nothing was going to change.

Drugs were my entire world and reason for existing, simple as that.

Nicky's arrest did put a damper on my dealing, however. Although I continued to sell drugs for numerous people over the next few years, it would never be at quite the same level that it'd been in Bridgeport.

The days of unlimited availability of cocaine and heroin had come to an end.

sixteen

2007

U.S. opioid deaths: 18,516

-

In the absence of a large-scale supplier, my group and I resorted to buying drugs on the street. We collected money from other users, bought coke or dope from people selling it on the street, and then sold it back to the users at a premium. That way, we could get our own fixes for free. I spent a lot of time over the next couple years playing the role of the middleman so I could support my own habit.

One cold December night in 2006, I was making just that kind of run. I'd picked up a friend who wanted to buy drugs. A girl I was dating sat in the front seat and my buddy in the back seat. The three of us drove to Bridgeport to purchase heroin, then returned to Milford.

Once we were back in town, I pulled into a gas station to buy a soda. I spotted some cops searching another vehicle but figured they were too busy to notice me.

Unfortunately, they weren't some beat officers searching that car.

They were the Milford Narcotics Team.

Because I was a known drug dealer, the narcotics team immediately noticed me. They dropped what they were doing and let the other driver go.

Before I could open my door to get out of the car, a detective was at my window.

"Hey, Mike," he said, motioning to the front window of my car, "looks like you got a crack in your windshield there. Why don't you get out of the car? Let's talk."

My heart sank. Although I'd been operating mostly out of Bridgeport for the past few months, the police in my hometown were not in the dark about my actions. My travel through Milford had become heavily scrutinized. It had been only a matter of time before this sort of situation presented itself.

I heard the rear passenger door open. The kid who'd just bought heroin got out and ran. I was fucked.

The cops pulled me from the car. I knew in that instant that my life was about to change.

The detectives handcuffed me and placed me in the back of their police cruiser. They swarmed around my car, and within minutes, found what they were searching for: bags of heroin and a folded bill loaded with cocaine.

I was taken to the police station, fingerprinted, and placed in a holding cell. I was officially charged with possession of narcotics and drug paraphernalia, and then released on promise to appear in court.

I called my father and told him what'd happened. The news barely registered with him. He was already so resigned, so worn out and tired from trying to help me, that my arrest just added to his disappointment.

I didn't even call my mother.

Take a breath. You will get through this.

At that moment, I had an inkling of what drugs were doing to my life. Everything that I'd ever valued was gone. My family had all but given up on me in order to save themselves more heartache and pain.

Most of my friends were drowning in a pit of addiction. My friends who didn't use were so disgusted with me that they'd stopped answering my calls. On top of all that, I was due in court on criminal possession of heroin.

Still, with all that stacked upon my back, I wasn't yet ready to change. To me, it seemed all part of the game. The life of a drug addict is a constant, unrelenting grind. Days passed, nights became morning, and the story never changed. My life had become a tunnel of dark, saddening events. But instead of learning from my mistakes and choosing to find a way to prevent them from happening again, I just chalked up the constant problems and harrowing debacles as part of the game we were playing.

A week after my first arrest, I was pulled over in my friend's Lexus en route to selling ten bags of heroin. The same narcotics detectives approached the car, pulled me out, and began searching me without providing a reason. I later found out that it had been a sting operation set up by a local snitch.

The same detective who'd pointed out my cracked windshield a week earlier was the one searching me again. "So, what do you have on ya tonight, Mike?" he said. "Let's see."

"Get off me," I yelled. "I didn't give you consent, and you have no cause for this!"

Within thirty seconds, the detective found a bundle of heroin in my pocket. Once again, I was on my way to police headquarters to be

processed. And once again, I was charged with possession of narcotics and released. In accordance with Connecticut law, the two charges were called on the same docket.

I was now facing two counts of felony possession of narcotics.

My life had spiraled completely out of control.

Sometimes when people described their own downfall, they said, "It all happened so quickly."

They weren't fucking wrong.

It was early 2007. Four years had passed since I'd graduated high school. Many of my childhood friends were putting the finishing touches on bachelor's degrees and entering the workforce. They were looking forward to home ownership, new marriages, families, and bright futures.

Whereas I was awaiting trial on felony possession charges. My family had understandably disowned me. My life was consumed with drug use and criminal narcotics distribution. All I cared about was where I would get my next fix. All the important moments of my life—birthdays of family members, caring for sick relatives, working toward goals, celebrating milestones—meant nothing compared to my addiction. I was a slave to the drugs, but I wasn't ready to admit it.

In March 2007, I took the little money I had and hired a lawyer to defend me against the pending possession charges. In criminal court, my attorney was able to argue that the police did not have reasonable cause to allow a search on the second possession arrest, and it was thrown out.

The prosecutors were willing to offer me a probation period in exchange for a guilty plea to one count of felony possession of narcotics. My attorney told me this would be the best offer I could expect. I reluctantly accepted.

On March 7, 2007, I was found guilty of possession of narcotics and sentenced to two years of court-supervised probation.

I was now officially a convicted felon.

Although it didn't shake me enough to change my life, the arrest and conviction did affect me.

It awakened an awareness inside me that what was happening to my life was detrimental. Unfortunately, the drugs had such a grip on me that it made committing to any real change exceedingly difficult.

I knew the first major obstacle to overcoming an opioid addiction would be getting past the physical withdrawals. It seemed to me that people on the outside never quite understand what it felt like to "hurt." I'd tried to explain it like this:

"Imagine the worst case of the flu you've ever had. Picture tormenting body aches, excruciating cramps, relentless sweats, terrorizing night tremors, and uncontrollable shaking. Your nose gushes fluid, your eyes sting and burn, your skin crawls with the sensation of a thousand insects. You are unable to eat or hold down liquids without retching uncontrollably. You have explosive diarrhea that won't quit. You can't even imagine getting a minute of sleep. Now multiply that feeling times ten."

The thought of having to overcome those terrible withdrawal symptoms is what keeps so many addicts running in place, including myself. I very much wanted to stop using opioids, but the fear of withdrawals rendered me unable to take the first step.

After my conviction, I began to hear stories about a clinic that had opened in a neighboring town. People were apparently going there and being prescribed a medication that was reducing the pain of opioid withdrawal. This medication—a legal drug—helped people remain clean of illegal opioids. Over time, I met hundreds of people

rejoicing in their success with this newfound substance.

Little did any of us know that it was just the beginning of a new threat that lurked in plain sight.

My group and I had seen methadone in small batches around town. We'd heard about it in music and movies. We'd also heard terrible stories of people waiting in line outside methadone clinics, nodding out and drooling on themselves.

Because of the spotlight of law enforcement, arrests, and recent crackdowns, it was becoming more difficult to find a way to get high. When my friends and I learned about this new methadone clinic, it seemed like the answer.

At first, I didn't believe it. Was there really a place that dispensed a powerful opioid to drug addicts to keep them from getting sick? Could we really just stop in to a clinic, get the drug legally, and be on our way? I didn't understand how it was possible.

I decided to check it out for myself. Sure enough, it was possible. After a short intake meeting with a counselor, a nurse, and a doctor, I became a client at the local methadone clinic.

It seemed like a brilliant idea. I would go to the clinic every day, receive a dose of liquid methadone, and start a life free of drugs and alcohol. It seemed easy enough.

But what I didn't realize was that in order to stop using drugs and alcohol, I had to *truly want to stop getting high.*

Initially, I thought I wanted to stop. In the first few months I was on methadone, I abstained from using any street drugs. I went to the clinic every morning and got a dose of the powerful narcotic, which satisfied my urge to use. The nurses at the clinic would congratulate me on "clean time" when I tested negative for illicit substances. They gave out gifts and "bottle privileges" to people who repeatedly tested

clean, which meant those patients could take home bottles of methadone and go to the clinic less often. Some patients even racked up enough clean time to only go to the clinic once a month.

Unfortunately, what everyone seemed to overlook was that methadone itself was a narcotic. I may have been abstaining from the use of heroin or OxyContin, but methadone got me high too. In fact, it got me higher than any other drug out there.

Methadone was a pharmaceutical-grade opioid. Like OxyContin, it had no fillers or cutting agents or additives. What separated it from Oxy, however, was its availability. Instead of having to scrounge up money every day to find drugs, a patient could just pay a monthly fee to the clinic to get a daily fix. The clinic also gave clients the ability to raise their doses to whatever levels they felt they "needed" to hold back the withdrawals.

During my daily morning doses of methadone, I said hello to my friends who were also coming or leaving with their drugs. They were the same honors students, ballplayers, and ordinary kids who'd gone to Nicky's to score heroin. Now, like me, they were also being legally prescribed methadone.

Soon, the clinic was also supporting the habits of Kenny, Jeff, and Alex. By now, our appearances resembled those of homeless men. Our clothes were tattered. Our shoes had holes in the soles. Some of our faces were bloated and others were skin and bones. It was difficult to understand our slurred speech. There was no way to avoid the fact of what we'd become: junkies.

Before drugs, we were regular kids with regular lives. Now we endured a bleak existence of pain and suffering.

The methadone acted as a crutch for a while. Eventually it became just another addiction.

Despite good intentions, the methadone clinic was set up for failure from the beginning. Maybe it was due to a lax attitude toward failed drug tests, or dosage-raising at client request, or not enough oversight. In any case, it didn't work.

The only difference between the medication offered at the clinic and the heroin purchased on the streets was that it was prescribed by a doctor and paid for by insurance carriers. The methadone clinic eventually become a state-authorized heroin dealer.

As I watched what had seemed like a solution to my problem fade away, I was back in the same place I'd been. Except now, I was addicted to methadone. Anytime I tried to break my habit, I ran into the same sort of withdrawals. Only now, the withdrawals seemed even stronger and longer lasting.

Even with the "help" of methadone, I fell back into active addiction. The circle of friends around me, the other addicts in my life, and my inability to break old habits continued to push me down.

I was twenty-two years old and began to ask myself some hard questions. *Have I done something wrong in life to deserve this kind of struggle? Have I been a bad son? Did I cause my parents to divorce? Maybe I'm a bad person who deserves this. Maybe this is all I have or will ever be.*

Until then, I'd always reserved a glimmer of hope that deep down I was a good person and that things would get better.

For the first time in my life, that glimmer was growing faint.

I had no one to turn to.

I'd stopped fearing death. My life was just a cycle of pain, day after day. It seemed there was nothing left to live for.

Somehow, though, I dragged on. That minuscule, barely flickering light told me to keep going. It was far away and out of reach, but it was still there, if barely.

I somehow got to all my probation appointments, and I made it to all my group meetings at the clinic. Every day was a laborious undertaking, a struggle beyond words.

Despite it all, a voice deep inside me whispered, *Do not give up. Don't ever give up.* It was all I had to propel me forward, one arduous step at a time.

The days were long. They seemed to drag on forever. The winters were colder than I'd ever remembered. But I knew I had to keep putting one foot in front of the other. If I couldn't walk, I crawled. No matter what, I just kept pushing forward.

By late 2007, my attempt to rid myself of illicit drugs had failed. With a new addiction to prescribed methadone, I continued to regularly abuse cocaine and heroin. I also continued to sell drugs to support my addiction, though in smaller quantities.

On New Year's Eve, Kenny and I rented a hotel room in Milford and planned to party there until the end of the night. Kenny was deep in his own addiction to drugs, and we continued to spend a lot of time together getting high like we always had. Around 11 p.m., we invited two girls, intravenous drug users who liked to "boot up," or inject drugs directly into their bodies, to come hang out in our room. We now only hung out with girls who used drugs. I didn't know these particular girls very well, but I didn't think much of letting them crash there for the night.

While I'd never injected drugs intravenously, I'd reached a point where I had no problem watching other people do it.

So on the last day of 2007, I watched two girls shoot needle after needle of heroin into their bodies.

It didn't faze me. It was a special occasion, so we all took ecstasy in combination with the other drugs we were using.

The ball dropped. I didn't even notice until it was over.

Another fucked-up year had come and gone. There was no celebration. No champagne bottles popped open. No calls to my friends and family wishing them a happy new year.

Just more drugs. Just more sorrow and destruction.

seventeen

2008
U.S. opioid deaths: 19,582

As New Year's Eve came to an end and the dawn of 2008 began to filter through the hotel room curtains, I finally dragged myself to the bedroom. I felt beaten, fatigued, and depressed as I came down from the ecstasy.

I turned to the group still partying in the living room and said, "Don't fuck up the room." They didn't hear me. I closed the door and lay down on the bed. Sleep had become my only reliable escape.

At 7 a.m., I was shaken awake by Kenny. His eyes were wild and sweat beaded his forehead.

"Where's your wallet?" he said.

"It's right here next to me, man," I said, grazing my fingers across the top of the nightstand.

I sat up, instantly wide awake.

My wallet, with its large amounts of cash, was gone.

"I fucking knew it!" Kenny shouted. "I saw those bitches sneaking around in here, man. I asked them what they were doing, and they

ran."

"How long ago?" I said.

"They just left."

"Go fucking get them!"

Kenny was one of my best friends, but he was also my enforcer. When situations got too hot for me to handle, I sent him in.

He dashed from the room. I threw on my shoes and followed. I flew down the stairs to the parking lot, where I saw the girls getting into their car. Kenny was already there.

When I caught up to him, he had jumped into the back seat of the girls' car before they could get away. They were trying to reason with him. They didn't see me coming up behind the car. I wasn't going to be so easily reasoned with.

"Open the fucking door, you little bitch!" I screamed as I smashed my fist on the driver's side window.

The girl at the wheel whipped her head to look at me, her eyes widening in fear.

Then she hit the gas and took off with Kenny still in the back seat. I rushed to my Jeep, jumped in, and set out in hot pursuit.

The girls' old car flew down Milford's busiest street, racing through red lights. It was 7:15 a.m. on New Year's Day, with early-bird families going about their business. Soon I caught up, doing 70 in a 35 mph zone down Route 1.

As I approached the girls' rear bumper, I flashed my high beams repeatedly.

Without warning, she flipped a swift U-turn in the middle of the street and headed in the opposite direction. I did the same. When I caught up, she again turned and drove the other way.

This happened over and over. Every time I caught up to the thief,

she slammed on her brakes and flipped a U-turn. I finally got tired of this little game.

I sped up, raced past her, and cut in front of the car. I slammed on the brakes, *hard*.

The girls' car crashed full force into the back of my Jeep. The impact lifted the back end of my car up over their vehicle's hood.

In a rage, I jumped out of my car and raced to the driver's side of their car. I bashed my fists against the window, screaming as I tried to pry open the driver's locked door.

The thief and her friend cowered in their seats.

I gestured to Kenny in the back seat. "Bro, unlock her fucking door!"

Kenny unlocked the door and threw it open, shouting. "She called 911, man!"

Fuck.

I screamed at the girls to return my wallet and the cash.

"We don't have it!" they shouted.

Sirens sounded in the distance.

I turned to Kenny. "Bro, I'm outta here. Get my wallet back."

"I got it handled, man," he said. "Get out of here, *now*!"

Since Kenny had no drugs on him, I knew he'd manage the situation. The girls had needles and drugs, though. They wouldn't be willing to talk to the police. Kenny would stay with them until he recovered the money.

The sirens came closer. I drove off.

When I got back to the hotel room, I went straight to the bathroom. I splashed water on my face to calm myself down. I stared at myself in the mirror, my mind whirling as I tried to take inventory of what had just happened.

I grabbed a white towel off the counter to dry my face. Something caught my eye.

My Coach wallet sat on the bathroom counter, previously hidden by the towel.

Shock jolted me.

Had I made a serious mistake?

Were the girls telling the truth?

With shaking fingers, I opened the wallet.

Nope, all the money was gone. I'd had $2,000 sandwiched between the interior folds. It was all missing.

Just then, the door flew open. Kenny rushed in with a look of panic and terror.

"There's a hundred cops out there," he shouted. "They're fucking everywhere, man!"

He handed me $600 that the girls had given him, telling him it was all they had.

Later, people would ask me if there was any chance that Kenny had been in on the scheme or had pocketed some of the money. I quickly shot down those accusations. "He would never. That kid is my *brother*."

The cops never did find us. They milled about outside the hotel for a while, then finally went on their way.

I went to bed that night unsure of what the morning would bring. The next day, I got a call from the mother of one of the girls. She sobbed while asking if I knew where her daughter was. She told me the cops had recovered the girl's cell phone records, which showed her daughter had been in contact with me before the 911 call.

I told the woman that I had no idea where her daughter was. I could hear the fear and pain in her trembling voice. For a moment, I

felt as if I were talking to my own mother. Guilt punched my heart.

It would be days before either of the girls would surface and return to their grief-stricken families. When the cops finally caught up to the girls to interview them, their story was one of pure fiction.

They told the police that they'd hidden my wallet as a joke, and that I'd chased them down in a drug-fueled rage. They said Kenny and I had assaulted them and tried to kill them. At first, the police believed their story.

After talking to the girls, the police interviewed both me and Kenny. I pleaded with the cops, asking them to call me first if they were going to arrest me. I promised I would drive down to the police station and turn myself in immediately. I begged them not to come to my mother's house. They agreed.

At home, I gave my mom a whitewashed version of what'd happened on New Year's Day. I wanted to prepare her in case the cops broke their word and contacted her. I promised her, once again, that I was done dealing and using drugs and that I'd learned my lesson. I also convinced her to allow me to live in her home again.

In April 2008, four months after the New Year's incident, the doorbell rang. It was 1 a.m. I opened the door to a squad of officers standing on the doorstep. They barked loud, commanding orders at me.

My mom woke up and rushed out to see what was going on. The cops, in purposeful defiance of my request, poured through the front door of our home, handcuffed me in front of my sobbing mother, and took me away.

As the police car drove me to the station, despair flooded my heart. I was haunted by the memory of my mom's devastated face. I was furious at the police who'd pretended they would let me turn

myself in, but there was nothing I could do. The cops were showing me who was boss, punishing me for all the crimes I'd slipped away from. My innocent mother was collateral damage.

Once again, I was back in front of a judge in Milford Superior Court. Only this time, there would be no simple slap on the wrist.

I was charged with twenty separate crimes, ranging from attempted assault to strangulation to reckless driving. The authorities threw the book at me in every way they could. They even hit me with two counts of felony unlawful restraint, a form of kidnapping in Connecticut's legal system. It seemed this was their chance to punish me for all the wrongs I'd ever done, in one fell swoop. I was already on a five-year suspended sentence for my previous crimes, so these added charges sealed a fate I didn't want to face.

Things were as grim as they could get. These were major violent crime felony charges that each carried a ten-year sentence. If convicted, I would do 80 percent of my time in jail. This time, it wasn't a matter of if I was going to prison, but when and for how long.

However, luck was on my side for once. During preparation for trial, the authorities found many inconsistencies and fabrications in the girls' stories. Time and again, the girls missed court appearances and failed to respond to inquiries by the state's attorney. The court then learned that they were wanted in other towns for credit card fraud. Eventually, the charges against me were dismissed. It felt like some sort of miracle.

In August 2008, I pled guilty to one charge of reckless driving and was placed back on probation.

It was the biggest sigh of relief I'd ever breathed. I couldn't believe I'd actually skated away from this one and had my life back. I was supposed to be behind bars, and it was a huge stroke of luck that I

wasn't.

Even with a righteous victory, the damage had been done. The case had taken its toll on everyone involved. My family had been certain that I would face jail time if I was convicted. My mom was disillusioned and heartsick. Once again, she'd believed in me. And once again, I'd let her down.

I was back on the streets. This time, I didn't have my buddy Kenny by my side, at least temporarily. Since he'd also been charged with various crimes, his mother blamed me and vowed to keep us apart. As usual, our separation didn't last long, and soon Kenny and I were hanging out again, away from the prying eyes of our parents.

As the year went on, my life continued its downward descent. Every "rock bottom" was found to be shallower than I'd thought. Things just got worse.

But the story wasn't only about me. My small, tight-knit town continued to reel from the outbreak of addiction and drug-related crimes. Everywhere I looked, I saw another distraught mother or father or sibling, helpless to save their beloved family member's crumbling life.

The ages of the kids experimenting with drugs continued to get younger. Teens in our community continued to lose classmates to overdose. The biggest wake-up call for the town came in the form of a beloved girl named Ashley Kaufman, a former classmate of mine.

One afternoon, she was dropped off alone at the emergency room. She was nonresponsive with a pallid complexion. The doctors quickly figured out that she was dying of a heroin overdose. They tried valiantly to revive her, but it was too late.

The news of Ashley's death spread quickly.

When I heard, I assumed it was just a rumor. I'd known Ashley in

both middle school and high school. She'd always been a great kid—a strong athlete and student with her head on straight.

"How could this happen to her?" I asked. "It's impossible."

But it was possible. At twenty-three years old, Ashley was gone.

Unlike other overdose cases we'd seen in Milford, Ashley was not a longtime user. In fact, I'd never once known her to use drugs. She'd graduated from Foran High and gone on to attend the University of Connecticut, graduating with a bachelor's degree in communications. The last thing I'd heard, she was about to start law school.

The story just didn't make sense.

Details began to emerge about the night Ashley had died. I learned from friends that she'd fallen in with the wrong people and had begun to experiment with cocaine. That had eventually led to heroin.

It was difficult for me to imagine how someone with so much to offer the world could get involved in the ugly, desolate world I'd learned to call home.

One night in 2008, two men from Milford had gotten a hotel room with Ashley across from the town's bowling alley. I knew one of the guys, but barely. I'd heard his name and seen him around at a few parties, but that was it. Both guys were older than me and intravenous heroin users.

While Ashley was with the two men, they either injected her or helped her inject cocaine and heroin into her veins. The mix, commonly known as a "speedball," had notoriously sent some of even the most experienced drug users to an early grave. The dose was too much for Ashley's small, intolerant body to handle.

The story around town was that the two men didn't notice until the next morning that Ashley was pale and nonresponsive. Instead of

driving her to the hospital to save her life, the two men did nothing. Maybe they thought she would come to, or maybe they were afraid of being arrested.

In any case, they didn't call for help. Instead, time ticked by. They went to breakfast, then returned to the room to use more cocaine and heroin next to Ashley's lifeless body.

Hours later, the men dropped Ashley's body off at the emergency room. It was 1:30 p.m. By that time, it was too late.

The news hit the town like a ton of bricks. Everyone knew Ashley as a sweetheart. She was a college grad, a cheerleader, a hard worker. She could win over a room with her beaming smile.

Ashley Kaufman's story was all over the news. It became the tipping point for a town that had already lost so much.

A year after Ashley's death, both the men she'd been with that night were charged with manslaughter. One of them had the charges upheld in court and was sentenced to ten years in jail, which was eventually suspended after five. Many people felt the penalty wasn't harsh enough, and the town debated what had happened that fateful night.

The town was finally awake. Parents, teachers, and community leaders had had enough of the drug epidemic that was paralyzing the community. Milford went into lockdown, and 2008 became the year that ended many careers for users and dealers alike.

The courts stepped up monitoring and penalties for possession. The cops began cracking down harder on anything drug-related. Parents began taking a firm stand with their kids early on. Schools started putting more effort into education and prevention. The community wasn't going to allow any more kids to fall through the cracks.

Unfortunately, there was an entire generation who already had.

After Ashley died, something in me permanently changed. My mind was no longer the same. Ashley's death, in conjunction with all that had happened to me and all that I'd seen, caused me to take a step back and reflect on what my life had become.

But all that reflection still wasn't enough to force change in me. I could dwell on the pain, trauma, and waste as much as I wanted, but I was still unwilling to commit to fixing the problem. I still refused to take the difficult, necessary steps to create a new life for myself.

Another year marched on as I continued my downward spiral with no end in sight.

eighteen

Memorial Day 2008 started
out like the many others before it. I picked up twenty grams of
heroin, bagged it for sale, and went to a friend's house in West Haven
to handle my calls. I hung out at his house, eating, drinking, and
sniffing large amounts of heroin and Xanax bars.

Although the amount of product I was selling was even smaller
now, I continued to sell heroin to support my addiction. Through my
years dealing, I had acquired many customers…and a few enemies
along the way.

That day, my cell phone was ringing off the hook as usual. I was
about halfway through $2,000 worth of product when I received a call
from another dealer in the area. He explained that his supplier was
out of town, so he needed some dope to hold over his customers.

It was not out of the ordinary for me to assist a fellow dealer.
When we weren't at each other's throats competing for the large
client base in the area, we sometimes helped each other out. I handled
the call just like I did any other. I rounded up Jeff and Kenny, and we
got in my new Infiniti G35 coupe, a car I wished I could have bought
myself rather than sniffing all my money up my nose. Instead, my

grandma had once again jumped in to pick up the slack.

Our plan was to drive over to the buyer's neighborhood, make the sale, and return as quickly as possible.

As I approached the house, the buyer sauntered toward my car. He was shirtless and wore a gold chain around his neck. He smirked as he drank beer from a red Solo cup.

I hated people from this area. They radiated a sense of trash and betrayal. But money was money, and besides, I had Kenny and Jeff with me in case anything went wrong.

I rolled down the window as the buyer approached.

"You know the deal," I said. "Cash first."

My goal was to just make the sale and get out of there. But as always, there was a problem. That was just the way things worked in this business. The buyer was either short on the money or the bag was too small or there was some other issue…always something to jam things up.

Assessing me with his darting beady eyes, the buyer said he wanted two grams of heroin for $300. That wasn't a large sale, but it wasn't a ten-bag of weed either. He grilled me at length about the product before he would hand over his money. I assured him that the bags were weighed and on-point and that everything was good to go. His skepticism grew.

"Just give me the shit first," he said. "You think I need to beat you?" He pulled out a wad of cash to prove he had the money.

I knew he was trying to "flex," or show off. I'd already been bickering with him for about two minutes, which was way too long in my book. The tension was growing. I had two choices: Either give him the product or walk away from the sale.

I was idling in the driveway between two suburban homes. It was

the middle of the day. Men mowed lawns, women called to their kids, and the smell of barbecuing meat wafted through the air. An innocent world surrounded my devious dealings. No one knew the danger that was brewing.

I stared the buyer in the eyes. He gazed back, unblinking. Neither of us made a move.

With the clock ticking and my boys sitting with me in my car, I finally decided to give him the bags. Before I got my hand fully out the window, he grabbed the dope and trotted away.

"You're beat, bitch," he said snidely over his shoulder. He sauntered off with a drunken air of arrogance and accomplishment. Not only was this a way for him to rob me of my product but also a way for him to break me. He was testing me to see how far he could push me before I retaliated.

I was out of the car in about ten milliseconds. I rushed after him, my eyes fixed on my product. At the same time, I saw a different man—the buyer's compadre—jump out of the bushes on the side of the house. He'd clearly been waiting for this moment.

The second guy ran at me full speed and tackled me from the side at the waist. He'd picked the ideal time to attack me, just as my foot hit a deep hole in the gravel driveway. My assailant's weight drove me hard toward the ground as my right leg jammed in the ravine.

Crack! Something gave way in my leg. The sound was unmistakable. White-hot pain shot through my ankle. I fell to the ground.

I lay there stunned, trying to figure out what'd just happened. My attacker pummeled me with his fists and feet. I was immobilized due to the blinding pain in my leg, so I couldn't move or defend myself. The buyer joined my assailant and began savagely beating me.

Kenny and Jeff rushed to my defense and took the men down. As

Jeff threw blows at the buyer, Kenny wrapped his massive arms around my main attacker and choked him unconscious.

Spasms of agony seared through my ankle. I glanced down at it to take visual account of the damage.

My shattered ankle was twisted at a 90-degree angle. The fibula bone poked through the jaggedly torn skin, a white knob against a raw, bloody background. For most people, that would've been the time to call for help and wait for the ambulance to arrive.

Unfortunately, people in possession of large amounts of narcotics didn't have such luxuries.

"Get in the fucking car!" I screamed at Kenny, my voice hoarse with pain.

Kenny grabbed my product back from the assailants, then jumped into the driver's seat of my black sports car. Jeff hopped in the back. I dragged myself across the gravel driveway G.I. Joe style until I reached the front passenger door. Gritting my teeth in agony, I managed to open the door and pull myself into the car using the handle above the jamb as a handhold.

As Kenny struggled to shift the six-speed manual transmission into reverse, the neighbors of the buyer came out and saw him lying motionless in the street. Assuming that we were the aggressors, they ran toward my car while simultaneously writing down my license plate number.

"Hit the gas, fucking go, man!" I yelled.

We sped away, leaving the man lying unconscious in the street. My mind raced between two repeating tracks. One was fear of what would happen if the cops pulled us over, and the other was horror at the sight of my mangled ankle gushing blood with the bone protruding through the shredded skin. My stomach churned.

Take a breath. You will get through this.

I'd been in dire situations before and survived. I knew I could make it through this one, just like I had all the others. Although the urgency of my situation was dizzying, I was somehow able to maintain a stoic, military-like vigilance. It was as if all the past years had been training for this moment. Somehow, despite the fight-or-flight adrenaline coursing through my veins, I was able to make calm, measured, rational decisions in the middle of chaos. My ability to think clearly in the middle of pain or horrifying events had become well-honed after years of trauma. I'd already dealt with a ruptured spleen, internal bleeding, shattered bones, and the pain and struggle of withdrawal. Now, tasting my own blood or seeing my flesh torn down to the bone barely affected me anymore. A mangled ankle was just another casualty of the drug game.

I urged Kenny to take me to an out-of-town hospital. I was too well-known in the community to take a chance at the local hospital. In the back of my mind, though, I knew I wasn't going to escape so easily this time.

Before we headed onto Interstate 95, I convinced Kenny to stop by his house to stash my product.

"Hide it good," I said. "I might not be back for a few days, so keep it safe."

Kenny dashed into his house and stashed it in his sock drawer before we started on our way again.

As we raced through side streets in the direction of the hospital, I felt relieved that I no longer carried enough heroin to put me in prison.

As the highway entrance beckoned ahead, two hundred feet from the on-ramp, any sense of security went out the window. Suddenly,

my car was surrounded by an entire squad of the West Haven Major Crimes Unit, undercover detectives, and the city's narcotics team.

Time slowed down. As the police executed their "felony stop procedure," I sat in the passenger seat, numb, with my hands raised toward the sky. There was constant commotion around me, but I was nearly catatonic, barely aware of who or where I was. My leg throbbed. Mentally, I knew my time was up.

That sense of unflappable military awareness was now gone. My heart pounded and my breaths came out in shallow gasps. I sat motionless, like a scared kid waiting for instructions…or better yet, for someone to physically carry me out of the car. My shattered leg pulsated with harrowing pain.

The cops surrounded the car, shouting orders. "Get out of the car! Get on the ground, face down! Interlock your fingers behind your head. Do not fucking move!"

My friends were the first to follow the orders.

A cop, no more than twenty-two years old, peered in at me through the open passenger side window. His face was mere inches from mine. It crossed my mind that he and I were the same age, and yet we were worlds apart. His path was one of dignity and promise. Mine…not so much.

He pointed a 9mm handgun at my face. He looked terrified, gripping the gun nervously with trembling hands. He'd clearly never done anything like this before. It wouldn't take much for his finger to pull the trigger. Chills raced down my spine. A wrong move on my part, a slip of his hand, a misfire…in an instant, I could be gone. Dead.

Things slowed down more, the effects of both physical and emotional shock taking hold. I looked around, trying to process the scene

happening around me. It was complete chaos. More than twenty officers swarmed the middle of the busiest intersection in the city, some directing traffic around my parked car, others surrounding me and my friends.

Jeff and Kenny lay facedown in the middle of the road, hands cuffed behind their backs, begging the officers to give me some sort of medical assistance. Everything moved slowly, surreally, without sound. The effects of shock were quickly bearing down on me.

The rookie officer leaned in, screaming orders in my face. "Get out of the fucking car! I'm not going to ask you again!"

I pleaded with him, trying my best to explain that I was incapable of getting out of the car.

"I don't care if your leg is fucking *gone*!" he shouted. "Jump out now and get facedown on the ground!"

Somehow, I managed to throw myself out onto the hard pavement. Gravel skinned my knees and bloodied my elbows. The officer's boot pushed hard into my spine before he cuffed me.

While I lay prone on the ground, uniformed officers searched every inch of my body. The narcotics team pulled apart my vehicle looking for the drugs and gun that my assailant's neighbors had told police I possessed.

I was thankful I'd stashed my heroin at Kenny's house.

I was not so lucky that I still had $3,500 cash in my pocket.

The police immediately confiscated the cash and began speculating among themselves why anyone would carry around that kind of money. The guessing ended when the narcotics team revealed to the uniformed officers exactly who I was.

The officers searched me repeatedly while I lay whimpering on the asphalt in pain, my mangled bloody leg hanging off my body.

Finally, one of the officers propped my foot up on a golf bag pulled from the trunk of my car.

I lay facedown for more than an hour, with my splintered ankle resting on the makeshift prop as terror and confusion swirled through me. The pain was agonizing, but it was overshadowed by my fear of what was going to happen to me legally.

Eventually, an ambulance arrived and took me to Milford Hospital. I was admitted to the emergency room and given X-rays. After that, I was handcuffed to a hospital bed and quarantined in a small room surrounded by police officers.

As the shock wore off and my sense of reality slowly returned, the pain in my leg got worse. My entire body trembled in pure, unmedicated agony. I was unable to focus on anything but my hellish suffering.

Whereas most patients would have received kind words of support and heavy medication to suppress that kind of pain, I was denied all relief.

Instead, I was met with looks of disgust from both the police and medical professionals at my involvement in the drug trade that had crippled the community.

"He deserves it," I could see them thinking.

Even though I understood the town's anger, I couldn't understand why I was being treated so inhumanely, so cruelly. I was a human being, after all. Hadn't the medical professionals taken an oath to put aside their personal feelings and care for the patients who needed it? What had I personally done to these people that I deserved to be so invisible while in the throes of obvious suffering?

Because of my connection to drugs, I was no longer seen as a person, deserving of even the most basic care. I was a throwaway.

It was only years later, after fully realizing the error of my ways, that I gained the perspective to understand the nuances and scope of the situation. I learned that every day, doctors and nurses treated victims of drug abuse, overdose, and drug-related injuries. They were on the front lines of addiction tragedy and understood it firsthand. In their eyes, I was not just another person being destroyed by this disease, I was one of the main perpetrators of this menace. They saw innocent people being harmed and killed because of individuals like me. In their view, I was the cancer that plagued my town.

Because of that, my humanity was erased.

My X-rays came back, and the doctor explained that my tibia and fibula bones were completely shattered. In short, my ankle was fucked. The physician told me that I needed immediate surgery. It was the kind of news I'd hoped to never hear again.

This time, there would be no attentive family hovering by my bedside. There would be no well-wishers checking in on me. There would be no flowers or get-well cards brought to my room.

I was alone.

I left the hospital several days later with two metal plates and more than twenty screws holding my ankle together, along with a fresh set of criminal charges pending against me.

As much as my family had given up on me, they still were unwilling to let me live on the streets with such a physical handicap. I left the hospital and started down another lengthy road to recovery at my mother's house.

Whenever I'd encountered this type of trauma in my life, I always went into a deep seclusion. I lay in bed and thought for hours about how far my life had gone off track. This time was no different.

After so many problems, returning home wasn't easy. For the first

few weeks, my travel was restricted. I was forced to endure a high dose of verbal "shelling" from my family for my poor decisions. My mother begged me daily to go to rehab and address my drug addiction. She pleaded with me to get rid of my cell phone and to stop talking to people who she thought "brought me down."

Instead of taking to heart my family's hopes that I would see the light and change, I continued heedlessly with my destructive lifestyle.

The rest of 2008 continued to be a drug-addicted blur, just like previous years. "Bad luck" and trauma continued to follow me. The only thing I took away from my terrible circumstances was a belief that I had a family who, despite all odds, would be there for me no matter what I did or how many times I did it.

Little did I know how close I was to losing them forever.

nineteen

As 2008 marched on in a drug-fueled madness, I again found myself on the streets. A new friend, Ramon, took me in and let me crash at his house. My latest home was now in an infamously rotten part of New Haven called "The Hill."

Ramon was a short Puerto Rican kid from a rough part of town. I'd met him through friends on the scene and eventually developed a close friendship with him. He hadn't had the easiest life, and we saw eye-to-eye on a lot of things. We definitely understood each other's pain.

While living in New Haven, I began getting my supplies from new connects, since Nicky's house had been shut down by the feds. Unfortunately, the area was even hotter with police presence than Bridgeport had been, as clamps tightened on the narcotics rings running in southern Connecticut.

One night I drove my Infiniti to a small New Haven housing project to pick up a "finger" of heroin. A finger was ten grams of rock heroin that I would blend to powder in a coffee grinder.

After picking up the product, I sat at a table alone in a hotel room I'd rented for this sole purpose. Like a twisted scientist, I spread out

all my tools on the small wooden table: a digital scale, hundreds of wax paper bags, and a trimmed straw to move the powder.

For two straight hours, I methodically ground up the dope and bagged three hundred and fifty $10 bags of the drug. I then stacked and rubber-banded those bags together into packs of ten called "bundles."

While I bagged up, I treated my nose to heaping piles of the product. Although I'd always used more than everyone else, by now the quantities were atrocious. I'd sniff through a normal addict's entire week of heroin in one sitting. I'd fade in and out of consciousness as I put rubber bands around the final bundles.

When I was finished with the bagging, I piled the thirty-five bundles of heroin into a Ziploc bag, put the bag in my cargo pocket, and walked out the door.

This was substantially more product than I usually carried on me at one time. In combination with the five-year suspended sentence I already faced if I was charged with *any* crime, this could easily put me in jail for twenty years if I got caught.

I climbed into my car, threw it into third gear, and started mashing the gas as I flew toward the highway. At that point, I didn't give a fuck. I didn't care about my life, the law, anything.

I wondered if I'd ever truly cared.

Sirens blared behind me. I pulled over.

My heart raced.

I can't breathe. Stay calm. Roll the window down. Don't panic.

…How can I not panic?

"Good evening, Mike," the cop said. "Where you headed tonight?"

How does he know my name?

"Evening, officer," I said, as calmly as I could. "I'm just headed

back to my mom's house."

"Oh, really, back to your mom's? Do you have your license and registration handy?"

I wasn't going to pull any argumentative bullshit. Not tonight.

"Of course, officer. Hang on one second." I reached across to my glove compartment. My hands visibly trembled.

"Mike, are you aware that your license is under suspension?" the cop asked.

Fuck.

"I'm not, sir. I must not have received the letter from the DMV."

Please don't ask me to step out of the car.

"Why don't you go ahead and step out of the vehicle, Mike?"

Motherfucker.

I stepped out of the car. My legs shook so hard the cop must've heard my knees knocking together.

"Turn around and face the car," the officer said. "Put your hands up on the roof."

I'd been searched so many times in the past that it was a familiar scenario. But never had the fear been so palpable inside me as it was now. I wanted to scream.

The cop's hands slowly patted down my shoulders. He moved to my abdomen, and then patted my waist. He reached into my jacket pocket and pulled out $5,000 in cash, wadded in two rubber bands.

"What do you do for work, Mike?" he asked in a jovial tone. Clearly, he already knew the answer.

"Just odd jobs around the house for my grandmother, mostly," I blurted like a moron. As soon as the words came out, I wanted to take them back.

The cop gave a nod to another officer who'd just arrived on the

scene. The new officer picked up his radio and walked back toward his car.

I was completely fucked. I knew it. The cops knew it. I was one second away from spending the next quarter of my life behind bars.

The officer resumed the search, and I felt his hand sliding close to the cargo pocket that contained three hundred and fifty bags of heroin.

As his hand brushed over my clothes, I thought of being back in the cell. *No. I can't do this again.* My heart pounded. I swallowed against a dry throat. The officer's hand moved down and passed across my waist again. My mother's sad eyes rose up in front of my mind. *God, please, no.* His hand slid over the pocket containing the drugs. My heart stopped. *This is it.*

His hand kept moving, down to my bare ankles and then to my socks.

When he was finished, he said, "Okay, go sit on the curb over there. We're going to search the car now."

Wait. What?

I couldn't move. I almost fell over in relief, right there in the street. But instead, I dragged my legs over to the curb and watched as the two police officers searched my car. They found nothing.

One of the cops approached me. "Mike, we're gonna cut you a break tonight. Do you have someone who can come pick you up? You're going to have to leave your car here in the parking lot."

"Um… sure, officer. I can call my friend to come get me."

I sat on the curb for twenty minutes more, with enough heroin hidden in my pocket to put me away until the age of forty-five. When Kenny pulled up, I immediately sprang up to get into his car.

As I walked over to what looked like the promised land, one of

the officers grabbed my shoulder from behind.

My heart dropped.

"Don't forget your money, Mike," he said, handing me the wad of cash. "Or your license. And get that straightened out with the DMV, okay?"

"Oh, right, thanks, officer," I said. "I'll get right to the bottom of it."

I couldn't believe what'd just happened. I told Kenny the story as he drove me back to Ramon's. We celebrated with a night of nonstop coke-bingeing. Before the next evening swung around, I'd sold off the thirty-five bundles for almost $4,000 in cash. I picked up my Infiniti from the tow lot a few days later.

I never did get my license situation straightened out.

A few nights later, after getting high on cocaine and Xanax all night long in New Haven, I fell asleep at the wheel and drove my Infiniti into a wooded area off the highway. After plowing through two metal light-posts and a guardrail, I hit several trees, flew off a cliff, and came to rest at the bottom of a deep ravine.

After lying in the car stunned for about ten minutes, I kicked my door open and rolled out. I looked up at the massive hill behind me and saw numerous motorists yelling down to me. "Hey! Are you alive down there? Help is on the way!"

My car was now on fire and black smoke barreled onto the highway.

None of the concerned citizens had any idea how I'd gotten into such a horrific crash. But of course, I knew how it had happened.

As the bystanders continued to yell to me from the embankment, I sat down on the cold ground and stared out into the woods. It was four o'clock in the morning. Nothing moved. I slowly exhaled. My

breath was illuminated against the night air in puffs of white clouds.

Once again, I found myself in a major predicament that I didn't know how to get out of…a problem of my own creation.

The paramedics and police soon arrived on the scene. Blood gushed down my forehead, over my nose, and into my mouth. I knew I was injured but didn't know the extent.

When I'd skidded off the road and into the trees, every airbag in the car had released and inflated. As I ping-ponged down the hill, bouncing off trees and rocks, I was cocooned in a protective pillow. But as I neared the bottom of the ravine, the airbags had begun to deflate. By the time I came to rest at the base of a massive oak tree, my face had smashed against the steering wheel numerous times. The result was a large gash on my forehead that pulsed blood.

When the paramedics arrived, they chalked up my slurred speech to the bad blow on the head. They didn't know I was slurring my words because I was messed up from a coke binge and sniffing Xanax all night.

After a few hours in the hospital, I was released with nothing but a pat on the back from the doctors and reassurance that things would get better.

Things didn't get better.

Not long after the crash, I was in a drug-ridden part of the inner city of New Haven so my dealer could sell a large amount of heroin. I no longer had a car since the crash, so a girl I often got high with was driving. My dealer and his friend were in the back seat. I sat in the front passenger seat.

As we rolled up to the dilapidated house, my dealer called the buyer from his phone.

"Yo, I'm outside," he said. "Hurry up."

The buyer exited the shack wearing torn clothes. He approached the car with purpose, his nose dripping with snot. I immediately sensed something was wrong. As he got closer, he picked up speed. He pulled out a large black revolver and pointed it at our car as he strode toward us.

I couldn't roll my window up in time. I shouted at my friend to drive away, but she'd pulled up too close to the car in front of us. A quick getaway was impossible.

The buyer was at my car window in an instant. He shoved the revolver against my forehead.

"Everybody, empty your pockets!" he shouted.

My dealer tried to reason with him. "You sure you wanna do this, bruh? I know you. I know your brother. You know me. You know I'm gonna come back, baby. Count on it."

The buyer yanked the gun off my head and pointed it at my dealer's temple.

The dealer paused and then gave in. "All right, go ahead," he said to us. "Give the man everything you got in your pockets."

We complied.

I was irritated with the girl driver. As a veteran of these kinds of window transactions, I knew to *always* leave enough space in front of the car for a fast getaway in case things went sour. Because of her rookie error, we'd had no choice but to hand everything over.

As we drove away, I glanced over at her. Tears streamed down her cheeks. Her seat was soaking wet, dripping with urine. When she'd seen the man run toward our car with his gun drawn, she'd pissed her pants.

Weeks later, my dealer told me that he went back to that house with his team and guns of their own. They got back everything that

was stolen, plus some.

To me, it didn't matter one way or another. I soon forgot about the whole thing, as if it'd never happened. I'd become less affected by events that would scare any normal human straight.

My life was now in free fall. Because my car had been totaled when I drove over the cliff, I had no vehicle. I spent the beginning of 2009 on the streets. Many of my fellow addicts in Milford shared a similar fate. We all suffered. Court cases stacked up against my friends and associates. We wandered with no purpose in a hazy fog of drugs.

One morning, the dealer who'd been with me during the New Haven robbery woke up and decided he was going to have some fun. He threw on a ski mask, grabbed his .45, and went out robbing street dealers in the area. I never heard from him again.

I never knew if he died or got locked up. He just disappeared.

Then there was the story of Ben Singer.

Long before I began using opioids, I'd met Ben at a party on the beach in Milford. After some time, I began selling marijuana to him and his friends. We lost contact, but a few years later, he called asking for Oxys, which I sold to him. Eventually, he began buying heroin.

Ben was an acquaintance of my family. He'd met my father while doing work for my uncle's construction business.

One day I heard Ben had stopped working because he'd been diagnosed with cancer. I couldn't believe it. It was shocking and tragic. He was so young.

Ben began coming to me on a regular basis to buy large quantities of heroin. He said he needed it to numb his pain. I had empathy for his situation because I knew what it was like to live with constant pain. When I sold him heroin, I justified it in my mind by telling myself that I was easing his suffering.

Whenever Ben came to see me, he had IV lines in his arm. He told me horror stories of dialysis and the excruciating pain of chemo. He had very little hair and wrapped bandannas tightly around his head. He looked feeble and pale. He had open sores dotting the length of his arms. The cancer was clearly taking its toll.

Ben told me how much the heroin helped with his pain. He said it was the only way for him to get through the day. Because of my deep compassion for what he was enduring, I went out of my way to cater to him. I sold him whatever he needed, and as much as he required.

He was dying, so instead of buying a few bags of heroin at a time for $50 to $60, he brought me $500 to $2,000 a week. He was a drug dealer's best friend.

After a while, he told me he'd burned through all his savings. His parents were now giving him money to live on.

I didn't care much about where the money came from. Every time Ben came to see me, I made hundreds of dollars plus heroin I could keep for myself. It was a never-ending flow of money. Part of me loved it.

Sometimes, though, I thought of Ben's family and his girlfriend. I felt guilty about selling him the heroin. I rationalized that I was helping him, but that didn't stop me from feeling horrible about being the supplier of narcotics for a person living out his final days on the planet.

Ben bought heroin from me every day for months straight. One day, I stopped hearing from him. I worried that his cancer had taken a turn for the worse. Had he died? While I was sad, I tried not to think about it too much. I did what I normally did and pushed it out of my mind.

Days later, I got a call from Ben's girlfriend, who had never been a fan of mine. I prepared for the worst, thinking Ben had died of cancer. I heard anger in her voice the moment she spoke.

She told me that earlier that day, the police from the next town over had raided Ben's house and arrested him for bank robbery. All the money that he'd said was from his savings or his parents was in fact money he'd stolen from Milford banks at gunpoint. In his desperation to purchase heroin, Ben had resorted to donning a ski mask and robbing bank tellers in broad daylight. His girlfriend was furious that I'd been selling him heroin. She believed that practice was what had forced Ben into robbing banks.

After his arrest, I continued to worry about Ben's health. I knew he was in great pain from the cancer and that he would never get the medical care he needed in jail. I felt terrible for fueling Ben's addiction, which had led to him being put behind bars. Guilt washed over me like a flood of dirty water.

Not long after, I got a call from my father that sent me reeling.

"Mike," he said in a tense voice. "I just got off the phone with Ben's girlfriend. He's been lying to us all along. He doesn't have cancer. He had us all fooled the entire time."

I was stunned, flabbergasted. I couldn't believe this news.

For the first time, it struck me how far ordinary people turned addicts would go to get drugs. Ben had told his entire family, his girlfriend, and all his friends that he had terminal cancer.

He'd gone to extreme lengths to feed his addiction. He'd shaved his head and told everyone he knew that he'd had another round of chemo. The IV lines he carried in his arm 24/7 for supposed dialysis were instead there for easy drug access to his bloodstream. After picking up heroin, he would simply screw needles into the female end

of the IV line and dump heroin into his blood without ever popping a vein.

By the time Ben was sentenced for armed robbery, there was no one left by his side. The grief he'd caused his family was too much for them to bear. They'd thought they were losing their child to cancer when instead it was to lies, betrayal, and drugs.

The last time I heard about Ben, he was facing multiple felony sentences, sitting in a courtroom alone with not a soul in the world to lean on.

I knew from experience that the main thing that gripped an addict so tightly was the thrill of instant gratification. I compared using drugs to shopping on credit. People could buy whatever they wanted and get all the pleasure associated with the purchase, along with the option to pay for it later.

Unfortunately, like with credit, there always was a catch. Instead of paying a high interest rate to borrow money, addicts paid in additional pain and suffering. That instant high ended up costing much more than they ever originally thought.

In my own journey through drugs, I'd come to realize that the shelf life of an addict was short. Most addicts either died of their addictions, got locked up, or—possibly, and against all odds—found a way to correct their course before it was too late.

In 2009, I looked around and noticed that there weren't too many of us left. Many addicts I knew were either dead or locked up. My friends and I were still around, but barely, as we wallowed in abject misery. We floundered, too far gone to get help, while our clean peers succeeded in their jobs, got married, started families, and created promising futures for themselves.

I told myself that at least I was still alive, even though I'd been a

full-fledged addict for seven years. I wasn't incarcerated. I was still hanging on.

Still, everything in my life had fallen apart. My goals and aspirations had vanished. I'd battered my body. I was pale and worn-down.

My family had continued their lives without me.

My sisters were gone. My extended family was gone. They no longer believed that I would ever be able to swing it back around. Only my mom, dad, and grandma still hung in there, but barely.

For years, my grandma had enabled me in the belief she was helping me. My dad had been there every time I'd needed him, despite the endless disappointment. My mom had taken me back home, time and again. She'd begged me endlessly to get treatment. Her cries fell on deaf ears.

Now I could see that they were all losing hope. They were giving up on me.

To be honest, so was I.

I was hurtling through darkness, alone in a world of addiction and despair.

twenty

2009

U.S. opioid deaths: 20,422

"Can you go out and meet some buyers outside?" Ramon asked. "I don't feel like going out there."

As friends and roommates, we sometimes did favors for each other. Ramon sold, too, and although I didn't know his customers, I trusted that he wouldn't send me into a situation I couldn't handle. After all, we were close friends who'd shared a lot of pain. We had each other's backs.

"That's straight, man, what are they buying?" I said.

"Just a $60 bag of yay. No big deal," Ramon replied. He strictly sold "yay," or coke.

As I ran the bag outside for him, the buyers—six fresh-faced kids who couldn't have been more than eighteen—pulled up in an old, beat-up Buick. They were scrunched in the car like sardines. In some ways, they reminded me of my crew when we were a little younger.

Since I'd just sniffed just over a gram of coke, I felt paranoid as I approached the car.

The driver rolled down his window. "Let us look at the bag," he said.

I laughed. "You've gotta be kidding me, right? Gimme the fucking money or go fuck yourself."

There was some back-and-forth heckling, so finally I agreed to show them the bag. I opened the rear driver's side door to the car, thinking they couldn't get away easily. I held out the bag.

Without warning, the passenger snatched it. "*Go!* Fucking go!" he screamed.

The driver hit the gas.

Without thinking, I jumped onto the door jamb and held onto the top of the Buick as it took off. Part of me figured they were young kids who would stop before anything serious happened.

They didn't stop.

The driver sped down the street at top speed, weaving back and forth to try to knock me off. I gripped the car tightly, my heart pounding. The driver took a sharp left that threw me off the car and into the middle of the street. I hit the ground with a crashing thud, then rolled and skidded on bare skin until I finally came to a stop. I lay there for a few seconds, my heart pounding. I was still alive. I was in severe pain, though, and barely able to move. I finally pulled myself to my feet and assessed the damage. I was covered in road rash. My entire body oozed with blood. But there were no broken bones, and no damage to my head or face.

I hobbled back home to recover and used whatever was around the house—old bandages and socks—to apply pressure and treat my wounds. I spent the next few days writhing in pain but eventually recovered. That event left deep, visible scars on my body and set off a street feud that would lead to further violence between ourselves and

the older members of the crew the kids ran with.

The violence around us in New Haven continued to grow as well. I slowly inched up the chain of connects in the area, just like I had in Milford and Bridgeport. One of my new connects, known as "Toper," was near the top of the chain. He would often drive his BMW 7 Series to New York to pick up kilos of coke and then cook them into crack, which then supplied many of the street-level dealers in New Haven.

Toper was a Puerto Rican dude in his early thirties who strongly resembled the rapper French Montana. He wore all black, had an extremely unpleasant demeanor, and moved in circles where bringing automatic weapons to drug deals was standard procedure.

One day Toper came to meet me with his neck and leg swathed in bandages.

"I need to borrow your car," he said, referring to my current vehicle, a BMW 3 Series that had yet to be totaled like every other car I'd ever owned. "I want to take it for a ride."

I let him borrow my car, only to learn later that he'd used it to pay a "little visit" to some people who'd shot up his vehicle a week earlier in another town. I didn't want to know the result of Toper's confrontation or what it entailed, just like I didn't ask questions when I saw the left side of his BMW 7 Series riddled with bullet holes.

I didn't want to know shit. The less I knew, the better.

As the year pressed on, I fell in with a new group of nefarious people. I'd had a falling-out with Ramon, so I found another place to crash. I packed my small knapsack of belongings and moved into a dingy loft apartment in my hometown.

As always, with new people came new addictions—and new pressures. One night, while partying with these "friends," one of them turned to me and asked, "Hey, man, have you ever smoked hard

before?"

I was already so high; I just didn't care anymore. In that old, dirty loft apartment, I took my first hit of crack cocaine.

The high was instantaneous and intense.

It felt like cocaine but a thousand times stronger. My mental alertness was immediately heightened. My jaw clenched, and my teeth involuntarily ground against each other. I felt a sense of euphoria and energy. But just as quickly as the high came on, it left. It was replaced by intense feelings of paranoia and guilt. My heart raced, and my brain felt clouded and dirty.

The only thing on my mind, however, was "How can I get more?"

-\/\/-

Crack cocaine was often considered an "inner-city problem," but it had found a way to slither into Milford. My city was once again alive with a new addiction.

In the months after I started smoking crack, I lost the last iota of control in my life. From then on, my only daily goal was to score crack on the streets. My addiction to heroin had subsided because I was still getting a daily dose of methadone, which took care of my dependency on opioids. My only penalty for failed drug tests at the clinic was the loss of bottle privileges. Although I had to go to the clinic every day, that didn't bother me. It had become part of my routine for getting more drugs.

My addiction to crack also increased my use of Xanax, which I began taking to "come down" after a long night of smoking or sniffing blow.

The daily grind of buying drugs on the street and supporting an addiction weighed on my body. With addiction, I was mentally in a prison of chemical enclosures. At times all seemed lost, but that ironically made things easier. Feeling as though I'd reached rock bottom was strangely freeing. There was almost a sense of peace in knowing I had nothing left to lose, where nothing more could be taken from me.

Still, I kept trying my best to beat the addiction's tightening noose. At one point during 2009, I made a half-hearted attempt to go back to school. I'd always wanted to get an education, but there was no way to balance a rigorous college workload with a full-time addiction to drugs—so I quit what mattered less to me. It wasn't the drugs.

All I had left was a tiny bit of faith that things might one day get better. But as my attempts to get clean repeatedly failed, all hope faded.

During that time, my mom was not only grieving her son's drug addiction, but she was also the sole caretaker for her father, who was in late-stage Parkinson's disease, cancer, and dementia. He'd suffered through the effects of these diseases for a decade, but his condition had recently worsened.

My grandpa, whom we called Pop-Pop, was a World War II veteran who'd raised his children alone after his wife, Jane, had left. He was a compassionate, loving man who lived for his family. He and my mom had formed a deep, unbreakable bond, and their love for each other was undeniable.

While I was growing up, Pop-Pop was at all my birthday parties, baseball games, and class plays. I loved him dearly, but in my addiction, I'd grown apart from him, just as I had from everyone else

in my family.

One day, out of sheer desperation, my mom asked if I could help her with Pop for a bit. I had nowhere else to go, so out of my own desperation, I agreed to temporarily stay with Pop to help out.

At my grandpa's old 1900s house, I was responsible for handling basic duties related to his care. I tried my best to do a good job. But…I was still first and foremost a drug addict.

One day, while Pop lay convalescing in his bed downstairs—at a time when I should have been caring for him—I sneaked up to the attic to smoke crack. As I blew acrid smoke out the tiny window, with the bitter aftertaste of drugs and shame coating my throat, I thought, "I'm the shittiest human being on the planet." I realized the addiction was my primary love, above every person in my family, including the most honorable man I'd ever known.

It was the lowest moment of my life.

Once it became clear to my mother that I couldn't balance caring for my grandfather and my drug addiction, I was back on the streets. The demon now had me fully in its stranglehold.

My family stopped talked to me and checking up on me.

I now operated off the grid, with no monitoring and nobody to tell me what to do. I was a freight train with no brakes, on old rusty rails, just waiting for a day to skip the tracks.

My life was completely out of control. I was in crisis. And I was alone.

I'd given up all hope for my life. I began wandering the streets with no purpose.

I contemplated dying. I thought about leaving the world and all the problems behind. I didn't have a concrete plan to end my life, but I pictured what the world would be like without me. I wondered

who, if anyone, would miss me when I was gone.

As 2009 dragged on, another Christmas passed without my family. Another New Year's and birthday slid by. I'd endured such great pain, but nothing was different. Wasted days passed in a slow, excruciating blur.

I was completely defeated. No matter how much I wanted to get off drugs or how much the thought of dying scared me, I was even more frightened of stopping. I was terrified of the physical pain that would come along with cleansing myself of opioids. I was scared of what my "friends" would think if I told them I was getting clean. I was unable to face myself or be honest about the problems in my life.

More than anything, I was petrified that I would fail.

So I continued on my path, the drugs flogging me toward my grave.

The addiction had finally won.

twenty-one

2010
U.S. opioid deaths: 21,089

Just when everything seemed too far out of reach and impossible... something happened that afforded me a flicker of hope.

In early 2010, I was assigned to a new officer at my court-ordered probation office. Her name was Ellen. My other probation officers had treated me like I was just another loser criminal to pass through their doors. But something about Ellen was different. She was stern but compassionate. She recognized that I was struggling. She began offering me sincere help.

Ellen turned out to be the person—the ally—I needed in my life.

She understood my story and still saw potential for change in me, even through the layers of tragedy and pain that showed in my eyes and face.

Ellen's greatest strength was her ability to see through my bullshit. As an addict, I had become a master manipulator. During my time on probation, I had been able to fool all of my prior officers with

every excuse in the book. When a urine test came back positive for illegal drugs, I claimed I'd had a rough week. I would tell them about my problems at home, or the physical pain, or the mental anguish I suffered, and that I'd "slipped up" as a result. The probation officers would tell me, "This is the last time," but when it happened again, I would find a new excuse. They might have thought I was going to eventually get it together, but I would have just kept on making excuses forever.

The first urine test I gave during Ellen's tenure came back dirty for opioids and cocaine.

"Mike, don't let it happen again," she said.

I shrugged it off as just another empty warning. Two weeks later, I returned and gave another dirty urine. Two days after that, I got a phone call.

"Mike, this is Ellen."

"Hey, Ellen, what's up? Is everything okay?"

"So here's the deal," she said in a calm yet direct tone. "Your last urine came back positive for opioids, cocaine, and benzodiazepines. You have two options. You can check yourself into detox today, or I will report that you violated your probation and you will serve out your entire five years in prison. Your choice."

Ellen sounded impassive. It was as if she'd given this speech a thousand times before.

I was speechless at her ultimatum. I fumbled for words. "Well, I don't know what to say…I…I…haven't even used any drugs in weeks."

She listened as I rambled with my usual excuses.

At her non-response, my tone turned defiant. "The test is wrong. I want to come back and pee again."

"Mike," she finally said in a level tone, "those are your choices. I need a decision by tomorrow at 10 a.m. I'll talk to you then." She abruptly hung up.

I stared at the phone in my hand.

What just happened? What the FUCK just happened?

What happened was that on June 18, 2010, my probation officer pulled my fucking card. It had all finally caught up to me. There was no more running. All my wavering back and forth and reluctance to change was halted with one phone call.

This was my first true intervention from the outside, and it happened at just the right time. I was finally ready to stop. I was worn out, and I couldn't go any further. I still had trouble imagining a life without drugs, but deep down, I knew that freedom from my addiction was what I truly wanted. Most addicts needed to come to the decision on their own for it to be effective. I was the rare case who just needed a little extra nudge from someone to activate my desire to stop. And I got it.

Still, I had never been so scared in all my life. Within a few days, I would be violently withdrawing from opioids…and I knew what that meant.

I stood on the precipice of a cliff looking down into the frightening chasm of the unknown. Everything in my life was about to change. Could I do it?

I was familiar with the usual MO of addicts. Many entered detox centers with no plans to actually change their lives. Some did it to satisfy a court order, and others did it to get off the streets short-term for "three hots and a cot," or three meals and a warm bed to sleep in.

I knew one thing for certain: I had no choice but to go into the treatment facility or I would go to jail, simple as that. The thought of

going to a long-term rehab away from everything I knew filled me with fear and trepidation. But it was the mental change I needed to make most.

I stood at a fork in the road.

I could either continue down the path I was on or make this change and alter my life forever. I could stay comfortable and remain on the road leading to my demise…or embrace this difficult decision that could save my life.

I decided to leap off into the terrifying abyss.

With my decision, though, I soon learned I would not have to take this arduous trek alone. As soon as I agreed to enter a facility for care, my family came back into my life. In the midst of my confusion, pain, and fear, they opened their arms and drew me in to support and comfort me.

The family who had every reason to turn their backs on me did the exact opposite. My mother's eyes filled with tears when I told her I was going to get help. My sisters hugged me and told me they loved me. My father told me that he would be there for me no matter what, and that he believed in my ability to change. Ellen called and offered encouraging words to boost my spirit.

On June 22, 2010, I entered into the Southern Central Rehabilitation Center in New Haven, Connecticut, and started the journey that would forever change my life.

As I waited for hours to get seen, my mother sat loyally by my side.

When I was finally admitted, the nurse asked what specifically had brought me there.

It was difficult for me to answer that question. I had been on methadone for years, I was a longtime user of synthetic opioids and

heroin, I had acquired a terrible cocaine habit, I drank out of control, and I abused prescription Xanax.

After I told her about my history, the nurse called in a doctor to evaluate me to see if I could even be treated at the facility or if I needed a higher level of care. The doctor and nurse conferred at length about my situation. They wanted to make sure they would have enough supervision on hand as I would likely need twenty-four-hour monitoring due to my plethora of addictions and dependencies. After an hour in the office, I was finally admitted into the facility.

Over the next five days, I endured the gruesome pain and suffering of opioid withdrawal that I'd dreaded for so long.

For five interminable days, I writhed in bed, moaning and bathed in sweat as my body spiked with fever. My body trembled and convulsed uncontrollably. I vomited every few hours, retching in agony. I struggled to sleep. When I did doze off, the nightmares were scenes straight out of a horror movie. I bolted awake in puddles of cold sweat, unsure of where I was. My skin crawled and danced with invisible bugs.

It was the worst kind of hell. Terrible, dark thoughts invaded my mind as I fought a personal battle with the single-minded demon that was used to coming out victorious.

On the rare occasions that I was able to, I phoned home. I told my mom about the physical and mental pain I endured. "I don't know if I'm going to make it," I said through sobs.

She was always there for me on the other end of the line, soothing me and being my support.

"The pain won't last forever," she said. "Just hang in there, Mike. Stick it out and you will come out the other side. You can do this."

She was right. The pain didn't last forever. After five days of with-

drawals and medical monitoring, my suffering finally came to an end. I was worn out and traumatized, but I'd made it.

When I was released from the detox facility, I felt as though I'd just been on the front lines of a battle and survived.

Ordinarily after withdrawal, a patient would then transfer directly to an inpatient rehab facility. But Ellen had only ordered me to go to detox and then maintain a drug-free lifestyle. Although she strongly urged me to admit myself to a long-term facility, she was unable to compel me into one.

The day I left SCRC, I went back to my mother's house. I didn't call my buddies or any of the people I usually hung out with. I sat in my room and dug deep into my soul.

I'd been clean from drugs for only five days and was still having intense withdrawals and physical pain. The doctors had warned me that the effects of years of opioid dependence would not disappear in a week, but rather would take months and months to fade away. I had a long road ahead of me. I began to consider using the services of an inpatient rehab facility. I could use the help. But did I really want to voluntarily enter a hospital where I would be locked down and unable to leave for thirty to forty-five days, or even longer?

Once again, I had options. In the past, every time I'd been given a chance to take control of my life and make a wise decision, I'd failed myself. I'd always taken the easy way out.

As I sat in my room in the long days after leaving detox, I felt as though I could possibly go down that same route again. But there was one thing that continued to tear at my soul—my mother.

She so badly wanted to believe that this was it, this was the time when I would finally give her what she'd been hoping for all these years. For so long, she'd hoped against hope that I would finally be

ready to change.

Mom sensed I was struggling and urged me to voluntarily enter the inpatient rehab facility.

"Michael, please go to rehab," she said. "You need to get away from everyone and everything for a while. It's what's best for you right now."

I tried to assure her that I didn't need it. "Mom, this time is different, I promise. I'm clean. I feel really good about it this time. Please trust me. I don't want to go away for so long, Mom. Please…" I was like a scared child asking not to be left alone in a dark bedroom after a bad dream.

I looked in my mother's eyes and saw someone who was also torn between two options. She wanted to believe that things would get better, that her son could figure it out and turn his life around and stop the pain and heartache that had lasted for so many years. But she was also realistic. Even as she smiled with hope at my words, her eyes filled with a sharp tinge of pain. I watched her hold back tears as she remembered all the times I'd told her the same thing in the past and had not followed through with my promises.

It was the middle of the summer. The weather was warm, and I often went outside to the back deck and stared up at the sky. I was doing that one day when my mom came home from work and asked, as usual, how it had gone for me that day.

I lied and told her I'd spent all day calling different rehabs and setting up appointments.

In truth, I hadn't. I was still pondering whether I was ready and able to commit to all the life changes that would come with long-term sobriety.

When I saw the glimmer of optimism in my mother's eyes, I

couldn't imagine hurting her again. I couldn't bear dashing her hope for the last time, as I knew in my heart it would be.

Three days after I left detox and eight days clean of opioids, cocaine, alcohol, and Xanax, I decided to voluntarily enter a forty-five-day residential rehabilitation center in central Connecticut. I'd made attempts to get clean in the past, but this was my most serious drive for sobriety.

I felt a sense of purpose for the first time that I could remember, a feeling I'd lost long ago.

I packed my ripped jeans and stretched-out shirts in a duffel bag and then made the long drive to the facility with my mom and dad. Even though my parents' relationship was strained from mistrust and betrayal, they always came together in my time of need.

During the drive to Connecticut Valley Hospital, it was as though a veil was lifting from my eyes. I saw clearly for the first time what had been happening to my life.

I'd spent years looking for someone to blame for my problems or searching for an escape or an easy way out. I had watched while counselors and therapists had placed the burden of my addiction on others. I had sought out every shortcut possible to solve my problems.

For the first time in my life, I knew what I had to do.

It was time for me to accept what my life had become, to take responsibility for my actions and stop blaming everyone else. The only way I was going to get clean was to realize that I was the only one who could truly fix me.

It was time for me to do something I had avoided doing for so long.

It was time to grow up.

twenty-two

When I arrived at the massive inpatient hospital, the reality of the situation began to sink in. This was really happening. One of the worst fears for every struggling addict is a long-term stay at an inpatient rehabilitation facility…and here it was, unfolding before me.

We parked the car, and I walked into the hospital lobby with my duffel bag. The staff searched me for drugs and weapons, and then I signed myself in. With fear pinching my heart, I turned to say goodbye to my parents.

It would be weeks before I would be allowed to see anyone from my family again.

As I walked through the heavy metal security door, a strange sense of calm washed over me. As scared as I was, I felt for the first time in a long time that I was going to be okay. A team of dedicated doctors, nurses, and counselors were there to help me through this next treacherous period of my life.

When I met the hospital physician, I was oddly at peace and even cracked a smile. The first thing on his agenda was to give me a full physical and well-being exam.

I couldn't remember the last time anyone had asked me how much I weighed or how tall I was. My entire life, I had been tall and slender. Even through high school I had been called "skinny" or "lanky." But after years of drug abuse and a poor diet, I had lost that frame.

I wasn't sure what to expect when I stepped on the scale. The doctor turned to me and told I weighed 280 pounds.

"You're dangerously obese," he said.

The news floored me. What had happened to me?

It struck me how much my health had been adversely affected by all those years of drug abuse. When I was in the throes of using, I'd had a one-track mind. All I'd cared about was drugs. I'd gone years without a medical exam, physical test, or dental screening…and it showed.

I'd always heard that prevention was the best way to fight disease. Instead, many addicts around me had ignored their health, with catastrophic results. Some died not as a direct result of their addiction but because of undiagnosed health issues stemming from their drug use. As I listened to the doctor talk, I realized I'd been well on the way to an early death outside of my drug addiction, just for my health issues alone.

At 280 pounds, my cholesterol was through the roof. I risked major damage to my heart and brain due to my poor diet and lack of exercise. The weight also put excessive strain on my already battered body—the damaged bones and muscles that I'd acquired from the various traumatic injuries. Pain shot through my leg with every step on my surgically repaired ankle and femur. I wheezed after walking up only a few stairs and felt fatigued and dizzy after minimal exercise.

The health of my teeth and gums had also degenerated. I'd been

blessed with beautiful teeth as a child, worn braces, and had been taught to care for my teeth. Unfortunately, during my years of addiction, I'd completely neglected my teeth. Most of them now had cavities as a result of the methadone's softening of teeth and bones. Some of my teeth had decayed completely. My dental health was at an all-time low.

The drug addiction and resulting poor health had taken its toll in every way.

Luckily, most of the physical damage I'd done could be corrected. With proper diet and exercise, the doctors were confident that I could lose at least some of the weight I'd packed on over the years.

At the rehabilitation center, the main focus was on maintaining my sobriety. I was housed with three other addicts of various backgrounds in a small college-style dorm room. We were awakened each morning at 6:30 to make our beds and clean our rooms. We weren't used to the level of order and discipline that was imposed upon us, but that structure was the only way that any of us would have a chance to move forward. We didn't realize that there was a method to the strict military-like expectations, and we chafed against the rules.

Each day was filled with meetings and group discussions. We sat in giant circles and talked about ways we could battle our addictions once we got out of rehab. We spent hours talking about coping skills, triggers, and addressing our past mistakes. There were one-on-one sessions with counselors and doctors, along with guest speakers who ran Narcotics Anonymous meetings from the hospital.

All this structure and group discussion brought me to a personal epiphany. While such groups had always proven statistically beneficial for addicts, I knew that they were not going to be what kept *me* clean.

I felt in my heart that each addict's journey and road to sobriety was his own, and that I was going to need to define it for myself in a way that worked best for me if it was going to stick. However, I knew this was in stark contrast to AA and NA rules, which mandated that we follow the program for the best chance at success. All I could do was hope that I was on the right track.

At the treatment center, one of my favorite places to go was called the meditation room. It was a small office with no windows, two large leather couches, a lava lamp, and most importantly—a radio. During my stay at Connecticut Valley Hospital, I spent much of my free time in that room. I listened to a local rock station that played classic songs by The Rolling Stones, Pink Floyd, and The Doors.

In my quest for sobriety, some of the same songs that I'd gotten high to now offered me peace and serenity instead. They were a salve for my physical and mental discomfort.

Most importantly, the room offered me a quiet place to begin my personal crusade against my demons. I spent hours recollecting, piecing together, and processing the immense pain that I had suffered through.

I started a journal. As I began to get in touch with some of the feelings that resided deep inside me, I realized that the process of getting sober was a process of getting to know oneself again. It struck me that everything I'd been for the past eight years had been built on lies. The person I'd been would have to be systematically broken down and rebuilt.

I spent many hours pondering the decisions I'd made. I thought about the people I'd hurt and the bridges I'd burned. I began to come to terms with the guilt I felt for the years of endless pain I'd subjected on my family. I thought, also, of the damage I'd done to myself. It

haunted me that I'd wasted so much time—precious years—in my addiction.

I was committed to repairing the wrongs I'd done. I was doing my best to fix the damage to my relationships, remedy my host of medical issues, and repair my credit and financial problems. But one thing I could never get back was the time I'd let slip away while I was getting high.

I never got to experience university life or build tight friendships during college years. I hadn't prepared myself to join the workforce. I'd never set or achieved goals in my early twenties that would allow me to lead a better life down the road. It seemed regret would be the familiar and suffocating sweater I was destined to wear for the rest of my life.

As much as I thought I could face the battle alone, I was in a hospital with hundreds of other addicts—and things didn't always go smoothly. Many of the patients inside CVH were in a situation similar to mine. Most were court-ordered to be in long-term care. Some wanted to change and were taking advantage of the opportunity, but others were bitter and looked only to fulfill their court order so they could return to the streets and their old ways. Fights were common. Like prison, everyone maintained a hyper-vigilant demeanor and fighting stance.

One day as I sat in the community TV room with a group of addicts watching a news program about the Deepwater Horizon oil spill, another patient sauntered up and stood behind me. Ironically, the kid was from my hometown and had gotten tangled up in the same problems that I had. It was pure coincidence that we ended up sharing the same rehab together.

"What's up, Mike, you remember me, man?" he said.

"Yeah, Brian, what's up, dude?" I replied, half-wishing he would leave me alone. Brian had always been one of the grimier kids, known for stealing and beating other addicts. In a way, I felt he was beneath me.

"Oh, you know, just trying to be a good boy so I can get back to *my* city," he said in a challenging way.

He was drinking out of a water bottle and pretended to trip. He spilled a small amount of water near my feet.

"Oh, sorry, man, my bad, my bad," he said with a smirk. "I didn't mean to do that."

It was clear he was trying to test me. The other men in the room perked up. All attention was on me. I could feel the anticipation.

Brian leaned in and tilted the water bottle over my head. "I would hate for some of this to spill on you, Mike…" The water crept toward the bottle opening.

"Listen, man, I'm here for the courts," I said. "I just want to make it thru the next thirty-five days. But if one single drop of that water falls on me, I'm gonna stand up, and I'm gonna beat the living fuck out of you."

"Oh, damn, Mike, I wouldn't want that to happen," he said sarcastically. He tilted the bottle a bit more, and the water inched closer to the edge.

I said nothing. I sat there looking straight ahead. When a drop of water hit my hair, I sprang into action.

I grabbed Brian by the throat and smashed the back of his head into the wall. People jumped up, excited for a break in the stale rehab routine. Cheering broke out as Brian and I wrestled.

At one point, he pushed off the wall and shoved me back hard. I instantly got behind him and wrapped my forearms around his neck,

cutting off his breathing.

Just then, alarms began to sound, echoing around us. A robotic voice poured from the speaker system: "Code Blue, Code Blue. D Wing. Code Blue, Code Blue. D Wing."

Within seconds, five guards rushed in and broke up the fight. As I was dragged away to an isolation room, Brian lay on the ground struggling to catch his breath.

While normally this would have been grounds for removal from the facility, Brian and I were only reprimanded by the head counselor and security. But we were warned that if it happened again, we would be removed.

I wanted to change my life for the better. I didn't want to stop my progress or go backward. But I wasn't a bitch. I never would be.

It wasn't until years later that I found the power in walking away from altercations.

After rejoining the general population of the facility, I found myself reverting to the class-clown role I'd had my entire life. I relished any opportunity to make the group laugh or to start some innocent banter. Because of this, I was viewed as someone who didn't take my recovery seriously. Some of the counselors sneered at me, acting as if I wasn't someone worth investing in.

Their doubt only recharged my determination to make the necessary changes in my life.

Every day my clouded brain cleared a bit more. The feeling of complete sobriety after years of being under the influence was without parallel. It felt as though I was waking from a deep hibernation. I was regaining a sense of clarity that I hadn't had in a decade. I was like a blind person being given the gift of sight for the first time. I loved seeing things for how they really were, and it stuck with me.

After two weeks, my family members were allowed to visit me. On Tuesday nights, families would gather in the cafeteria and wait for their patient relatives, who were marched down as a group.

When I walked in with the other guys, I immediately spotted my parents sitting with a large group of visitors. My mom began to cry. I walked up and gave her a long hug. My dad shook my hand and patted me on the shoulder. Then he said something meaningful that I hadn't heard in a long time: "Mike, I'm proud of you."

After a few more visits, two more weeks of group discussion, and many more hours of personal meditation, my stay at CVH came to an end. I was given a sobriety coin upon completion of the program—a token to celebrate my milestone.

I had a final meeting with a staff of counselors and doctors, some of whom still remained skeptical about my readiness to enter back into society. One of them was the head of the center, a woman named Bernadette. She took me into her office for a one-on-one meeting right before I left, looked me in the eye and expressed her lack of faith in me.

"We've seen people like you before," she said with a sneer. "You'll be back soon, you can be sure of that."

I met her gaze with a sinking heart. *Is she right? Will I be back?* The cynicism of an important figure in the recovery center who was supposed to offer encouragement—the top person, no less—caused me to question myself, my ability to heal, and fueled latent doubts. I couldn't believe that a person in her position wasn't offering support and encouragement to a vulnerable addict under her care instead of undermining me.

I left Bernadette's office and went to pack my bags for my discharge. As negative as that woman's words had been, there was one

thing she couldn't take away from me: the profound feeling of clarity and determination I felt as I walked out of the hospital that day. It was indescribable.

My family smiled buoyantly at me as I walked out the door.

I was on the road to recovery, an addict successfully battling my treacherous temptations. For that, I was considered a survivor.

Unfortunately, that wasn't the end of the road.

Instead, it was only the long, hard beginning of the journey that would reshape my life.

twenty-three

The rat race that we call life doesn't exactly account for or include a "time out" for recovering from an addiction that most people have had the luxury of not experiencing.

Immediately after my release from rehab, it became painfully obvious how far behind I was.

I was twenty-five years old.

I had no job, no real-world work experience, and I had not completed college.

I was a convicted felon and had built a terrible reputation for myself.

My credit was shot and, to add insult to injury, my car had been repossessed during my stay in rehab.

I had no way to get around and no real prospects for employment or my future.

I was forced to sit back, take inventory, and truly comprehend the amount of work I had in front of me.

In addition to the problems in my professional life, my health issues continued to present huge challenges.

Despite it all, my primary goal was to stay clean and sober from drugs and alcohol. In and of itself, that was a full-time job.

After I left rehab, my mom allowed me to move back into her house. After losing me to years of drug abuse, she looked forward to spending some time with her son again.

During my first weeks at home, I experienced all the feelings expected of an addict. I was ecstatic to be able to tell my family that I was clean. They said it was good to see me smiling again, something they hadn't witnessed in years. I regularly attended Narcotics Anonymous and Alcoholics Anonymous meetings.

My mother wanted nothing more than for me to attend ninety meetings in ninety days, something that was strongly encouraged by the groups and medical professionals. I felt I owed it to her to put my best foot forward, so I decided to give it a shot.

Behind closed doors, while my family was gone, things were much more difficult than I let on.

When my mother left for work, I spent the days alone, flooded with waves of deep depression, loneliness, and regret.

I spent hours in my room ruminating over the people I'd hurt, the damage I'd done to my body, and the time I'd wasted in my addiction. I thought about my childhood best friends, Jeff, Kenny, and Alex, who were still lost and struggling with the insidious tentacles of addiction. I grieved for the boys we'd once been, before addiction had stolen our dreams. Those feelings would lead to the urge to use again.

Those were the days I was thankful for NA and AA so that I could talk to other recovering addicts who were dealing with similar feelings and problems. Those meetings in my early recovery gave me unparalleled help. I couldn't imagine how much harder the struggle would be without the compassion of fellow addicts who truly

understood what I was up against.

Even with the help of others in the months after rehab, life remained a struggle. I was advised to stay busy, as that was one of the most essential parts of recovery. I found this to be true. I could see how idle time could easily become the enemy for an addict trying to keep his mind off drugs or from associating with old friends. With that in mind, I decided to search for a part-time job and other activities to fill my day.

Unfortunately, my job hunt would prove to be a fruitless battle. I had a felony conviction, no car, and a poor employment history. After pounding the pavement day after day, my inability to find work lowered my confidence and already battered self-esteem.

Through my hardship, my mom noticed what the rejection and regret was doing to me. She tried her best to do little things to cheer me up and drove me to group meetings every night for those ninety days.

"Take it slow, Michael," she said. "Nothing is going to happen overnight."

Her confidence in my ability to make positive changes in my life kept me going when things got difficult. She was my biggest supporter.

"If you just keep doing the right thing," she always said, "good things will happen to you. That's just the way the world works, Mikey."

Unfortunately, my mother was going through struggles of her own. Her biggest supporter, her dad, was losing his battle against Parkinson's, cancer, and dementia. His condition had dramatically declined.

While my mom did her best to support me in my recovery, she

also tried to mask the immense pain she felt as she watched her father deteriorate.

As Pop-Pop's health worsened, my mother frantically searched for a way to deal with the host of issues related to his care. She refused to place him in a convalescent home because she worried about the kind of care he might receive. She also didn't want to move him from the home where he'd lived his entire life. The burden of his care was entirely on her shoulders. She was overwhelmed, frightened, confused, and didn't know where to turn.

One day, she got an idea for how to simultaneously help her recovering son and her ailing father. She saw that it was proving difficult for me to find a job with my lack of transportation and felony record. She also knew that it wasn't financially feasible to pay for a live-in nurse to stay with my aging grandfather. Even with his pension and Social Security, hiring around-the-clock caregivers would be too expensive.

So, in what would become a chariot of hope for everyone involved, my mother asked me to move in with my grandfather to care for him full-time.

At first, it seemed like a bad idea to me. I didn't know if I was up to the task, and I still carried tremendous shame and guilt for smoking crack in Pop's attic when I was supposed to have been caring for him.

"I don't know, Mom," I said reluctantly. "Pop-Pop and I aren't really that close...I don't know if he even likes me that much."

"Give it a shot, Mike. You'll have a place to stay and maybe you guys could become friends."

I was hesitant. For one, I knew nothing about how to manage a sick old man, especially one who required the highest level of care. In

Pop-Pop's fight against Parkinson's, he'd become immobile, erratic, and unable to use the bathroom on his own. The daily tasks in nursing him were endless.

"I'll think about it," I said. I considered refusing the job altogether, but after some thought, I realized I owed my mother a debt. She'd put up with so much of my bullshit. She'd stuck by me through the lying, the dealing, the arrests, the fights, the surgeries. This was my chance to pay her back for always being there for me. With all the regret I felt in my life, I was not about to make another mistake that I couldn't fix.

Soon after, I made the commitment to move in with my aging grandfather. I would have a bedroom in the attic and would be responsible for every aspect of his daily care. I would feed him all his meals, give him an array of medications throughout the day, take him to and from the bathroom, shower him, dress him, and monitor his general well-being. Even though I was unqualified for this job on so many levels, I had confidence in my ability to get it done.

I did my best with Pop-Pop's daily care, along with preparing meals and keeping the house clean, but I think my mom knew exactly how well two ailing men were apt to do on their own. She stopped in every day to mop floors, bleach the tub, clean the toilet, wash clothes, cook meals, or vacuum. I began to understand how hard she worked to keep her father in his own home where he was comfortable and received the attention he needed and deserved.

When my mom came by to check on us, Pop-Pop's bad days were very difficult for her.

"Dad, can I get you anything?" she would ask. "Do you want some soup or a glass of juice?"

He would just stare at her, unable to comprehend or come up

with a response. On those days, there was no way to get through to him, and I saw deep pain in my mother's eyes.

Because of Pop-Pop's dementia, he also had trouble understanding simple commands and tasks. He often saw things that weren't there, and occasionally would throw temper tantrums for no reason.

It was difficult for me to watch him go through such pain and agony, but it was even harder on my mom. I did my best to provide her with comic relief. I'd never been good at telling people that things would be okay, and I didn't give a very convincing pep talk. But for some reason, I'd always been able to make people laugh. Sometimes that made all the difference. Despite everything I'd been through, the class clown had somehow found a way to survive. It felt good to be able to bring a smile to my mother's often-sad face.

One of the ways that Mom and I were able to bring some happiness to Pop-Pop was to help him maintain his traditions and ways of caring for himself prior to his illness. My grandfather had always worn suspenders, slicked his hair back, and dressed in freshly pressed slacks, so we tried to provide him with those simple comforts and dignity.

Pop had other traditions that weren't so easily kept. Every week for years, he'd met up with five of his lifelong friends at a local diner for breakfast. They discussed sports, war, and whatever else men of their generation talked about. It was the one time in the day that they all got together, away from their wives or kids, and were just able to be themselves. As time went on, though, Pop's friends became too ill to meet for breakfast. One by one, they began to fade away…and then pass away. In the end, Pop was one of only two friends left.

"How about you take me up to the diner to see the boys?" Pop would ask me with excitement in his voice. "That'd be something!"

"Today's not a good day, Pop," I'd say with a lump in my throat, not having the heart to remind him that all but one of his friends were gone. "Maybe next week, okay?"

I always hoped that when the next week came, he wouldn't ask me again to take him to the diner to see his beloved friends.

Caring for Pop-Pop gave me a new perspective on life and how precious it was. I'd spent the past eight years of my own life in reckless abandon. I'd sped down highways high on drugs. I'd challenged drug dealers at gunpoint. I'd lived with the belief that tomorrow would never come, and if it did, that it wouldn't matter.

Being with Pop-Pop awakened me to what was important.

For the first time in a long time, I was happy to be alive.

twenty-four

2011
U.S. opioid deaths: 22,784

Although Pop-Pop required a high level of care, his energy was very low. He napped for hours at a time, which gave me a chance to work on the things I needed to do for my recovery. While he slept, I searched for jobs on the Internet and found new AA meetings to attend. However, my lack of transportation made it difficult for me to get to meetings. I wished I could be more mobile on weekends, when I had more free time after my mom took over. Not having a car frustrated me. I felt as if I were stuck on an island with no means of escape.

"Why don't you take one of the old bicycles out of the garage?" my mother suggested one day. "You can get to your meetings that way."

"No way," I said. "I'm not gonna ride around on a rusty old bike."

I'd been babied for years, and I felt like I deserved a car. The last thing I wanted to do was tool around on a hand-me-down ten-speed.

But as time went on and I remained isolated, the idea of the bike

started sounding better. I was chomping at the bit for some mobility, so one day, I took the old Schwinn out of the garage. Slowly but surely, I began to ride everywhere.

At 280 pounds, cycling wasn't easy for me. I was constantly out of breath, and my legs ached. On top of that, the bike wasn't made for riding on pavement, which made things even more difficult. It was an old mountain bike with thick tires, not designed for endurance cycling on city streets.

I did the best I could. I rode miles downtown to AA and NA meetings. Sometimes while Pop was napping or when Mom came over, I would go out, plug some earbuds into my iPod, and just ride around. I found freedom and peace through cycling. It cleared my mind, relieved my stress, and loosened up my battered body. Most importantly, exercise helped ease my depression and anxiety, which I found to be one of the most important aspects of my recovery.

During my rides, my favorite soundtrack was by an artist named Mac Miller. His music was my escape. It was all about good vibes, rising out of shitty situations, putting on a smile, and persevering. It was just what I needed to hear, and his music made a deep impression on me.

By spring, I was riding twenty miles a day. By summer and early autumn, I was riding everywhere—as much as I could.

I also began to focus on eating better. During my time as a drug addict, I'd lived off fast food. My friends had made fun of me when I ate fast food three meals a day, seven days a week. After I started riding my bike, I no longer enjoyed the fatty nature of McDonald's and Burger King. I began eating grilled chicken, fresh greens, salads, and fruit.

I fell so in love with cycling that when January came and the

weather got colder, I was still out on the bike. For the first time since I could remember, I actually looked forward to what the new year might bring. For a third of my life, I'd been gripped by an ugly addiction and had seen and felt terrors that most people never would. I had buried friends and lost myself completely in a deep ocean of self-destruction. But as 2011 dawned, I felt a newfound hope for the future.

The new year brought new hope for my professional life as well.

One day while walking around downtown, I met a woman who was interviewing local business owners. I approached her to ask what she was working on, and we struck up a conversation. She told me that she was building a new website for AOL, called Patch. It was to be a hyper-local news website, with local reporters and business reviews. I told her that I enjoyed writing and knew a lot of people in town. She was new to Milford, having moved from New York, and I think she saw that I could potentially connect her with people she didn't know. She asked me if I wanted to be a part of the website, and I ecstatically accepted.

My mom was right when she'd said that with hard work, patience, and doing the right thing day after day, good things would eventually come my way. I was living proof.

For the last few months of 2010 and most of 2011, I helped develop Milford's Patch website. I documented businesses, tasted food, and wrote restaurant reviews. I sat in on local government meetings and reported on what took place. I attended charity events. I was given the chance to interview Indianapolis Colts coach Tony Dungy and ESPN reporter Dan Patrick.

My writing and reporting skills were praised by my editor. I learned to take photos, edit videos, and utilize social networks. The

experience was incredible, and for someone coming from the darkest depths in life, it seemed surreal.

Working for the Milford Patch was a major turning point in my life. It improved my self-esteem, showcased my talents for a broad audience, and gave me another way to fill my time during recovery. It was a great way to meet and interact with new people. Most of all, it helped repair my name in the town I'd wronged through so many years of drug abuse. As my self-confidence thrived, so did my outlook.

In contrast to my burgeoning mood and self-esteem, Pop's health continued to decline. Nights were a constant battle. My grandfather had never been one to admit his weaknesses or acknowledge his need for help. Even in his terrible state of health, he tried his best to be independent. He would wake up in the middle of the night and try to go to the bathroom or bathe himself on his own. When he took some falls, we had to bring in a bed with rails so that he couldn't get up and wander around.

Every day there was a new challenge, but my mother and I solved each problem as it arose. We worked well as a team to get things done, and we were fueled by the knowledge that we were doing right by Pop-Pop. Mom continued to cook for him although he wouldn't always eat, and she was there every single day to clean the house.

As the weather warmed and summer approached, I continued to ride farther on my bike and maintain the new diet I'd put in place for myself. By June 2011, my weight was down to 230 pounds. I started to feel better about myself and have more energy and stamina on the bike.

I was so busy I almost lost track of the fact that I was in recovery at all. It felt so natural to be doing positive things with my life that I started to forget the horrors of all I'd seen and experienced.

As time went on, I began to attend AA and NA meetings less religiously. For the first six months, I'd gone every single day. Then I started to miss a meeting here and there. By the one-year mark of my sobriety, I was only going to one or two meetings a week.

I continued to set my own plan for what individually worked for me in my sobriety, despite the fact that this strategy was against AA's rules for a lifelong healthy recovery program. I stayed occupied and tried to forget the terrors of addiction, which worked well for me. However, I never forgot the personal stories of tragedy and triumph from my meetings. They were a reminder that no matter how long a person was sober, addiction was never truly beaten. I knew the supportive doors of the recovery programs were always open to me should I ever need them again. Most importantly, I'd learned that I had the personal power to take control of my own life.

As the summer went on, I floated on a cloud. The freedom from my addiction was overpowering. There were mornings when I would literally cry for joy during my shower for somehow making it out of the horrifying existence of drug addiction. Every day seemed like a miracle.

It was then that I came to another important awakening in my life...my faith.

I was raised a Methodist Christian, but we were never regular churchgoers. My family and I attended church on major holidays and paid our $50 tithe, but I prayed only a few times a year. As I started to crawl out of the darkness of my addiction, however, I started to find more reasons to be grateful for the love of my God.

I treated the practice of my faith similarly to how I treated my recovery: "Do what works for you." Just as I believed that those in recovery should create their own plan for reaching long-term sobriety,

I felt that people should make up their own minds about how they practiced their religion. In the year following my cleaning up, I began a personal relationship with my God and started having a conversation with Him without the help of a clergyman or priest.

My connection with God became more than just showing that I was thankful; the relationship also made me more responsible for my actions. After years of selling drugs, taking part in violent acts, and operating with reckless abandon, I now saw the error of my old ways.

Any time I would get an urge to do something unworthy, I would ask myself, "Would your family, friends, or God want you to do this? With all that you've accomplished, all you've beaten, is this worthy of the man you have become?" This helped keep me solid and focused on my sobriety.

After a year of hard work in my recovery, however, I began to walk a very thin line.

It was right before summer, and I felt confident enough in my recovery to go out to a few parties. I was certain my willpower was strong enough to withstand any temptation.

At the first few parties, I walked around drinking water while everyone around me was getting drunk. Then, on Friday nights, I slowly began going to local bars.

In my recovery meetings, there was a saying: "Hang around the barbershop long enough, and you're gonna get a haircut." While it sounded like a corny slogan, I knew it was accurate. If I kept hanging around bars and parties with people drinking, chances were I was eventually going to have a drink myself.

Even though I'd created a recovery program for myself that I believed I could handle, I knew one thing wasn't up for interpretation in AA—recovering drug addicts should not drink alcohol.

There were reasons behind this logic. First, alcohol affects judgment. Second, it can lead to bad decisions. Third, it can potentially act as a replacement for drugs.

For these reasons, recovering addicts were encouraged to stay away from social events that involved drinking and were told to *never* drink themselves.

Even with all this knowledge, I decided to take a chance and have a drink after a party one night. I was with some girls I didn't know well, and I wanted to impress one of them. Against my better judgment, I took a shot of tequila. I didn't immediately drive to Bridgeport and buy cocaine after that. I didn't even have the urge to use drugs. But I knew I'd done wrong.

After that drink, I reflected on my decision and thought of ways to make sure it didn't happen again. I went back to focusing on being constructive and making positive things happen in my life going forward.

One summer day, a friend named Dan, whom I'd met in recovery, invited me to join him at the beach with some friends. I made Pop-Pop his breakfast, helped him bathe, and dressed him. When my mom arrived, I left for the day.

The bike ride to the beach was quite far. I'd unsuccessfully tried to ride there before. But after constant dedication, my ability to ride longer distances had improved. Now, riding fifteen miles to the beach was no problem.

I arrived at Lake Street Beach around 11 a.m. It was already 80 degrees. The guys in my group took off their shirts, but I was too self-conscious about my weight to do the same.

Dan and I threw around a football and listened to music for a while before lying down on our towels. Groups of college kids

laughed and talked around us, all gathered for summer vacation. The mood was relaxed, and everyone smiled as they soaked up the sun.

While surveying the beach, I noticed a group of girls nearby. They were stretched out on towels and drinking beers. One of them immediately caught my eye. Her white bathing suit set off her bronzed skin. I watched her smiling and laughing with her friends. Something about her grabbed my attention.

As I watched this girl, I remembered what the recovery programs taught addicts: Avoid new relationships of any kind for the first year of sobriety. The potential stressors of meeting new people or falling in love could drive an addict back to active use. Moreover, many addicts lacked self-confidence during their early recovery.

I certainly did. After years of being beaten and trapped by the addiction, after years of pain and suffering, I'd entered recovery with a flawed self-image.

As mesmerized as I was by this girl's beauty, I knew there was no way that I could ever have her.

But something about her smile invited me. Something about the way she laughed made me feel a bit more at ease. I wondered if I could say the right thing to grab her attention. I didn't really plan it out.

Sometimes the best words are thought of on the spot and are more organic in nature.

I stood up, brushed the sand off my back, and walked over to her.

"Just wanted to tell you I love your dimples," I said.

She was lying facedown and squinted as she looked up at me.

"I'm Melissa," she said with a laugh.

Sometimes things just happen like that. I'd set my target on the most beautiful, spirited girl I'd ever seen. As little as I thought of

myself, Melissa obviously saw in me what I no longer could. The encounter at the beach that day would eventually blossom into a romance that would change my life in more ways than one.

I was at a place in my life where I was caring for myself and caring for Pop-Pop.

Caring for someone new seemed like a feasible possibility.

twenty-five

Unfortunately, along with my new relationship came some of the stressors that were discussed in my sobriety meetings. Namely, how would I tell Melissa about my problem? I was twenty-six years old, and she was nineteen. I was unready and unwilling to be completely honest with her. She was in college and was just starting her own party days. She wanted to go out to bars and hang with friends and drink Long Island Iced Teas and dance all night and fall on the ground. In an attempt to fit in with Melissa and her friends, I regressed to doing some of those things with her.

For the rest of the summer, I fell into complacency with my sobriety by occasionally drinking beers as I hung around with Melissa and her group. I knew the dangerous line I walked, but I walked it anyway.

One night, while at a house party, I was drinking beer alongside Melissa when someone took out a bag of cocaine and dumped it onto the table. That person quickly sniffed the fine powder with a rolled-up bill—an activity with which I was all too familiar.

Partygoers began passing the bill around. The bill went to each person, one by one, until it got close to me. The person next to me

snorted a line, and then passed the rolled-up bill over to me. It was my turn now. Like a train collision in slow motion, I saw my world begin to tumble down the way it had so many times before.

I paused.

The guy next to me said, "Hey, man, you want some of this? It's good shit."

"No, I'm good, man, thanks," I said casually but with complete authority. It was a simple statement, but it was clear I wasn't going to waver.

He passed the bill to the next person.

That night, and that decision, had a profound effect on me. As I watched many of my close friends struggle mightily with maintaining abstinence from drugs, I seemingly did not.

After that moment, days passed that I didn't think about my history or feel the urge to use drugs again. If I did happen to think about lighting a dirty crack pipe or sniffing a crushed pill, I immediately felt sick to my stomach. Something had permanently changed in me—I now became disgusted with anything drug-related, enough to cause physical nausea. I came to believe that God had instilled this feeling in me to keep me on my path.

Nevertheless, I'd started to drink socially. For an addict in recovery, that was unacceptable, and it weighed heavily on me. I did my best to limit myself and abstained from alcohol for weeks at a time.

It was difficult to be around people who were drinking and not drink myself. During those times, I tried every tactic taught at meetings to ward off questions about why I wasn't drinking. I drank ice water in a chilled glass with a lime wedge. I told people I had to work early the next day or that I was the designated driver.

But, despite my efforts, I began to give in. Often, I found myself nursing a drink while hanging out with friends or at a social gather-

ing. I knew it was a slippery slope, but I thought I could handle it. *Just one drink…what can it hurt?*

I'd found myself thrown back into a world of people who functioned freely without the shackles of addiction. All around me, people went about their lives. They worked at their jobs, drove new cars, went home to their families. Most of them lived their lives with no knowledge of a terrifying alternate world that existed beneath their own stable ground…an underbelly where pain and agony, lies and regret were the only certainties. I wondered how any recovering addict could ever begin to explain to another person the horrors of this other realm.

Life went on, and soon I was presented with another opportunity to better my life. Lillian worked as a personal assistant in an affluent part of southern Fairfield county. She knew I was looking for more work, and since I'd just finished a year of sobriety, she trusted me enough to fill in for her at her job in Norwalk, Connecticut.

When Lillian went out of town, it was my job to care for a hardworking couple's home and pets. Every day for a month, I rode my bike to the train station in Milford and got off in East Norwalk.

My responsibilities were numerous. They included stocking the refrigerator with groceries, watering the massive garden, doing laundry, and making the beds. The household tasks I handled were menial but gave me a way to add continued responsibility to my life. The job taught me discipline and rigor, which were valuable skills.

While I was covering for Lillian, it was also my responsibility to care for the family's two Weimaraners, Haley and Bauer. They were big dogs, and I had little experience with pets, but something about the job came naturally to me. Once again, I was in the position of caring for a being that wasn't able to care for itself. And once again, I found solace in that duty.

During the time I commuted to and from Norwalk, a visiting nurse worked in partnership with my mother to care for Pop-Pop. But every night after work, I returned home to perform my duties as promised.

Unfortunately, Pop-Pop's health continued to get worse. As the summer wound down in September, Pop was limited in his functioning. We brought in an electric bed and recliner to help us and the nurse lift him up more easily. Pop used a walker or a wheelchair to move around. His appetite continued to diminish, and we worked feverishly to get him to drink, eat, and stay nourished. Even with all our efforts, my mom knew the end was near. I watched helplessly as the grief took an emotional toll on her.

I did my best to help her with her pain. I knew the best way I could help her was to do well in my life and to eliminate the worry she'd had about me for so long. I continued to feed and keep Pop clean at night and go to Norwalk to work during the day. I also spent as much time with my mom as I could, rebuilding the relationship I'd abused for so many years.

My life was filled with important activities from the moment I woke up to the moment I went to sleep. I now had a new way of living that had become part of my existence instead of my previous "do whatever" mentality. I would never again find myself without a schedule or set of responsibilities for the day. I was now utilizing the advice I'd gotten in recovery classes and which I now offer to others: Always stay busy.

But the most important part was to stay busy with the right things….healthy, productive pursuits that furthered one's growth.

My life was now on track. I was actively making good choices and moving in a positive direction.

Finally.

twenty-six

One rainy September day, I got a disturbing phone call from an old buddy named Jordan. His tone sounded panicked. He asked if I'd heard about what had happened to my childhood best friend, Jeff.

Since I'd gotten clean, I'd mostly lost touch with my old high-school buddies. It was very rare for me to speak to Jeff, Kenny, or Alex anymore since they were still battling addiction. But the bond we shared remained, never to be broken.

With all that I'd experienced so far, however—the overdoses, the violence, the arrests, the terrors of addiction—nothing could prepare me for what Jordan was about to say.

"What happened with Jeff?" I asked.

"I don't know the details," Jordan said, "except there are a lot of cops and ambulances in front of Jeff's house."

My heart sank. That didn't sound good. "I need to know what's going on. You don't know anything else?"

Jordan paused. "Mike, I think Danny killed Caddie."

I felt as though I'd been sucker-punched. The breath left my body. I dropped the phone to the concrete garage floor, my head reeling.

Caddie, murdered?

Jeff's mom had been like a second mom to me, the only constant in Jeff's life. We'd known she was in an abusive marriage. We all knew Danny, her husband, was unstable. But nothing could have prepared me for that phone call.

Within minutes of my conversation with Jordan, news began to break on Facebook and Twitter: *Possible homicide in Milford.*

The article went on to name Jeff's street. It was surreal. How many times had I played basketball with Jeff on that very street? How many times had I hung out at his house, the same house where this crime had occurred?

Details began to trickle in, but none of the stories listed the exact address where the crime had occurred. I hoped and prayed it wasn't Jeff's house and that there'd been a mistake…but I knew in my heart it was true.

I tried calling Jeff. No answer. I messaged him on Facebook. Nothing. He was in the throes of active addiction, so I knew it was a long shot to get ahold of him. Still, I tried.

It would be a few hours before all the nightmarish facts were revealed.

On September 23, 2011, in a scene straight out of a horror movie, the home in which I'd spent much of my childhood was turned into a grisly crime scene. In a tragic murder-suicide, Danny Foster had violently assaulted, strangled, and stabbed Jeff's mother to death. Danny then stabbed the family dog multiple times before tying an orange extension cord around his neck and hanging himself.

Before the events of that day unfolded, I thought I'd seen or heard just about everything this cruel world could throw at a person. But this tragic event reminded me how much worse things could always

get in life.

The news of Caddie's murder sent me reeling. Of all the people I'd met in my life, she was the kindest soul I'd ever encountered. She loved Jeff unconditionally and had been his greatest champion. She was the one person who had never given up on him.

Like me, Jeff had put his mother and the rest of his family through immense pain with his drug addiction. He'd been convicted of numerous robbery-related crimes and drug possession. He'd had a difficult time overcoming his problem, as did we all.

Before the drugs, Jeff had been a star basketball player, a baseball fanatic, and an aspiring sportswriter. Drugs had taken hold of his life and shaken every goal and dream from his mind and future. Jeff was another soul moved off his proper path, but he would have a harder time than most in trying to get back on track.

Through it all, Jeff had always had one person in his corner who never gave up on him—his mother. Caddie had fought tooth and nail, day after day for years, to keep her son out of trouble. While I had a large support group that had aided me on my path to sobriety, Jeff had only one person: his mother. She was his biggest fan, his strength to push forward through all the pain, and his crutch when all hope was lost. To Jeff, his mother was his only light in the darkness.

In August, just a few weeks before the tragic day, Jeff's stepfather, Danny, had gotten into a serious fight with his and Caddie's other son, Eric. Both had been arrested. While Danny was in jail, Caddie decided that she'd lived in fear long enough and wouldn't put her family through any more suffering at Danny's hands. She filed for divorce and began preparing for life on her own.

When Danny was released from jail, he learned of the divorce filing and that he'd been terminated from his job at Pepsi due to the

arrest. He snapped.

The murder-suicide quickly became the topic of every newspaper op-ed column in the area. Opinions were rampant about mental illness reform and tougher domestic violence laws. Everyone wanted to get in their two cents about what had happened.

But I was dealing with a much more personal issue. A woman I had adored with all my heart was dead. My best friend had gone missing after the crime. No one could find him. He'd lost the person he loved the most in the world, his only lifeline and sole emotional support. I was deeply worried about his well-being.

Jeff's brother, Eric, had lost both his mother *and* father. The family dog, Rocky, was in intensive care for the multiple stab wounds he'd received trying to defend Caddie during the vicious attack. Jeff was out in the cold world somewhere, a full-blown addict, grieving, and completely alone. The situation couldn't get grimmer.

Shortly after the tragedy, there was a wake for Caddie. That day was the first time since I'd gotten clean that all four of us friends— me, Jeff, Kenny, and Alex—were together again.

When I saw Jeff, I immediately broke down into tears. I didn't know what to say to him. There were no words. What could I say to someone who had just endured something so horrific? Nothing I could say would have been enough.

Instead, I walked up to my best friend and simply wrapped my arms around him. We stood there and wept together. I finally found the words to tell him how much I'd loved his mother.

"She loved you more than anything in this world," I said between sobs. Jeff just held me tightly and sobbed.

I spent hours in the funeral home with Jeff and his family, surrounded by pictures of Caddie, before I finally left.

That devastating event had a profound emotional effect on my life. I wanted so badly for Jeff to get clean and join me on my journey of sobriety. I wanted him to have a chance to experience some of the blessings that hard work and perseverance were bringing my way.

But after the loss of his mother, Jeff faded away into further addiction. It became even more difficult to reach him. An integral piece of him was lost forever.

He would never be the same again.

twenty-seven

2012

U.S. opioid deaths: 23,166

In the months after Jeff's tragedy, I made strides in my own personal and professional lives. I continued to cycle, work out in the gym, and maintain a clean diet. My relationships with my mother and the rest of my family showed signs of improvement as the trust and respect returned. My relationship with my girlfriend, Melissa, was still in its infancy but we were learning more about each other every day. Most of all, I focused on meeting people in Fairfield County, laying the foundation for a network that would later propel my career.

Unfortunately, my decision to drink socially continued to haunt me. I believed that I had enough self-control to drink in moderation and that it helped me loosen up in social situations. I was wrong. I began to see that alcohol was *not* actually helping me interact. Instead, it slowed my wit, humor, and ability to make comfortable, loose conversation. After a few beers, I changed from the funny guy who was always smiling and making jokes into a more reserved person.

Alcohol actually impaired my ability to socialize.

After taking this into consideration, I made the decision to stop drinking completely in January of 2012.

No one forced me into this decision. There was no probation officer or court telling me I couldn't drink anymore. While my family opposed my drinking, they'd looked the other way due to the growing success of my professional and personal lives. A beer or two on a Friday night didn't seem like a big deal if I was doing well in other areas.

When I made the independent decision to stop drinking, it was the first time that I truly believed that the completely sober me was a better person than the guy who had a few drinks. I made a promise to myself to steer clear of alcohol for the foreseeable future—and I had every intention of keeping this promise.

With a new dedication to achieving my own personal best, I started 2012 with a bang. Within weeks of dropping alcohol, I started feeling better than I had in years. My focus at work became sharper, and I had more energy to devote to new and creative ideas.

With a solid period of sobriety under my belt, I started to experience some of the things that others in extended recovery had always raved about. I was able to put away a few dollars and also buy things for myself. I was able to afford new clothes and shoes. I was doing my best to fit into the society that I'd looked at from the outside for so long. As a result, my sisters started to invite me to events where they were proud to bring their brother.

In February 2012, my sister Lillian offered me a taste of what hard work and dedication could earn a person. She'd won a ticket lottery and was able to purchase two hard-to-get seats for a highly sought-after upcoming performance at Carnegie Hall. For the first time in

history, a rapper would grace the stage of the iconic venue. The famous "stage of all stages" would host none other than Jay-Z himself.

Lillian knew how I felt about Jay-Z—about his struggle through turmoil, about his life as a hustler, and about his triumph over all the things that had brought him down. Lillian told me that because I'd worked so hard to get clean, she wanted to reward me with a trip to New York City to see my favorite artist at an unforgettable venue.

We dressed up and went out for steaks before the show. We shared seats in the audience with Steven Spielberg, Chris Rock, and countless other celebrities. I was ecstatic when Jay-Z walked onstage wearing a white suit, backed by a full orchestra, and started rapping to the songs I had sung along to in my car since I was sixteen. There, in beautiful midtown Manhattan, I got to experience a night that I could never have imagined in my wildest dreams.

As I watched the show, it struck me once again how profoundly life could change after giving up drugs or surviving other hardships. Throughout rehab and early recovery, people had told me how good life could be and how it was still possible to make all my dreams come true. I'd thought that it sounded like an infomercial. After all the shit I'd been through, I couldn't imagine how I could make it in life, but I figured I'd take a shot at it anyway. Now I was an example of a person who'd turned things around. I realized that anyone could have anything they wanted in this world. They just had to believe and take the necessary steps toward a better life.

If I was able to do it, so could anyone else.

As my life continued to progress, my grandfather's health did the opposite.

Pop's health had always been a roller coaster. There would be really good days and then really bad days. Sometimes he would wake

up in the morning with a big smile on his pale, wrinkled face and say, "Hey, let's go up to the barbershop and get me a haircut!" My mother would use those times to get Pop out of the house for a ride in the car or a walk around the neighborhood.

But as good as those days were, the bad days were worse…much worse. And they were becoming more frequent.

March came and went, and Pop's mental state, clarity and ability to function dramatically deteriorated. The anguish and physical pain from years of battling Parkinson's, dementia, and cancer showed in his face. He began to refuse food. My mother and I did everything we could to get him to stay nourished, but it was becoming impossible.

We brought in doctors and nurses to perform tests at the house. At first, we'd kept Pop home because we thought it would benefit him to stay in his preferred environment. Now we kept him there because we knew the shock of moving him to a new place would be too much for him to bear.

The stress was beginning to take its toll.

In recovery, I'd learned about the triggers and risks of stress. I was fighting to maintain the full life I'd put together for myself, but it often felt as though I was juggling too much. There weren't enough hours in the day to get everything done. I now had many important duties and responsibilities, and I didn't want to let anyone down, including myself.

To calm myself, I visualized that I was on my bike and had reached the steepest part of a hill just before it flattened out. I told myself that things had to level out at some point. I dug my feet in, put my head down, and just kept going.

Near the end of March, Melissa and I decided to take a quick trip to Burlington, Vermont. I'd spent a lot of time there as a kid with my

family. Melissa had never been, and I knew she would love it. I was faced with the challenge of finding someone to care for Pop-Pop for the three days that I would be gone, but as usual, my mother was willing to step up and help out. Despite all that she was dealing with herself, she knew how hard I was trying to better myself, and she wanted to help me in any way she could. I was awed by the depth of her strength and love.

For the first time that I could remember, I had a rare few days off. I was excited to spend the time with Melissa away from all the stressors of life.

I booked a beautiful resort outside Burlington that doubled as a culinary institute. We packed our bags, jumped in Melissa's car, and started driving.

The next three days were exactly the therapy I needed. We swam in the pool. We took in the beautiful Vermont scenery during long walks around the sprawling property. At night, we sat together in the outdoor hot tub, breathing in the crisp country air and peering up at the bright stars illuminated against the night sky. Melissa talked me into getting a professional massage while she got a "volcanic-ash facial." We ate at the local restaurants. We laughed and let go. The trip had turned into something even better than we'd expected.

A strange weather pattern was happening in Vermont that weekend, so the temperature in late March reached an unusually warm 80 degrees. We felt as though we were on a lazy, blissful summer vacation. On the final day, we packed sandwiches and rented bicycles. We rode for miles on the paths that circumnavigated stunning Lake Champlain just outside Burlington. We found a picturesque bluff overlooking the clear water and towering pine trees and sat down to eat our lunch. As the sun shone warmly down and a balmy breeze blew softly around us, I realized my life felt whole.

For the first time since age sixteen, I was truly happy.

After years of abuse and addiction, pain and tragedy, my commitment to hard work had led me to a place I never thought I would see again. The strength of my family had sustained me and pushed me to achieve my goals. My diet and dedication to fitness had me feeling better than I ever had. I'd learned so much about life and the way things worked. I finally felt positive about my future.

But no matter how happy and serene I was in the moment, I knew I could never live in oblivion or abandon the lessons of the past. Tomorrow was never a guarantee. Life was a gift.

When I returned home after our trip to Vermont, I stepped up my care of Pop-Pop. Both my mom and I could feel him fading. I spent my time trying to talk to him, cheer him up, and rouse him from what seemed to be a perpetual state of sleep. Every attempt failed, and I was just met with his blank stare. Pop-Pop was leaving us, but I didn't want to face it.

One day, when I asked how he was feeling and if he was hungry or wanted to go outside to feel the sun on his face, I saw a flicker of fear behind his eyes. It was as if he knew he was leaving us, too.

I told him I would be right back. I ran as fast as I could to my room, dropped to my knees, and sobbed. I cried, alone in my room, for a long time before I was able to return to him.

My mother was having a hard time, too. We both knew the end was near for Pop. We wanted nothing more than to be by his side for as long as we had him.

One day, my mother called me in a panic. She told me a bird had flown into her house. She'd heard it was an omen of a death in the family. I swallowed my shock and assured her that it was just a silly superstition.

During Pop's last days, I saw my mom in a new light. I already

knew about her inner strength by the way she'd battled through a difficult divorce and the devastating trials of having a drug-addicted son. But the way she cared for her father as he died was the true testament to her character. She spent hours by his side, holding his hand and talking to him while never shedding one tear despite her pain. I knew that every night, after she went home for the night, she would cry a river of tears. Strong people, it seemed, were often the most difficult to comfort as they show no signs of breaking down or needing help.

One April day, I prepared for work as I normally did. I showered, got dressed, and made myself a light breakfast. I went in and checked on Pop and, as I sometimes would, just watched him sleep. He lay in his bed with four blankets on him since he was always cold. I looked at his face and listened to his breathing.

His mouth was open, and he looked peaceful, as if he were dreaming of sailing a boat or ice-skating at Rockefeller Center as he once did. His breathing and heart rate had changed so much over the past few months that I didn't think much about his breathing being a little more rapid than usual today. He was sound asleep and seemed at peace, so I went to work knowing that soon my mother would be there to make him breakfast and get him cleaned up.

As I drove down I-95 in my old smoking Ford Explorer with a blown gasket—the first car I'd ever bought with my own money—I got a phone call from my mom. I heard sniffling and heavy breathing on the other end. She tried to say my name, but her voice cracked.

"Mike…" she finally said.

"Mom, what's wrong?" My heart clenched. I knew deep down what she was going to say.

"Pop's gone, Mike. He died."

twenty-eight

I immediately pulled my car over to the side of the highway.

Pop's gone.

I'd prepared myself to hear those words, but it wasn't enough.

I turned off the engine, turned on my hazard lights, and wept. I sat there on the side of the highway for what seemed like an eternity, flooded with an ocean of grief.

When I was finally able to pull myself together somewhat, I rushed home to be by my mother's side. My sister Lillian and my mom's brother, Glen, were already at the house. Gabby was on her way home from D.C.

I ran through the door and burst into Pop's room. Part of me couldn't believe he'd really died. But when I entered the room and saw my family huddled around his lifeless body, I knew it was irrevocably true. My family gazed up at me with tears filling their eyes.

There was no doubt. Pop was gone.

Thoughts pounded my mind. *Did I do everything I could to keep him comfortable? Did he know how much I loved him, or how much we're*

all going to miss him?

In the weeks leading up to Pop's passing, we'd all attempted to say some of the things to him that we'd always wanted to say but were too busy or too scared or too stubborn to say in the past. But still, I kept asking myself: *Was it enough? Did I get to tell him everything that's in my heart?*

I was overcome with searing regret that my addiction had kept me from my grandfather for so many years. I was crushed by the knowledge that I never got the chance to sit down with Pop and experience all his great wisdom, stories, and anecdotes before Parkinson's took him away. By the time I'd gotten clean and made amends with the people I'd hurt, it was too late.

I was on an emotional roller coaster. I'd been Pop's primary care-taker for all this time. I'd written stories about him saying how proud I was to call him my grandfather. I'd learned more about humility, compassion, caring, and patience during my time with him than I had in all the years before. I could see in my family's worried expressions at how I was going to handle this. They were scared that Pop's passing might interfere with my recovery.

Upon seeing the scene in the room, I broke down. My mother ran to me and hugged me tighter than I could ever remember. She whispered in my ear, "You did great, Michael. The only reason he made it as far as he did is because of you. Remember that. Be proud of yourself."

Her words made me sob even harder. Her praise of me for pas-sionately caring for and deeply loving her dad meant everything to me. I would never forget her words.

The days after Pop's passing were not easy. Gabby made the long trek up from Washington, D.C., to attend the wake and funeral and

to be with us. We all spent the first days together at my mother's house, sharing stories about Pop and comforting each other when the pain was too deep.

Pop was buried with full military honors at a cemetery in Easton, Connecticut, next to his parents. His one remaining friend, Milty, showed up with his wife. I shook Milty's hand with a lump in my throat. It pained me to see the old man's sobbing and grief-stricken face over the passing of his last friend in the world.

Gabby and I read short stories about Pop-Pop, which we both struggled to get through without being overcome by tears. After a twenty-one-gun salute and playing of "Taps," my grandfather was lowered into his final resting spot, beneath the softening New England soil.

After my grandfather died, I moved in with Lillian in Norwalk to be closer to my work. The move strengthened my determination to continue sober living, healthy eating, and maintaining a schedule at the local gym. I missed caring for Pop, though. Through helping Pop and during my recovery, I'd discovered great value in helping others. I made the decision that with any extra time I had, I would start giving back.

I began looking for ways to help other struggling people. Eventually, the chance presented itself.

Every summer, the Connecticut Challenge sponsored a cycling event to raise funds to benefit cancer survivors in the state. In order to take part in the 50-mile leg of the ride, participants were required to raise $750 for charity. I'd just bought myself a brand-new pro road bike, a Cannondale CAAD-8, which felt like good timing. Participating in this ride was the perfect opportunity to give back while also doing what I loved.

Right off the bat, though, I was unsure about my ability to raise the funds, let alone complete a 50-mile ride on one of the toughest, hilliest routes in the Northeast. Then I thought of Pop-Pop and his battle with colon cancer and Parkinson's. I decided to ride in honor of Pop-Pop. That decision gave me everything I needed to push forward and find donors.

I sat down to write a letter to my friends, clients, and family, asking them to donate. Within two months of sending out those letters, I had surpassed my donation goal. It filled my heart with gratitude to know that I had earned money to help cancer survivors. The only thing left to do was train for the ride.

In July 2012, I completed the 50-mile segment of the Connecticut Challenge. As I neared the finish line, my mother, my father, Melissa, Lillian, and her boyfriend, Pete, were all there to cheer me on. I was struck by the sight of hundreds of cancer-stricken children lining the sidewalk, waving and clapping as we passed by. Many of the kids and their parents had tears rolling down their cheeks. It took all my willpower to ride by without breaking down like other riders did. Just knowing that I was making a difference for these children meant the world to me.

The moment I crossed the finish line, I thought of my grandfather. I thought of the people I'd hurt in my addiction and the pain I'd caused my family. I thought of my childhood friends who weren't there to watch me finish as they continued to wrestle with the challenges of drug addiction. But more than anything, I thought of my recovery.

I thought about a return to the path I was destined to travel. I thought about inner strength, perseverance, and never giving up. But most of all, as that tape burst open and my family ran toward me with open arms, I thought about *redemption.*

twenty-nine

2013-2014
U.S. opioid deaths: 25,052-28,647

As the summer of 2012 wound down, my family, Melissa, and I decided to spend Labor Day in Cape Cod at the family home of Lillian's boyfriend and future husband, Pete. I liked Pete very much. He fit in well with our family, and I felt an immediate rapport with him.

All of us spent the entire trip bonding. Sometimes the women would go off to spend time together, leaving me and Pete to chat over a round of golf or a bike ride. Pete was like an older brother to me, and we ended up talking extensively about mortgages, stocks, and health insurance—all things I had no knowledge of.

During that vacation, I tried to spend time with each of my family members separately for some one-on-one bonding. It felt good to build back all that was lost during my addiction.

One sunny day, Gabby and I decided to take a day trip to Nantucket. For lunch, we found a small burger shack overlooking the Atlantic Ocean.

"How are you, Mikey?" she asked as we sat down.

"I'm good," I said—my standard generic reply. "Just riding the bike. Finding work to do. Everything is positive."

She studied me. "No. I mean, how are you *really*?"

It was clear she sensed I'd been keeping something to myself.

She was right. I hadn't wanted to burden my family, but as much as I was getting back on track and things were going well in my life, I was still internally struggling. Lately, my anxiety had been skyrocketing, as well as thoughts of guilt, regret, and sorrow. Maybe I hadn't been hiding it as well as I'd thought.

I took a deep breath and met my sister's eyes. "Gab, I'm going to tell you something. But you can't mention this to Mom. Promise me."

"Of course, Mikey. I promise," she said.

I paused for a moment before speaking. "I haven't been doing so good. I can't get my mind to stop racing. It happens every single day and I can't—" My voice cracked, and my eyes filled with tears. "I've been having these thoughts about sometimes not wanting to be here anymore."

It was hard to get the words out, but as I emotionally unburdened myself, Gabby listened with compassion and understanding.

I didn't know if it was okay to be feeling this way. Even though my life had changed 180 degrees for the better, I still had hard times. Was this normal? Would it ever get better? Or was I doomed to these bouts of suffering with no end in sight?

Gabby assured me that everyone struggled and that it was all part of the human experience. She let me know that I wasn't alone and that things would not always be a straight shot toward happiness. There were still going to be dark days, even with all the positive changes occurring in my life. I just had to keep persevering.

Her words made sensc, and I knew she was right. Luckily, my tenacity and determination through my past experiences had prepared me for this period. I'd earned a warrior mentality, and it was here to stay.

That conversation with Gabby on Nantucket had a profound effect on me. After that day, I never spiraled into that level of darkness again. While I continued to have bouts of inadequacy, insecurity, or anxiety, that deep form of despair was gone. It was almost as if the most destructive element of myself had needed to have the light shone on it—and like a cockroach, it went scurrying away. That offered an important lesson to me and to others whom I knew struggled: *In time, everything changes. One might feel extremely low at certain points in life, but it won't always be that way. Just hang in there. It will get better.*

It was important for people to remember this when they were in the throes of suffering.

The rest of my vacation in Cape Cod went by in a haze of relaxation. The weather was warm and beautiful, and we spent most of our time hanging out or lying in the sun. Due to my hard work and dedication to fitness, I was finally comfortable taking off my shirt on the beach. This was a huge step for me. The scars from the various traumas of my past remained, but I had done my best to get my body back into shape.

A few weeks after the trip, my mom was looking through some of the beach photos.

"How much weight have you lost, Mikey?" she asked.

"I have no idea," I replied. It dawned on me that I hadn't stepped on a scale since my first day in rehab more than two years ago. Later that evening, I weighed myself at the gym.

I couldn't believe the number. After weighing in at 280 pounds just two years earlier, I now weighed 184 pounds. Through dieting and exercise, I had lost almost 100 pounds of pure fat.

Others had also begun noticing the extreme physical change in me. They often asked for advice on weight loss. Although I wasn't an expert on the topic, I shared what had worked for me.

Friends started bringing younger buddies to me for advice on healthy living, and I discovered that some of those kids were newly starting on the path of drug abuse and addiction. After talking to these kids and feeling as though I'd helped them, I knew I'd found a calling. My interaction with struggling young people confirmed what I already knew—that the bond between addicts is like no other. We understood the unique brand of suffering that the lifestyle created: emptiness, loss, guilt, and pain.

Through this bond, I saw that I might be able to truly help these kinds of kids. I began working with teenagers and young adults of Milford who'd strayed down the same path that I once did, work I continue to this day. There was no greater joy than getting a text message from a nineteen-year-old who told me that my words were the reason he'd been clean for more than ninety days or a sixteen-year-old who said I'd inspired her to not take her life.

That sealed the deal for me.

One thing I'd learned from my journey, however, was that even with the greatest of triumphs, a fall can be waiting around the corner...

On a warm summer afternoon in August 2012, I decided to take a bike ride around the beaches of my old hometown. As I approached an intersection at an admittedly reckless downhill speed of thirty miles an hour, an older woman driving a Toyota failed to see me and ran into the front wheel of my bike.

It happened too quickly for me to react. I didn't even have time to brace for the collision.

After the initial impact of my body hitting the pavement, I didn't remember anything beyond that. The world went black. Witnesses later told me that I'd been thrown over the hood of the woman's car and landed square on my face in the middle of the intersection. The fall was especially treacherous because of the professional clip-in bike shoes that attached the bike to my feet; when I fell, the bike came with me.

Like the other traumatic accidents of my past, I remembered only bits and pieces of the ambulance ride to the ER. After regaining full consciousness at Yale New Haven Hospital, I learned of the damage to my body. My face had deep gaping wounds, my arms and legs were oozing blood through my shredded clothes, and my body was covered in extensive road rash. The worst part, though, was the major concussion on my head that produced a large, throbbing, painful lump and thick brain fog.

I thanked God that on a last-minute whim, I'd decided to wear a helmet on my bike ride that day.

Ever since I'd first started riding, my mother and father had urged me to wear a helmet. I'd always made excuses for not wearing one, saying I looked dumb or it was too hot or that I forgot. I assured everyone that I was a safe rider, had it under control, and that nothing would happen. I never considered the alternative.

The nurses showed me my bike helmet. The back rim had completely cracked in half. The medical staff told me that if I hadn't been wearing a helmet, I would have died from traumatic brain injuries.

The pain was intense and overwhelming.

But when the nurse offered me painkillers, I turned them down for the first time in my life.

This was a milestone for me. I knew that I could never again rely on medication to numb my physical or emotional suffering. It just wasn't worth it. The fear of relapse was real. Managing my pain in a healthy way without using drugs had to be a permanent part of my life.

After extensive CT scans, X-rays, and other tests, I was able to leave the hospital in a wheelchair. There were fresh scrapes and abrasions all over my body, including my face. It was difficult to move. My lower back throbbed in terrible pain, and my vision was blurry.

But I was thankful. I felt lucky to be alive.

After weeks of therapy and chiropractic visits, the pain finally lessened, and I was able to regain most of the movement I'd lost. But just like my other traumas, the scars, both physical and emotional, remained.

Besides the lasting damage to my body, my mental clarity never fully recovered after that concussion. I'd had too many traumatic blows to the head. There was only so much a brain could take before it eventually would have trouble healing itself.

As always, my support network was there to aid me in every part of my recovery. They continued to show me their unconditional love and prove that we as humans are only as strong as the people around us. It was painful for me to imagine others out there trying to get through their struggles alone. I knew that if everyone had the kind of support I had, the recovery success rate would be much higher.

In 2013, Melissa and I broke up. We'd had a wonderful, caring relationship, but it had run its course. Although she'd been an important part of my life and recovery, we had a basic incompatibility that wasn't going to work for the long haul. She was an introvert who liked staying in. I was an extrovert who wanted to be out in the world.

As the early sheen of our relationship began to lose its luster, we started to argue. After a year of dating, we parted ways with the promise to remain friends, which we still are to this day.

I wouldn't get into another relationship for seven years. Instead, I continued to focus on my recovery, my health, and my work.

I networked throughout the state and made connections. I enrolled in college and began taking classes and studying. I eventually obtained my associate degree from Connecticut Community College. It was a powerful feeling to finally reach a goal I'd always wanted to achieve, a dream that had been robbed by addiction. It was like closing a door that had been left open.

Over the next several years, I worked at a variety of jobs. I wrote for America Online. I worked for a large firm surveying the land of uber-wealthy Greenwich landowners. As a land surveyor, I learned the importance of precision, details, and getting things right.

I also worked as the head of a dog camp where I was required to drive around and pick up thirty to forty dogs from their homes and then supervise their playtime as they romped around a muddy backyard.

No job taught me more than my job running the dog camp. From the outside looking in, it seemed like a lighthearted, fun position, but in truth it was anything but that. It was the most difficult job I'd ever had. I endured frigid winter temperatures, an extremely abusive boss, a poorly run business, and severe on-the-job stress that sometimes entailed prying open the jaws of ferocious pit bulls as they viciously attacked German shepherds or Dobermans—or vice versa.

Most evenings, I would leave the chaotic dog yard at 7 p.m. covered in blood and mud, with my toes on the edge of frostbite, drive around to drop off the dogs, and then come back to headquarters to return the truck, only to find my boss waiting for me with a dark

scowl on his face.

"How did that fucking dogfight happen today?" he'd shout. "Are you a retard that you can't watch a few fucking dogs? I'm docking your pay for today, and next time you're fucking done! You can go back to being a homeless heroin addict, you dumbshit."

There were many times I wanted to quit. In hindsight, I *should* have quit. Even my family wanted me to leave. Most semi-normal people would have thrown in the towel after just one time standing knee-deep in December mud, covered in blood from dog bites, and enduring a verbal onslaught after a twelve-hour day. But for some reason, I stayed. I persevered through each day, determined to conquer it. I liked the feeling I had when I got home, took off my boots, and sat back, knowing I'd made it through another day. As much as I'd escaped the addict's war zone that was my life on the streets, part of me was clearly still drawn to the pain, the trauma, and the rush of a shitty situation. It was familiar.

Day after day, I learned tenacity and resilience in that job. I was proud of myself for not quitting, even in the worst of times. Those moments, like all the trials that came before them, were seared into my bones as a reminder: *I paid my dues to be where I am.*

Eventually, the dog camp company started to take on water and my paychecks started bouncing. I had no choice but to leave.

As I left work on my last day, I felt an enormous sense of freedom. I'd had tremendous pride in sticking out a tough situation, but that feeling paled in comparison to walking away from a toxic, dangerous, abusive environment.

Unfortunately, I didn't have another job lined up. Running that dog camp had been the job I'd held longest in my life.

I was nervous about being out of work. I was living with Lillian and her husband, Pete, in Norwalk and paying rent at a "friends and

family discount." I had to pay for health insurance and car insurance, plus car payments…and now I was back at square one, with no job and no serious prospects.

At this point, I'd made a whole new set of friends in Connecticut. Most of them lived in Milford. They were younger than me and shared many of my former troubling habits. They drank and partied to excess. But unlike my old friends, they had a core redeeming quality: They all wanted to win in life.

No matter how hard they partied or how little they slept, whenever those things started to affect their ability to sell mortgages or trade stocks, they would cut it off or at least cut back. At the end of the day, my new friends were all driven by the desire to be successful or make money or build businesses. They were productive and developing lives of worth. They weren't going to let partying get in the way of that.

I saw that my new friends were able to live with moderation and self-control, and I developed the same mindset. Now that I'd crawled out of the slums of darkness, I wanted to win. I didn't even know what game I was playing per se, but I wanted to be a champion. I wanted to be a success. If something I was doing got in the way of my business or my ability to network or my gym routine, I cut that shit out. That desire to make something of myself, of my life, continued to keep me away from the drugs that almost killed me.

One of my new friends was a guy named Pat. He was from a big Italian family. He was one of the hardest partyers in the crew but also had the strongest urge to succeed. For this reason, Pat and I became good friends.

Over the course of 2014 and 2015 we explored innumerable new business ideas. He got licensed to sell houses. We took stock trading courses together. We made business tutorials and tried to sell them

online. I wrote for online newspapers and even started a food blog, called The Essential Foodie, which did well. We didn't know exactly what we wanted to do, but we knew we wanted to win and that was enough.

One day, I saw a post on Craigslist that made me sit up and take notice. A brand founder was looking for a "social media expert" who could help blow up his personal channels. I responded to the ad with a bunch of exaggerated stuff about my brief time writing for America Online. I Googled brand-speak and terms like "brand awareness," "cost-per-click," and other marketing terminology that I didn't fully understand—and threw that shit in there as well. I didn't know what would come of it, if anything.

One day Pat and I had just finished a rough day of day-trading penny stocks. We literally had no clue what we were doing and had legit lost on about 98 percent of our trades. We decided to take a walk to the local Subway for a BMT sandwich. While sitting there chomping away, I got a phone call.

"Hey, is this Mike?" the man asked.

"Yes?" I said hesitantly. I was always reluctant to tell a caller who I was, since it might be someone I didn't want to talk to: Someone from my dealing days. A bill collector. The cops. Or even worse, a fucking telemarketer.

"This is Shawn Nelson," the man said. "I'm the CEO at Lovesac in Stamford. You responded to my Craigslist ad last week. I was hoping we could chat next week at my office."

"Yes, of course, Shawn," I said, outwardly calm as my heart began to pound. "Great to hear from you."

This was *it*.

I felt it in my bones…my life was about to change.

thirty

2015

U.S. opioid deaths: 33,091

"**What** days are good for you to meet next week?" the CEO of Lovesac asked.

"Can you hang on one second?" I said. "My assistant is checking my calendar."

In reality, Pat was blowing bubbles into his Coca-Cola and mouthing, "'Yo, who the fuck is that?"

I walked outside and stood next to the bike rack in front of Baskin-Robbins.

"Sorry, Shawn," I said. "Are you still there?"

"Yeah, man, no problem," he said.

We talked for about ten minutes. He asked me a bunch of questions and, shockingly, I had some good answers related to how I could market his brand. During the past few years, I'd gotten quite good at digital media and social media. I had a decent feel for how to drive brand engagement. My Instagram account already had ten thousand followers. I was driving business to local eateries with my

food blog, and then driving traffic to my blog with Twitter, Tumblr, and Instagram.

From a corporate perspective, though, I had absolutely no idea what I was doing…but Shawn didn't need to know that just yet.

Later in my career at Lovesac, he would say of me, "He was rough around the edges, a street kid. But you would've had to be blind to not spot the talent after a conversation with him."

Shawn and I chatted a bit longer, and then we talked about a time to meet.

"I'm free all week, man," I said. "I can work around your schedule."

"Perfect, brother," he said. "See you Tuesday for lunch. Pumped for this!"

I hung up and stared at my phone. *What the fuck just happened?*

I went back into Subway and told Pat about the call. I didn't understand what had taken place myself, but instinctively, I knew it was big. Once I got home and did some research, I realized what a break this actually was.

Shawn had been building the Lovesac brand since 1996, when he was eighteen. He started out by making the world's largest beanbag chairs in Utah and hustling them to friends in the Salt Lake City area. In the following years, he began producing Sactionals, a line of hyper-adaptable couches. Shawn and his company were adored by celebrities and tastemakers across the country. Everyone from Jamie Foxx to Rob Dyrdek to OutKast owned Lovesacs.

The company grew rapidly, and by the time I spoke with Shawn in 2015, Lovesac operated 50 stores nationwide with approximately $50 million in annual revenue. The company was in an aggressive growth phase, and Shawn had the foresight to understand the power

of social media to drive business. He was persistent and passionate about it, even when other board members and decision-makers were skeptical. That was at a time when many companies were still slow to understand the power of social media, and even slower to harness it.

Shawn got it. He knew that social media was the next wave, and so the following Tuesday I drove my 1999 Ford Explorer to meet him at an upscale lunch spot in a new corporate development in Stamford. I wore a faded, threadbare blue button-down Gap shirt that I'd worn to every business meeting since leaving rehab more than five years earlier.

"What's up, brother?" Shawn said as I walked in the door. He seemed genuinely excited to meet me in person.

Shawn had piercing blue eyes and wore his hair in a pretty tight buzz cut. I learned later that he styled his hair in massive gelled spikes when he was close with world-record holder Rob Dyrdek, gold medalist Ryan Nyquist and the entire X Games crew back in Lovesac's early days.

Most business meetings started with a handshake; this one began with a bear hug. Shawn's personality was a unique blend of relaxed, chill demeanor and explosive high energy. He had a way of transferring his optimism to whoever was in the room with him.

"Good to meet you, man," I said as I took off the peacoat I'd bought specifically for this meeting.

The server came, and Shawn ordered a steak salad. I looked at the menu and saw that the salad was $24. I couldn't believe we were spending that much on lunch. I followed his lead and ordered the same, medium rare. Later, I realized how ordinary all of this was in the business world, but I was so green at the time that everything seemed new and exciting—even a steak salad.

We talked for two hours, covering everything from Shawn's launch of Lovesac with its ups and downs, to some (not all) of my own personal trials and tribulations, to what we thought I could do for Shawn and his brand.

As we talked, it struck me that my ability to build rapport and connect with people was starting to heat up. Some would call this a unique brand of emotional intelligence. Others would call it charisma. In truth, it was simply a sincere openness to people and their perspectives. I was curious and eager to learn about others and what was important to them, and apparently, it showed. Every time I'd ever interviewed for a position I'd gotten the job.

Shawn and I left the restaurant and walked across the street to the Lovesac headquarters. Inside, I was impressed by the hub of busy workers, all focused on the same goal of building this brand.

As Shawn gave me a detailed tour, he talked about the creative process and how he planned to take over the market in this category while building brand awareness. While he talked, I couldn't keep my eyes off the workers. I was intrigued by how focused they were. Everyone had their own workspace, goal, and specialized skill set. Everyone was smiling, and they all looked as though they were having a blast. I'd never seen such a positive work environment. I immediately knew I'd found my new home.

After the tour, Shawn said he'd be in touch. We said goodbye, and I headed to my car. As I drove home, I prayed that things would work out. I hoped Shawn liked me and saw my potential. I worried that I might have appeared too rough around the edges. I wished to the stars that Shawn wouldn't do a background check on me.

As hours went by, I worried that I was too unrefined to get a job like that. Everyone in that office had been so cool. They'd branded

themselves so well. They all had new clothes. They were college grads. They had nice cars and good family lives. Many of them owned homes and had 401(k) accounts. They had their shit all figured out.

Negative thoughts consumed me. *This company is hot…it's blowing up. I may have some skills and talents, but why would they ever want me? Why would they take a chance on some street kid with a criminal record and no experience?*

I'd always struggled with negative thoughts and self-doubt. I battled dark regret over the past and crippling anxiety about the future. I sometimes considered giving up and moving back home. Some days I even had a hard time getting out of bed, too worn out and defeated by all that I'd been through and the relentless negative voices in my head.

But somehow, I always found a way to get out of bed.

No matter how dark I felt or how negative my thoughts were, I got in the habit of showing the fuck up.

And thank God I did, because a week later I got the call I had hoped for.

"Hey, Mike," Shawn said. "I spoke with the rest of the team. We're absolutely stoked to offer you a position. Welcome to the Lovesac family, brother."

What unfolded next would give me a platform for the rest of my life. After starting as Shawn's personal PR specialist and social manager, I quickly proved myself and was absorbed by the Lovesac brand in an official way a year after I started.

At first, I spent most of my time managing Shawn's social channels and trying to build relationships for the brand. I built out his social calendar for the month, responded to celebrities who Tweeted at him, and worked on getting him featured on news shows or in

articles. The Lovesac story and the product itself was so cool that it made my job a lot easier. I felt bad for people who did social media for nail clipper companies and shit. I couldn't imagine how different that kind of job would be from mine.

I quickly moved up the ranks from social media specialist to marketing manager and beyond. I was responsible for some of the biggest waves in Lovesac history, including a Facebook spot that became one of the most viewed branded videos in the first twenty-four hours in Internet history, with more than 43 million views the first day. The video went on to garner over 250 million views, and along with several other ultra-viral posts, secured my spot as one of the more successful social managers in branding history.

But at first, I was just the new guy. And in early 2015, it felt as though I was drinking from a fire hose. There was so much lingo to learn: brand awareness, conversion ads, diminishing return curves, CTAs, CPCs, CTRs, controls. I was completely lost. But between Shawn and his team members Pat Santangelo, Eric Allen, and Charlie Tubb, I had the best teachers I could ask for. I loved every second of it.

After the inception of the brand, Shawn won a competition on a TV show hosted by Richard Branson, who became the first-ever investor in Lovesac. Branson wrote Shawn a check for a million dollars, and the PR from the show gave Lovesac a great infusion of awareness.

Lovesac had many victories, and by mid-2015, Shawn and I were pretty inseparable. The only time we weren't working together was when he traveled, which was quite often. He was always back and forth between Connecticut and factories in China or Los Angeles or Salt Lake City, his hometown.

Eventually, he wanted me to start traveling with him. As a kid, I'd been to Orlando and Vermont, but that was it. Traveling had always seemed like an exciting, unattainable pipe dream to me. I'd gotten somewhat comfortable with the idea that I'd only ever be a big fish in a small pond.

One day, I walked into the office and took off my coat and backpack as usual. At the time, I was working in a tool closet. The company had grown so fast that there was no place for me to sit anymore.

As I settled down to work, Shawn poked his head into my tiny work space.

"Hey, Mike," he said. "What are your plans for the weekend of the twenty-fifth?"

"Uh, probably nothing," I said. "I should be free."

"Lock it down, okay? I'm going to L.A., and you're coming with me."

He turned and walked away.

Excitement raced through me. I couldn't believe this was happening. Since I was a kid, I'd had an obsession with California. Visiting L.A. was on every single bucket list I'd ever written, including the one that got me through rehab in 2010.

It seemed unreal that I was actually going to experience California. It didn't seem possible.

But it was possible, and it was real.

In October 2015, I stepped off a jet at Los Angeles International Airport. I was in L.A. at last, but I didn't know what to expect.

I'd heard so many things about the city: how it was filled with fake people and miles of traffic, how it was dirty and smoggy with an elevated chance of dying in an earthquake.

Yes, there were those things, but they were overshadowed by everything else…all the wonderful things about California.

During my first drive along the Pacific Coast Highway, I marveled at the way the cliffs ran out into the emerald waters of the Pacific Ocean. I'd never seen nature presented this way before. The weather was balmy and warm. Rows of tall palm trees stretched as far as the eye could see. The women were beautiful, with fit, sun-kissed bodies.

I wanted to drink it all in. I cycled the bike route from Venice to the Santa Monica Pier. I rode the Ferris wheel and gazed out over the hills that stretched up the coast toward Zuma Beach in Malibu.

I surfed in Huntington Beach. I lay on the sands of Manhattan Beach and watched content souls work on their tans or play volleyball.

I never wanted to leave.

The next week, as I boarded my Delta flight to return to New York City, I had a tight knot in my stomach. I couldn't bear the idea of going back to my old state and all that it represented.

As we accelerated down the runway at LAX, I promised myself I'd be back. And I kept that promise, every two months for the next three years until I moved there for good.

I couldn't get enough of California.

It was where I belonged.

thirty-one

2016-2017
U.S. opioid deaths: 42,249-47,600

Although I was enamored with California, I wasn't ready to move just yet.

After five days in the Golden State, I arrived back in Connecticut and back at my desk. The City of Angels quickly became nothing but a beautiful memory.

I dived back into work at the Lovesac headquarters, returning emails, taking calls, juggling tasks, and mastering my "third discipline" of multi-tasking. In the debate over which was more important to success, drive or talent, I felt that both were essential but there was a third factor that was paramount: the ability to optimize efficiency and master the art of working on multiple projects simultaneously.

While cranking away at work one day on my numerous tasks, my cell phone lit up with a text from an unknown Ohio number.

"Ayo, is this Mike?" the text read.

I eyed it warily, not knowing the sender.

"Yes," I typed. "Who is this?"

"I got your number from a friend. My name is Logan Paul."

I'd heard of Logan Paul. He was one of the biggest social media influencers in the world, but I didn't know the full extent of it.

In recent years, a whole new industry had emerged. While I'd been struggling to regain control of my life, the use of smartphones had skyrocketed, along with apps like Facebook, Twitter, Instagram, YouTube, and Vine.

At the same time, average people—mostly teens and young adults—were filming themselves with smartphones and posting content online for the entire world to see.

This new industry had started off slowly. Eventually, some of those "everyday people" began to amass followings that were larger than some of the biggest television audiences in the world.

This original crew of budding influencers was small. Some centered their content around video games, others around food reviews, and others around travel. As their audiences grew, their posted videos began to garner millions of views. Brands took notice and began spending advertising money on these videos and photos in order to gain an advantage over the traditional advertising market—one that had held a monopoly for many decades.

The era of the social media influencer had dawned. The top influencers became household names and earned millions of dollars. They became celebrities in their own right, with as much power and influence as any top media personality or businessperson.

On the day in 2015 when I received the text, there was no one hotter in the social media/influencer world than Logan Paul.

His next text went straight to the point. "What's the deal with these Lovesacs, man? Can you fuck on them?"

With my new corporate position, I didn't know the best way to

respond. I knew how I *wanted* to respond but I also didn't want to say anything that could get me in trouble. But in the moment, I took a chance—like I always had in life.

I texted: "Yeah, the covers are machine-washable so the cum washes right out, haha."

Logan's response was immediate: "Hahahahahaha ur funny, dude. Let's work together on something. I need a couple of these in my life."

Years later, Logan would tell media outlets that the reason we became immediate friends was because of how I responded in that first text exchange. He said that I bucked the trend of "normal marketing guys" he'd worked with. That little bit of risk secured a relationship that would help build a successful business partnership and friendship that endures to this day.

In the beginning, our Lovesac team didn't know what to expect from the influencer crowd or how it would affect our brand. In 2015, it truly was the Wild West on the Internet. There was no playbook. There were a few industry "experts" at the time, but it turned out they didn't know much. No one knew much. Everyone was just figuring things out as they went.

During my first year at Lovesac, Shawn and I had looked everywhere for ways to go viral on social media, without success. Shawn instinctively knew it was the next wave, but we underestimated how hard it was to make a splash. We made videos with athletes and traditional celebrities. We made animations. We spent money on stunts and events. We had people line up outside our stores and invited news crews to film it.

Nothing stuck. We garnered a few thousand views here, a couple thousand views there. But no major splashes. Every time we spent

$5,000 or $10,000 on a campaign that failed, the board of directors looked at our efforts with skepticism.

Still, I was willing to try anything to get Lovesac on the map. Shawn and I felt strongly that social media was the future.

During my text exchange with Logan the day he contacted me, I offered to send him three Lovesac beanbag chairs in exchange for a post on his Instagram and Twitter accounts. He told me that his normal fees were far higher than the value of the Lovesacs, but since he loved the product and liked my vibe, he would post this one time in exchange for the chairs.

A month after first connecting with Logan, everything changed. It was a Sunday afternoon, and I was at the beach in Rhode Island, drinking with some friends and hanging out by the water. A text came in from Shawn, just as the sun began to set.

"I've been trying to text you for hours!" his message read. "Where the fuck have you been?"

At that moment, all his other texts came streaming through as well.

"Sorry, man," I responded. "I'm right by the water. I haven't had service all day."

"Go check Twitter and Instagram right now. Something is happening. Site traffic is higher than it's ever been. Like it's-gonna-crash type traffic."

I immediately clicked off my texts and went to Google Analytics. Sure enough, the traffic on the Lovesac site was ten times higher than it had ever been. I went to Instagram and saw that our followers had increased by more than ten thousand since the last time I'd checked, which had been just a few hours earlier.

I quickly shifted over to Twitter and looked at our "mentions"

tab. Every single mention had @lovesac and @loganpaul in it. *Thousands* of mentions!

I immediately texted Shawn. "That kid I told you about who does the splits, Logan Paul—he just posted on Instagram and Twitter for us. I've never seen anything like it in my life."

I was overcome with pure elation. I put my phone down and just basked in the sunlight, knowing that the relationship I'd curated had spiked site traffic by hundreds of thousands of visits. Sales at Lovesac would soon increase proportionally.

What followed that fateful summer day would be one of the more fruitful relationships between a brand and an Internet influencer/creator in the early days of this new online industry. More importantly, it would be the beginning of one of the most important friendships and business relationships in my life.

Upon my arrival at the office the next day, I was greeted with hearty cheers and applause from the entire headquarters. My phone was filled with text messages from Logan's closest friends, such as Amanda Cerny, Juanpa Zurita, King Bach, and others.

Over the next four years, those early relationships in the creator realm snowballed into an influencer program that drove billions of impressions for the Lovesac brand, as well as millions of site visitors and immeasurable increases in top-line revenue. In the end, my efforts as marketing manager for Lovesac and the performance of the influencer program became the topic of case studies, panels, and magazine articles.

I was invited to speak on panels, where I was asked what I thought was the number-one factor that contributed to the success of the program. My response was always the same: "It helps to have a kickass product or a ton of expendable marketing dollars, but the real

key to a successful influencer program is who you have running it."

I learned that influencers were people, just like everyone else. They might be a little better looking than average, or a little more creative or funny or skilled in some way, but at the end of the day, they just wanted to have a conversation with someone who understood their needs. They wanted someone who could add value to their life. One of the most important tips I began sharing with up-and-coming influencer managers was the concept of *brevity*. Influencer-creators were so busy that they couldn't be weighed down by lengthy chats or long memos. Anyone working with them needed to get to the point, and quickly.

But from the beginning, I got it. I talked the talk, and when it came time to start meeting other influencers and celebs in person, I walked the walk, too. I worked hard to develop strong, honest, real relationships with the people I met. In the years since I started running the Lovesac influencer program, I've worked directly with everyone from Jay-Z and Beyoncé to Ariana Grande, Justin Bieber, LeBron James, and countless others in between. They've gone above and beyond for the Lovesac brand because of the strong and sincere relationships we've built.

At first, that little bit of gas was all we needed at Lovesac. The product began to sell like crazy. I would spend the next few years expanding my Rolodex with hundreds of influencers, content creators, singers, artists, and athletes for the brand, but my strongest relationship was with Logan.

In 2016, after months of texting back and forth, I finally met Logan face-to-face at Travis Pastrana's house in Maryland. Travis was one of the most well-known and well-respected people in the action sports community. As an insane daredevil, he was one of the first

people to backflip a motocross bike. He'd won multiple gold medals at the X Games and was responsible for the Nitro Circus television show and tour. In short, he was—and is—an action sports icon.

At the Lovesac headquarters, the team and I had dreamed up a crazy idea to have Travis jump his motorcycle off his biggest ramp over a massive airbag and have Logan Paul knock him out of the sky with a $1,500 Lovesac beanbag, shot from a gigantic slingshot. I pitched the idea to Logan, Lovesac covered his travel to Maryland, and soon we were on a brand activation at Travis's house.

I didn't know what to expect upon meeting Logan. Even though we'd built a friendship over text, it was still hard to know what he might be like in person.

I was already at Travis's house when Logan rolled in. It was early morning when he got out of his car and walked down the long driveway of Travis's estate. At the time, Logan had a wild blond puff of hair and looked like some sort of cartoon character.

"What up, Mike!" he yelled as soon as he saw me. "This place is fucking insane!"

He trotted down the rest of the hilly driveway and gave me the first dap, or handshake.

"Good to meet you, brother," I said. "How was the trip in?" I was slightly nervous and unsure how to act toward him. While I'd worked with some smaller creators in person, I was still green and getting my approach down.

"Great! I had a lay-flat bed in first class. Can't say the same for Mark," he said, laughing.

Mark Dohner, his videographer, had flown economy. Mark was tall, six-foot-four, so he hadn't had the best six-hour flight.

I later learned that Mark had been Logan's cameraman from the

beginning, following him everywhere when Logan had first starting vlogging. Within a few years, Mark accumulated a massive following of his own. He later split off from Logan to start creating his own content and making millions.

Mark's career was just one of many that Logan helped build by including him in his sphere. It was an indicator of Logan's power that nearly every person around him from the beginning became a successful influencer, actor, or businessperson with their original Internet awareness built by Logan's platforms. These were talented people in their own right, but most of them had no idea that they'd jumped on a rocket ship that was going to travel farther than anyone expected…except Logan. From the beginning, the kid just had it. His energy was infectious. He was good-looking, intelligent, and funny, and he knew how to control his audience. He had the sauce from day one. When everyone else in the industry was obsessing over how to make a few thousand bucks, he was already dead set on becoming the biggest entertainer in the world. For him, it was never just a pipe dream—he had the talent and the drive to get there.

During the weekend I first met Logan in person, another influencer-creator named Roman Atwood came out to the Maryland estate as well, accompanied by his wife, Britt. We spent the weekend rolling around Travis's playground of a property, skating, off-roading, just being boys. We all got a chance to bond. We got a kickass piece of content for Lovesac and left with a bunch of new friends.

Logan went back to California, but I had an important event to attend. My sister Gabby was getting married in Washington, D.C., just a few hours from Travis's house. She was marrying her longtime love, Jack, a graduate of Annapolis Naval Academy and a veteran pilot for the Navy.

I'd missed Gabby's college graduation along with so many other important events in her life during the years I was stuck in a cycle of abuse and addiction. I was elated to be able to share in my little sister's big day and see her walk down the aisle. She'd even asked me to give a speech in front of hundreds of guests.

I didn't have a date since I was coming straight from Travis's house, and neither did my mom. I was honored to walk her down the aisle and escort her to her seat before the ceremony. It was probably the first time my mother had seen me in a tuxedo since my high school prom.

I watched my mom and dad's faces light up with happiness as Gabby and Jack read their vows—a happiness that was compounded by the presence of their son. I'll never forget the pure joy I felt that day.

It was a sense of coming back to myself and all the good in my life…to the love that had been there all along.

I flew back from D.C. after an incredible week. I was on cloud nine. The shoot with Logan had gone great, and my little sister had married the love of her life. Work was going well, my relationship with my family was stronger than ever, and I was truly happy in my life.

But I had an anxious feeling in the pit in my stomach. Everything seemed too good to be true. It had to be.

After years of hell, I'd become conditioned to thinking the other shoe would drop. When was the rug going to be pulled out from under me? I often struggled with that feeling. For many years, I'd been accustomed to things going badly wrong. I'd gotten used to the terrible pain. It was hard for my brain to ever imagine things going right for long.

I began working in my mind, training it to think differently. Every day, I forced myself to wake up thankful and grateful for what I'd been given. I told myself that as long as I kept doing right by others, good would continue to come my way.

Despite my work, I still sometimes found myself in the shower, gripped by worry or anxiety. My mind whirled with fear: *This can't be real. Something bad is bound to happen, just like it used to.*

Any time I felt like this, I calmed myself again by finding solace in my continued strength. I told myself, "If I can control the outcome of a situation, then I trust myself to make the right decision and for the outcome to reflect that." I told others who were experiencing similar emotions the same. "Get in the habit of trusting yourself. You're smarter and wiser than you know. Believe that."

On the flip side, I realized that if I couldn't control the outcome of a situation, I'd think, "Fuck it." For years, I used to worry about such things as genetic disease and atomic war. Now, unless I was able to do something better to positively affect an outcome, I didn't give a shit. I believed that what was out of my control should also be out of my mind. Easier said than done, of course, but when perfected, I believed this mindset—a version of the Serenity Prayer, in a way— could save me and others a ton of mental and emotional real estate.

After all my self-work, that real estate and trust in myself had started to *bear real fruit.*

For that next year after meeting Logan, his view of me grew from a friendly acquaintance into a trusted confidant and advisor.

In early 2017, I led Lovesac into teaming up with Logan again. This time, we took a trip to the Sundance Film Festival in Utah. We rented a massive ski-in/ski-out house on the peak of Deer Valley. For someone who loved skiing as much as I did, I was elated. Logan

brought along a few other influencers including Chantel Jeffries, Alissa Violet, and his then-videographer Spencer Taylor, whom I met for the first time on that trip.

We partied in the theater at our insane $20 million mansion. We skied Park City and Deer Valley. We partied in town. We were brought onstage during a performance by an up-and-coming DJ named Marshmello, and the crowd went wild below us. Everywhere we went, we were ushered inside quickly, away from popping cameras.

Logan was used to the fame by now, but it was my first taste of the limelight. Even as just a temporary entourage member, I felt part of the "in-crowd," and I liked it.

Aside from all the hype, the Sundance trip also introduced me to the world of Logan's vlogs. I'd previously made a small appearance in one of his pieces, but this time I was front and center alongside Logan. Up until then, he'd primarily known me as a marketing liaison, but as the Sundance trip carried on, he noticed that I was able to convert my off-screen comedy and energy into an on-screen personality. We bounced jokes well off each other and were on the same page in terms of energy and culture.

Just like that, the era of Logan and Big Mike began.

Sundance 2017 was the first of many trips I made to collaborate with Logan that year. I would fly to California any chance I got and stay at Logan's for weeks at a time. Slowly, this began to eat away at my time with Lovesac. By the end of the year, I was bicoastal, going back and forth between California and Connecticut.

"Soon enough, you're gonna leave us," Shawn said one day after I got back from another L.A. voyage. "I feel it."

"Bro, I could never," I said. "You're the reason I'm here. You

believed in me. I don't think I could ever leave Lovesac."

In reality, I had already started negotiating with Logan's Team Maverick management to put together a contract for employment. Logan had driven over $30 million in clothing sales in 2017, and his team was actively looking for ways to scale up and hire an influencer team to get other influencers wearing Maverick clothes. That was where I would come in.

On top of that, Logan was collaborating with The Rock, Kevin Hart, and other A-list celebrities. In October 2017, he appeared on *Jimmy Kimmel Live!* He was months into a relationship with a talented Hollywood actress by the name of Chloe Bennet.

As the year drew to a close, Logan Paul was on top of the world. He was one of the most googled celebrities in 2017 and everyone was watching to see where the rocket ship would go next. There were a ton of guesses, but not a single person in the world could have predicted what would happen next.

As I went to sleep early in the morning on New Year's Day, I was grateful and excited for the future. I was excited for Logan, for me, and for a potential future with Team Maverick.

I had no idea what was in store...

thirty-two

2018
U.S. opioid deaths: 46,802

My phone buzzed incessantly, forcing me out of my slumber. My eyes struggled to open. It was New Year's Day 2018, and my notification alerts were going crazy.

"Must be standard 'Happy New Year' texts from my friends and family," I thought. I turned off the notifications without reading the messages, rolled over, and went back to sleep.

When I finally woke up around 11 a.m., I looked at my iPhone screen. There were 226 missed texts and 32 missed calls. Way too many. Something was up.

I scrolled through the messages.

"Yo, are you fucking seeing this?"

"Hey mike, this isn't good."

"Not the best way to start off the New Year."

"Logan is a piece of fucking shit for this, and so are you for being friends with him."

"Mike, call me immediately."

As I read down the never-ending list of texts, my heart dropped to the floor. What the fuck was going on?

I opened a text from a girl who Logan had dated previously, and who had become a close friend of mine.

"Mike," she texted. "Please call me when you wake up. Are you seeing all this?" She sent a link to an article from a news website based in New York City. The headline read: *Logan Paul Posts Suicide Forest Video on YouTube.*

When I clicked on the link, the video was gone. It had already been taken down.

But the damage was done.

On the evening of December 31, 2017, Logan had uploaded what would become arguably the most infamous video in Internet history. He'd been in Tokyo with friends for the holiday. While visiting Japan's Aokigahara Forest, nicknamed the "Suicide Forest" for the staggering number of people who kill themselves there each year, Logan and his team had happened upon the body of a man who had hung himself from a tree moments before. The man dangled in plain sight, just a few hundred meters from the parking lot.

As Logan walked toward the body, he instinctively did what he'd done for years: He directed his videographer to start filming.

His initial reaction to the dead body was uncomfortable laughter, a common reaction documented by psychologists in some situations where humans are unable to properly process strong emotions.

After some debate with his video team, Logan edited the piece and uploaded it to his YouTube channel. The video contained a call to action from Logan with the promise to raise suicide awareness in Tokyo and abroad.

As Logan and his team slept, the video attracted over six million

views and the resoundingly negative attention of the world.

When Logan awoke in Tokyo on January 1 and saw the extreme backlash to his video, he promptly removed it from his YouTube channel. It was too late.

Over the next week, Logan Paul was digitally eviscerated. Celebrities from America to Australia expressed their outrage and anger toward him. Every news organization from CNN to MSNBC to Fox News reported on what the majority of people agreed was one of the most heinous acts the Internet had ever seen. The story trended globally at number one on every social media platform. It seemed the entire world was obsessed with Logan Paul's instant fall from grace.

In the days after the video was posted, Logan posted sincere apologies in both written and video form, but they did little to calm the massive uprising of rage toward him. People from around the world were calling on YouTube to permanently remove Logan's channel. Logan's business deals were killed by marketing teams. His show that had been scheduled to air on YouTube RED was immediately canned. The Rock and Kevin Hart quickly distanced themselves from Logan and their relationships with him. The world wanted blood.

And at the receiving end of this massive funnel of hate was a twenty-three-year-old kid from Cleveland. He'd spent years posting videos that were judged solely on view count. In an attempt to shock and engage, to drive more of those views, he'd had made an extremely poor decision. He'd gone too far. He'd made a mistake. A grave mistake, but a mistake nevertheless. In Logan's case, that mistake was reviewed, discussed, and debated by millions of people on the world stage.

I texted Logan the night of January 1: "How are you, brother?"

"Not good, dude. Not good at all."

"When are you coming back?"

"We're leaving tomorrow for L.A."

"Listen, man. For what it's worth, it'll blow over. It'll be the hottest thing for a week until some elite asshole cheats on his wife. Keep your head up."

We texted for a few minutes longer. By the time we signed off, it seemed he had a bit better mindset than when we'd started. All my pain and struggles had put me in a unique position to give words of encouragement to people in their own times of hardship and peril.

I also felt strong anger at the situation. Of course, Logan was at fault for posting the video on his channel, but my background in the brand world had taught me that there should have been layers of review first. That is standard operating procedure for brands that generate millions of dollars of revenue a year. The scandal immediately revealed to me that Logan, while young, reckless, and hardheaded, was also being mismanaged (or undermanaged, at the least) by his current team.

By the time I flew to L.A. a few weeks later, Logan was embroiled in another scandal, this time for using a Taser on a dead rat on his balcony. Now I was livid.

"I fucking told you last month," I said. "Get a review system in place. How the fuck did this happen?"

I texted Logan, his manager, even his parents. The dead rat scandal cost him more sponsors and led to the demonetization of his YouTube channel, which meant he was ineligible to collect ad revenue. It also made his "Tokyo was a singular mistake" defense harder to believe.

Over the next week, I sat with Logan and offered advice on his current business structure and the way I saw the Maverick brand

being run and managed. I didn't expect him to act on any of my advice unless he wholeheartedly agreed. For me, this was not a play to further my own placement on his team. I was simply trying to help a friend I cared about.

Together, Logan and I hammered out a working structure on how Team Maverick would handle the scandals moving forward. That trust became the bedrock for our current working relationship.

Over the course of 2018, Logan, his team, and I worked diligently to repair his image and rebuild the struggling Maverick brand. We worked through months of infighting in a power struggle between parents, management, lawyers, investors, and accountants as a brand that had driven over $50 million in revenue the year before now struggled to stay afloat.

The effects of my advisory position began to show. Every single piece of content that went out, no matter how big or small, would now be reviewed by a multiple-person team to ensure it was appropriate for public consumption. People who were toxic to the business were pushed to the sidelines. Strategic meetings that should have been commonplace years earlier became a weekly occurrence.

More than just working with Logan on his business and content, however, I worked with him on *him*, just as I'd spent years working on myself.

I encouraged him to build bridges with other influencers, as opposed to burning them. I pushed him to ditch the cocky-jock image he'd risen to fame with. In an attempt to age him up, I urged him to watch movies, listen to music, and align with a culture that I hoped would one day embrace him again. I offered him advice on how to be a more effective leader to his team. Both of us learned together about the new approach he'd have to adopt in order to move past the

scandals that had almost ended his career.

As time passed, I watched Logan grow as a businessperson and human being. He became more grounded, and his life began to take on new meaning and substance.

During that time, Logan's romantic relationship with Chloe Bennet also had a profound effect on him as a person. During the months Logan and Chloe were together, their love for each other had softened Logan and made him embrace concepts like empathy and compassion more intimately. While Logan and Chloe split later in 2018, he credited her role in becoming the man he is today, and they still maintain a friendship.

As Logan's career began to swing back upward after months of hard work behind the scenes, I faced a momentous decision about my own career.

One day, in September 2018, Logan and I had a serious conversation about his future plans and the direction of my career. We sat, ironically, on a couple of Lovesacs in his garage—the same beanbag chairs I'd offered him in our original partnership—as we discussed my role in his company and a potential podcast we might do together.

Logan said, "It's pretty obvious how important you've become to this team, Mike. If we're going to try this podcast, you're going to have to move out here full-time. I've made a request to the business team to get you an official offer with Team Maverick."

I was excited, but I was also at a difficult crossroads.

I'd lived in Connecticut my entire life. I was close to my family in case I needed them or they needed me. After years of torturing them with my addiction, I was finally on the right path and loved spending time with them. With Lovesac, I'd created a nice little niche for

myself in the brand world and had begun to build a healthy 401(k). I had stock in the company, and we'd just brought Lovesac public on NASDAQ. I'd made strides in fixing my terrible credit and had been able to secure a mortgage to purchase a beautiful condo in South Norwalk, right on the water. I'd finally set up a happy life for myself after years of destruction and self-sabotage.

But the opportunity with Logan was a dream come true.

While I wrestled with my decision, a tragedy rocked the world that would make the choice a little easier to make.

One day while at Lovesac HQ, I walked out of a meeting we'd had regarding a collaboration with the video game Call of Duty. It was going to be our biggest collaboration ever, and I was completely focused on the project. I hadn't looked at my phone all morning.

As I came out of the glass meeting room into the large open-concept office, I was approached by my manager, Charlie.

"Yo, Mike, did you hear?"

I instantly knew the tone. Someone had passed.

"No," I said. "What happened?"

"Mac Miller died. Overdose."

My heart went into free fall. My knees buckled and tears welled up.

Mac Miller's music had made a deep impact on me during my recovery. It had been my solace and escape as I rode my bike and found my way back to myself. It had given me hope.

As I mourned the passing of Mac Miller, I remembered all the times I'd listened to his mixtapes and gone to his shows up and down the East Coast. I remembered his albums *Blue Slide Park* and *K.I.D.S.* and all the songs that had affected me so much.

His death hit home in so many ways. He'd also been an addict.

He'd started out as a recreational drug user, but his mental demons had led him down a path to other hard substances.

On September 7, 2018, he'd accidentally overdosed on a bad batch of cocaine mixed with fentanyl. At twenty-six years old, his staggering talent and potential as an artist and a human being was stripped from the world forever.

Mac's death took a piece out of my heart. The fact that he'd been unable to escape his struggles filled me with deep sadness and pain. His music reflected how hard he'd struggled with his mind and interior suffering.

Mac Miller's death brought the fentanyl problem in America front and center. Over the past few years, the number of overdose deaths linked to the illicit narcotic used to cut opioids and cocaine had spiked tremendously. If I'd continued using heroin, I have no doubt I would have already perished as a result of fentanyl.

In the weeks after Mac's death, I sat in my condo in South Norwalk, drilling my mind on what to do about the decision I was faced with.

It was hard to imagine taking a leap of faith and moving away from everything I'd put together. But on the other hand, I knew what I had to do. I knew there was so much more for me out there. I knew there was so much I owed the world, and so much the world could offer me back. All I had to do was make the jump.

Plus, I was in fucking love with California.

Mac Miller's death crystallized in my mind how short life is and how important it is to live one's life fully, productively, and from a place of truth because one never knows when it will end.

I wrestled with the decision for weeks. But in the end, my heart wouldn't let me go any other way but west.

My mom gave me her blessing to leave.

"All I ever wanted for you is for you to be happy," she said. "I love you, and I'll miss you every day, but if it makes you happy, then do it."

We hugged each other and cried. My mom's love had been my strength for so long, and now it was time for me to fly. It had been a long journey for both of us, but now here we were.

Breaking the news to Shawn was also emotional. "This isn't easy for me to say," I said, "but I'm going to be moving in with Logan next month and officially joining Team Maverick."

Shawn was the most intelligent and respectful of any CEO I've ever met. His response showed his professionalism and good heart.

"I obviously can't say I didn't see it coming, brother," he said. "While I'm sad that you're leaving, I couldn't be more excited for you. You're gonna do great things."

Leaving Lovesac was extremely difficult for me. Shawn had given me so much for during my years at his company. He'd taken a chance on a street kid, and it had changed the course of my life.

I'd learned too many things to count and still carry many of his now-famous "Shawnisms" with me. Here are a few that stand out:

"When is the best time to plant an oak tree? Five years ago."

In other words, get off your ass and start moving. Whether it's a vlog channel, a book, a painting, or learning a new craft—just get it started. It may suck at first. No one may watch it or read it or listen to it. But eventually you'll look back at a catalog of work, a catalog of *growth*, and that will be your legacy. Don't waste time thinking about "if and when." Just get off the couch and go.

"Work hard, play hard."

We lived by this at Lovesac. It was part of our company ethos. But I keep it in the back of my mind. The pace at which today's world

demands you move can sometimes push you into a cycle of work that isn't balanced with an outlet for stress. Find a way to let go and unplug. Force yourself to take time for you. There is just as much risk in being overworked as there is in being lazy. Find your outlet.

"Be transparent. Always."

The management team at Lovesac led with transparency and honesty. They overshared in a good way. When sales were down, the entire company worked harder to make it up and hit goals. When revenue was up, bonuses came in and the company celebrated. No matter what, that feeling of being "in the know" was an extremely powerful culture play. Furthermore, I'd always believed in honesty anyway, so it resonated with me.

More than anything else, Shawn told me that the most valuable thing I had in my life, and the most valuable takeaway from my time with Lovesac, would always be my relationships. My "Rolodex," as he called it.

From the beginning, I put an intense amount of work into relationship-building. I focused my attention on building bridges, forming unlikely alliances, and creating new partnerships. At times, it took everything in me to put aside my ego to create every possible relationship along the way. I learned that nothing will pay off more than building strategic and sincere long-lasting relationships. And that means being a good friend, a good listener, and just being good to people.

Always.

That philosophy was a long way from who I used to be. During my many years of addiction, I'd been focused only on myself.

Now, after harnessing the power of those principles, I'd made them a permanent part of my being.

thirty-three

In November 2018, I officially left Lovesac. I left Connecticut, my family and friends, and moved across the country and into the Team Maverick house in Los Angeles.

Since then, Logan, his team, and I have spent much of our time building the *Impaulsive* podcast into the success it is today. We've had everyone on the show from Alex Jones to Ben Shapiro to Russell Brand. The practice and repetition of being on set a few times a week helped calm my nerves, and my anxiety eventually got better.

Logan focused his attention on his newfound love of professional boxing as well as other business endeavors. Throughout 2019, he stayed relatively controversy-free. In 2020 he began to take back the YouTube throne.

All our hard work is starting to bear fruit. Sponsors are back. Movie studios are having conversations with us. As long as we stay on track, the bad decisions of 2017 won't slow down the freight train that is Team Maverick.

In mid-2019, I made the decision to start my own YouTube show called *The Night Shift*, which was received extremely well by fans. Upon writing this, *The Night Shift* has more than one million

subscribers and tens of millions of views. It was never my intent to start my own channel. In fact, I first did it as a joke. I soon realized that with the format I'd created plus my love of comedic expression, the show had serious staying power. Today *The Night Shift* represents one of my main responsibilities and has the potential to become one the biggest shows on YouTube over the next couple years.

However, along with all the success I've found, I've also discovered that Los Angeles is filled with temptation.

"Are you doing one of these?" the girl asked me, holding up a rolled-up bill. I was at a gathering in the Hollywood Hills. I sat atop a marble countertop between "his-and-hers" sinks. It was 4 a.m., and I was at the second after-party of the night. Floor-to-ceiling windows offered breathtaking views of the city below. The lights of Los Angeles looked like tiny diamonds, sparkling in the distance.

Five feet away from me, three of the biggest porn stars in the world sniffed lines of cocaine off the spotless marble surface.

One of them smiled at me, encouraging me to join her. "C'mon."

"No, I'm good, babe," I said.

Earlier, before this after-party, I'd attended another party, at the home of Dan Bilzerian, a well-known Internet personality and actor. Years ago, when I'd been in the early stages of getting clean, I'd stumbled across his Instagram. Dan's whole feed was of him hanging out on private jets and partying in hot tubs with Instagram models. I'd never in my wildest dreams thought that I'd meet Dan, let alone

hang out with him. This was the kind of shit I was used to now. Nothing blew my mind or surprised me anymore.

Now here I was, partying with porn stars in a $100 million-plus house in Bel-Air and taking shots of 1942 with entertainers Marshmello, Chris Brown, Tyga, and others.

The party we were at now was smaller than the previous party, with a much more intimate vibe. In my experience, the after-party crowd was always more twisted.

The girls sniffed line after line of powder off the counter. The speaker outside the door played The Weeknd album loud enough to be audible in the bathroom.

"Are you *surrre* you don't want one?" another porn star asked, elongating the "sure" in a sexual way. She caressed my leg through my ripped jeans.

"I don't do coke anymore," I said. "I used to have a bit of a problem."

"Oh, wow, I'm so proud of you," she said, leaning back over the lines, holding the bill to her nose. "At least you recognized that and were able to stop."

This kind of statement was commonplace. There was always someone sniffing a line while congratulating me on being clean. Sometimes they would say, "You're a better person than me."

The other two porn stars began making out and taking off each other's tank tops. More lines were snorted. Everyone was high and happy.

While the situation didn't shock me, it struck me that I should walk away from the fire I would have so eagerly walked toward in my youth.

As I got up to leave the room, one of the girls pushed me back-

ward toward the sink. She unbuckled my belt and swiftly pulled down my pants. She took out my dick and began sucking on it. Within seconds the other girls joined in. Soon, they were all taking turns, with one licking my balls and another stroking my shaft and then changing positions. Several minutes went by as they switched on and off.

"I'm about to cum," I said.

One of the girls pushed the other two back and took over. I gripped the counter and came in her mouth while the other two porn stars stroked my balls and rubbed my legs.

When I was finished, the first girl wiped her mouth. All three girls giggled conspiratorially, in a mischievously wicked sort of way that I'd become accustomed to in this city.

I pulled my pants up and left the bathroom.

"Where are you going?" one of them yelled after me as I pushed through the crowds of people hanging around the marble foyer.

"It's 4:45 a.m.," I shouted back as I pushed open the massive wooden front door. "I'm going home."

"Lame, we were just getting started," one of the girls shouted behind me with a devilish cackle.

My Uber was already waiting. I got in and closed the door behind me.

The scenarios that most men fantasize about their entire lives and never attain offered me no satisfaction whatsoever anymore. Sexual deviance, wild partying, gambling—all vices I still struggled with brought back vivid memories of a time not too long ago when my vices controlled my life altogether.

The type of event described here is an illustration of the life I live now. No longer do I worry about being robbed at gunpoint by fellow

addicts. I don't need to figure out where I'm going to get my fix before I start withdrawing. The cops aren't knocking at the door with a warrant for something I may or may not have done. But I have other challenges. I still have to manage temptation, and I still have to manage my sobriety. It's just on a different stage.

That being said, the concerns I have now pale in comparison to the woes of my past.

I work hard to keep my state of mind balanced. People around me always ask, "Dude, what do you think of all this?" or "How does it feel to be where you're at?"

I'm never able to answer those questions properly.

It's important that I let people know that my life is not all glory. I still struggle every single day with the pain and trauma of my past. My addictive personality gets the best of me at times, whether it be infidelity, overeating, or just getting stuck in a cycle of unstoppable negative thought patterns.

Sometimes I feel detached from my emotions. I struggle to commit to relationships and have ongoing intimacy issues that will take years of continued work to get past.

Still, I keep trying.

In January 2020, I started dating one girl exclusively. Okay, fine, it wasn't just "a girl," it was Lana Rhoades, the number-one adult film star in the world.

On my birthday, Logan surprised me by introducing me and Lana for one of his new vlogs. His channel was taking off again after years in limbo following the Tokyo scandal, and the whole world was watching, so it was time to put on a show.

Lana had held the number-one spot on Pornhub for years, even though she'd retired from porn nearly three years earlier. She's now a

successful businesswoman and influencer in her own right, with a thriving merchandise line and a new YouTube channel with safe-for-work content. I'd initially thought Lana was unattainable, but I was able to break down her walls just enough to create a nice little lead-in to a relationship for us. What I discovered upon getting to know her was that she was an incredibly sweet, intelligent, grounded, driven, loyal, and supportive partner.

We traveled all around the country, went to dinners, appeared in each other's content (no, I didn't do porn), and captured the hearts of millions on the Internet. While I had already started tiring of the L.A. party scene, dating Lana further removed me from it and the temptations that it brought.

A lot of people have asked me, "How are you able to get over the fact that she had sex on camera with all those men?"

My answer is simple: "It was her decision, and I don't judge her for it. More importantly, if anyone can look beyond someone's past and appreciate them for who they are now—it's me."

Besides my new relationship, I continue to work on myself every day with all of the things that I have learned.

My addiction and surrounding trauma have taught me endless valuable lessons about empathy for others, perseverance through hardship, and patience in all things. It taught me that many things that feel good in the moment can have damaging effects far beyond the moment. It reminded me how important family is and that, if you have one, you should never take it for granted. I also learned that in order to become a truly healthy and successful person, there are things I live by that I hope will help others:

- Free yourself from harmful evils because the clarity and

motivation you will experience from getting clean and sober will be the bedrock for your real route to success.

- Sweat. The natural release of "feel-good chemicals" in your brain that comes from exercise will help you fight depression or anxiety.

- Lean on your people. Talk to friends, family, or therapists…whoever you can. The feeling I get when I leave my therapist's office is second to none. It feels like someone has lifted a fucking rock off my back.

- Believe in yourself. It might sound corny, but it's everything. Even with a catalog of quality work, I still question myself at times. But I'm getting better. Whatever you choose to do, believe in your ability to do good. Fuck that…believe in your ability to be the *best ever.*

- Fake it 'til you make it. Don't just try new things, *be* new things.

During my time in Hollywood, I learned other valuable lessons that I hope others can apply to their lives:

- Not everyone is going to be your fan, and that's okay. People are more vocal than ever before about things they don't like. Take what constructive criticism you can but leave the hate. Let people's negative thoughts be more ammo for you to succeed.

- Not everything deserves a reaction. This was something I should have enacted in my life a lot earlier. If someone hates you, instead of asking why and trying to fix it, just keep on moving. You'll spend so much time trying to fix other people

that you'll lose track of what you need to do in order to make yourself the best possible version of *you* that you can be.

- More than anything else, take comfort in knowing who you are. People will have misconceptions about you. As long as you are strongly rooted in who you truly are, you'll never get too tied up in what others think of you.

- Your journey is your own, and it makes you who you are. The person I am today, while unrecognizable in comparison to the person I once was, is rooted in the lessons I have learned through my struggles. Your hard days teach you more than your easy days. Don't forget that. I would not be the man I am today without my struggles and painful journey through addiction. And I'm proud of that man.

These lessons may seem too general or too simple…maybe they are. I'm no guru. I can't magically turn people into winners or give them the lives they want. But I can say that these things were all important components in my journey, my recovery, and in building me into the person I am today. Maybe they'll help others, too.

I could have spent another five years writing about my life in Hollywood or with Logan or Lana. There are a hundred stories to tell, and that list refreshes every week. Similarly, I could have spent more time sharing the minute details of my recovery or career. But many of those stories are the ones I already tell online that anyone can hear. This book is about telling the backstory. This book is about painting the picture that not only can you dig your way out of whatever rut you're in, you can flourish in your life afterward. This is me telling you that you can escape addiction or mental illness or whatever you're facing and get to the highest levels in this world and within yourself.

If you have the power to keep fighting when so many others give up, then you have the power to do anything you want in life. I know because I lived it myself.

No matter what, I can't shake the feeling that I am unarguably and undeniably blessed. Sometimes it feels impossible to believe that I was somehow able to take myself from where I was to where I am now. When I look back at the trail of absolute destruction, carnage, and death, I thank God every day *twice*, once in the morning and once before I go to bed, for giving me a second chance. I thank Him with everything that I have for granting me a second go-round on this carousel we call life.

And that second chance, that gratitude, is what drives me every single day. It wakes me up and gets me moving. Even on days when I struggle, whether with accusations of an expanding "ego" stemming from my newfound "fame" or with self-doubt or anxiety, that gratitude elevates the one rule I'll live by for the rest of my life:

Be good to other people. Take a second to make someone's day. Smile. Talk to the lonely. Help the elderly. Do something to make someone else feel good. Anything.

I'm not holding myself up as a role model, even though I don't regret my past because it's made me who I am. I'm simply telling my story for those who need to hear it, in the hopes that it will encourage those who are suffering to know that they are not alone and to find the strength to go forward. I hope to inspire people to discover what's good in their lives and in themselves.

After all that I have been through—all the bad I've done, the comeback, the money, the sex, the "fame"—the only thing that truly feels good is the good that I can help create in someone else.

I hope this book creates some of that good.

afterthoughts

Even with all the pain I've endured, I can't begin to express how blessed I feel to have made it to this stage of my journey. Looking back, I can truly say there were many, many times I could have or should have been taken from this life. For whatever reason, God decided to allow me a chance to continue on and to redeem myself. My family was and continues to be there to pick me up, even after all I have done to them. For that, I am eternally grateful.

I am currently in the process of clearing myself of all criminal charges that I was convicted of by the State of Connecticut. Through the length of time I have spent crime-free and in sobriety, and due to my continued work in the community and with various charities, I am confident the Board of Pardons will rule in my favor. I was even able to secure a recommendation from the mayor of Milford, the town I had so badly wronged, to permanently remove the crimes from my record. The hard work I've put in to better myself has inspired people in the community to offer assistance to help me continue to grow beyond my past mistakes. It's hard to explain how good that continued support feels.

The physical pain of my injuries continues to be a daily battle for me. The pain in my femur from the skiing accident makes things challenging at times, as do the residual injuries from my bike accident. But the pain in my shattered ankle causes me the greatest discomfort. With over twenty screws and two metal plates holding my ankle together, rainy weather will always be a torturous enemy. With every step I take, I'm reminded of the traumas of my past. My only option right now is fusion surgery, whereby doctors would remove my ankle joint and fuse the lower leg bones to my foot. They have told me this will limit my motion but will also greatly reduce the pain and inflammation. I am reluctant, but also hopeful that I will one day walk pain-free again.

Even on days when the physical pain is less daunting, the scars remain. My body is a road map of tragedy and despair. Even the minor scars contain a story of pain. They are the reminders that will never be erased by a change in my lifestyle or the passing of time.

Through all of this, my abstinence from drugs will always remain the most important priority in my life. On January 1, 2020, I committed to stop drinking alcohol as well. As much as alcohol wasn't a problem for me, it didn't add anything to my life either. On days after I had a drink or two, I found myself to be moving more slowly and slightly less motivated and productive. I understand that the only thing that allows me to continue growing and bettering myself to the highest degree is complete abstinence. ***There is just no other way for me.***

It hurts me deeply to know that there are so many of my child-hood friends, and so many people young and old out there, who still don't understand how important this is to me. In the time since I've been clean, I've tried to get in contact with my Milford friends to tell

them how good life can be if they put down the drugs.

I was able to find some of them, but not all. Some were able to change, some were not.

I learned that Alex is still going to the methadone clinic. He has been clean for over five years, works for a land surveyor, and just bought a house with his girlfriend in Connecticut.

Kenny also works as a land surveyor. He's married to a surgeon and has been clean for more than six years.

Jeff still struggles with his addiction to drugs. Upon writing this, he is currently in a long-term treatment program.

The sad truth is that there is no way to force an addict to change their ways. You can aid them, assist them in their journey once they make the choice to change, but you can never make that decision for them.

That's the biggest lesson that all parents, administrators, and counselors need to learn—the change needs to come from within. Until an addict has that epiphany to change, he will continue to use. As badly as many people out there want to get their loved ones back, to rip the addiction from them, unfortunately the waiting game continues until the moment of true inception when the addict realizes, like I did, that they are going to die if they don't stop.

But even with that moment of inception, it's not always enough to induce the change. There is always going to be "back and forth" on whether addiction is a disease or a choice. While the medical world has defined addiction as "a chronic, treatable medical disease," some people still believe it's a choice when someone uses for the first time, and even maybe a choice to continue using. What they don't take into consideration is the mental illness or physical ailment that someone might be suffering from that may have pushed them to use drugs as a

way to lessen the pain…and then are unable to stop.

I don't ever try to argue the point. We can all agree to disagree. The only thing we need to agree on is that addicts are people—human beings who are hurting badly. We need to do a better job of helping the more than two million brothers, sisters, mothers, teachers, veterans, and friends who continue to struggle, like I did, every single day of their lives.

Simply forgetting them is not the answer.

Unfortunately, the horrifying cycle of addiction that I experienced continues in my hometown and every city and state in the country. Addicts are still being born every day in high schools. Lives are still being ruined. Young people are still dying in droves. My story is not mine alone, but that of every addict who struggles through this painful journey and makes it out the other side…if they're lucky enough to survive.

The road I've traveled has been treacherous and plagued with obstacles. By the time I turned twenty-five, I'd been through so much. Now I'm thirty-five and my mind is bent from the stress and the painful experiences I have endured. Still, I never feel sorry for myself. No matter the struggle, I know that things could always be worse. No matter how hard things have been in my life, I know that someone out there is going through something much harder.

I'm not immune to getting caught up in sorrow. It's difficult to not look back with regret after so much turmoil and pain. It's easy to wonder if things could have been different. Without contact with any of my old friends and very few friends now that can relate to my story, I sometimes feel alone in my pain. But I'm always able to think back and put things in perspective, to look at where I was, and then look at where I am now. I tell myself, "If you were able to get here, you can

get wherever you need to go next." That gets me through.

There were many times along the way when I felt like giving up. Life can get so hopeless at times, to the point that it's difficult to see a way out…so many tears cried after trying everything, nothing working, and the tragedy continuing day after day. The world can become a dark and rainy place, and it's possible to imagine never seeing the sun again. I have been to this place. I can remember it when I close my eyes.

Sometimes I try to imagine how I could explain the hell of addiction to someone who has never tried drugs. Many people look at addicts as people who continue to make poor decisions instead of correcting their lives. That may be partially correct. I was given a ton of chances to change my life and correct my addiction. But to be honest, my biggest mistake was trying drugs for the first time. For many addicts, that first drug is enough to send them down a dizzying spiral that they may never get back under control. I can accept chalking up the first use of drugs to poor decision-making, but addiction truly is a disease and should be treated as such.

Instead of trying to explain addiction, I try to explain what it feels like to be an addict. There is the terror and agony of unrelenting pain, sorrow, and regret, day after day. I ask people to imagine the worst day they have ever had or the worst mental or physical pain they ever felt. Then I tell them to imagine this pain lasting for eight years, or ten or twenty years. That's how it is for countless addicts. Of course, we all have it in us to stop the pain, but many are too depressed, too worn-out, too beaten up, or too scared to stop. Over time, drugs become all we know. No matter how uncomfortable and painful addiction can be, nothing is more terrifying than facing the change that is required in ridding oneself of the drugs and getting rid of

everyone and everything that comes along with the addiction.

One thing I have learned is that everyone struggles. No matter how our friends, family, and the people we see every day appear on the outside, everyone faces difficult challenges. Cheating spouses, financial burdens, or family members fighting sickness or disease plague the lives of those around us.

What makes one person's battle more painful than someone else's? At the end of the day, pain is only relevant to the person who experiences it. The most painful tragedy I have ever experienced in my life is only as painful as the most painful tragedy experienced by someone else. Whenever I start to feel sorry for myself, I try to remember that those around me suffer just as I do. We're all just trying to do whatever we can to make it through the day or the week or the year, and to be happy.

Whenever I speak to an addict now, I always remember to remind them of one important concept that I almost lost in my own dependence: *Addicts are people too.* Many times during my sobriety, I saw people kicking addicts who already have so much working against them. People say they have no sympathy for the addicts who have all the power to change their lives but don't do so. I have even heard some people say they don't feel sorry for the boy or girl who pays the ultimate price and dies in their addiction.

Sometimes I am quick to become angry at these people. I ask them, "How would you feel if that was your brother or your sister, and their life was cut down by addiction? Would you make the same heartless statements if that was your best friend who lost a battle that burdens the lives of so many?"

I ask, what really separates those who deserve sympathy in their vices? Most people would never turn their noses up at a person who

died of lung cancer and say they deserved to die from smoking too many cigarettes. Most people wouldn't say that those casualties of heart disease from eating fatty foods "got what they deserved."

Since I have gotten sober, I have witnessed some extraordinarily heartless dialogue directed toward the active user. That is why I feel it's my duty to remind those people that addicts are people too. Addicts have dreams, goals, and aspirations for excellence too. Hopefully, their ambitions are just temporarily interrupted by the drugs. With strong support from others and the will to better themselves, some addicts achieve true greatness, even in the face of powerful adversity.

Sometimes I find myself questioning it all. Am I on the right path now? I know that I've done everything I can to fix myself, but where would I have been if I'd never become an addict? Why did I make it to where I am today when so many good people continue to struggle miserably in addiction?

I suppose everyone questions life from time to time. We all fight daily battles for balance. We struggle to work and support ourselves and our families. We wish we had more time to do the things we love—to ride our bikes, hug our kids, travel the world. We think of the past and question how things *could* be now. What if we hadn't made that move across the country, or if we had asked that girl to prom, or if we had stayed on course and gone to a good four-year college? Our minds rove over the past, over our mistakes and our regrets.

Through my journey for redemption, I have learned that we will never get things exactly right. We will never look back and say to ourselves, "Wow, I can't think of one thing I would have done differently." There will always be something that led us off course, off

what could have been our true "path" in life. In that realization, I have come to an even greater truth—there is no "path" set out for our life. We create our destiny as we go. And no matter how far away you are from where you feel you should be, it is never, ever too late to change.

In closing, I offer the following words…

To those who have never known the struggles of addiction or mental illness:

You are the truly blessed.

May you never know the agony that those suffering feel on a daily basis. May you never feel the guilt, the regret, the embarrassment, the hopelessness of the addict or the unstable human being. I pray that you understand the blessing that is the landscape of your life. I pray also that along with your prosperity comes an empathy for those less fortunate. I pray that you find those stricken ones and shower them with the bright light that radiantly illuminates your life, the same light they so badly need themselves in order to continue on through their own darkness.

More than anything else, I pray that one day every person struggling with mental anguish or addiction gets to feel as free as you do.

To the families, friends, and caregivers of those who are struggling:

You are our everything. You are the reason we live.

I can't even begin to imagine your pain. I struggle immensely now as I type this, my face, shirt, and hands covered with tears, imagining the helplessness you feel watching someone you love stripped of their humanity, their

dignity, and their will to go on.

Please understand your perseverance is what keeps us going. Your commitment is the promise that wakes us up in the morning and the hope we take with us to bed at night. We understand that this commitment will cost you a piece of your life, and it will be a cost we unfortunately can never pay back. Please understand, without this investment, we would be bankrupt of life. Please understand, we are more grateful than we could ever show in this lifetime.

For those families, like mine, who supported loved ones through addiction or mental illness: You are our heroes. Everything we have now is a result of what you did then. Take great pride in watching as we grow, improve, and excel—all of it a product of your hard work and perseverance.

For those families who continue to support someone in the struggles of active addiction or mental illness: Be strong. Your continued support will be the deciding factor. Whether you feel you must coddle or show tough love, your commitment will be the ray of light that guides them through the darkness.

For those families or friends who have lost someone to overdose or suicide related to addiction or mental illness: May you know peace. May you find solace in understanding how complex, and at times without solution, these problems are. May you hold your head high in knowing you did everything you could to help. May you find joy in the memories you had before the onset of these issues. May the desires of your own life be filled now that your loved ones are at peace.

And most importantly, to those of you who have found yourselves caught up in the endless struggle of addiction, mental illness, pain, chaos, and despair:

I am you and you are me.

Our stories, while surely dramatically different, share very similar truths— that tremendous pressure you feel on your heart and in the pit of your stomach, the heaviness that chokes the air from your lungs, and the anxiety that ravages your mind to madness. I have felt that same terrible pain. You are not alone. You never will be. Revel in knowing there is someone who feels just like you.

If you have people who support you, take advantage of your extreme blessing. Lean on them. They will be the ones who carry you on days you cannot carry yourself. And on days you find yourself alone, burdened, unable to run or walk, beaten down and ready to give up...crawl. As impossible as it may seem, pull yourself through the mud. Scrape for every single fucking inch until one day you find yourself able to walk again. Against the strongest of tides, keep moving forward. Never stop. Never be pushed under.

However dark things are, and however dark things get, I urge you to find your light. Find that one glimmering remainder of hope that continues to push you forward. It will dim. It will be obscured by obstacles in your path. It will flicker in a breeze of uncertainty, fear, and tragedy. But no matter how faint your light gets, please never let it extinguish completely. For one day, that dim little flickering lifeline of hope will burn brighter than the sun, and will illuminate your world beyond what you could ever imagine.

And to **anyone** who is in over their head and who feels as if they will never swim to the surface again, I offer these words **from experience and with absolute certainty...**

Take a breath. You will get through this.

280

Collage credit: Maclin Bilski

Collage credit: Maclin Bilski

acknowledgements

To my mother: Thank you for keeping your light on, even when darkness smothered you. You are my rock and my reason. I'll love you forever.

To my grandmother: Thank you for your unconditional love when everyone else had to take the tough-love route. You were a shelter and a warm, comforting meal on the rainiest of days.

To my dad and sisters: Thank you for your forgiveness. Your patience and dedication allowed me the time to recover and have a chance at redemption. Without you, I wouldn't be the man I am today.

To Shawn Nelson: Thank you for taking a chance on the street kid with potential. Your belief in me was my big break. Your bet paid off.

To Logan Paul: Thank you for your trust. Your confidence in me during your own dark times forged our comradery in steel. You are the brother I never had.

To Amara Maple: Thank you for smashing down my walls and helping me learn how to love and be loved again.

To FaZe Bank$, Adam22, Bradley Martyn, and True Geordie:

Thank you for carrying the torch. Maybe it's because you're all a little older like me, but you guys made me feel like it was okay to be a YouTuber and still be authentic as fuck. Never, ever change.

To Jim Jordan: Thank you for being so kind as to postpone the writing of your own incredible story so that Riley and I could work on mine.

To Riley J. Ford: Thank you for your blood, sweat, and tears (mostly tears). You took a lump of clay and helped me create a testament of life. Without you, the book would not be.

To Purdue Pharma: Fuck you.

additional acknowledgments

Thank you to the best readers in the world: Christy, Josh, Kathie, Manny, Perry, Sherry, and Tina. Your impact is felt.

Much gratitude to our editor, Amy: Your talent, hard work, and keen eye are unparalleled.

Thank you to my author assistant, Tina R., and my management team for all your dedication over the years.

For Camille, Aria, JD, Finn, and JJ: Thank you for being my family. I love you.

A special thank you and big shout-out to @JimJordan Photography and @WhiteCrossManagement: You make things happen.

To Mike Majlak: Thank you for the gift of who you are and for the opportunity to be part of this life-changing, profoundly meaningful project. You put your truth and heart into this book, and it shows. I honor you. Keep being the light.

—*Riley J. Ford*

letters to Mike

From Mike's mom:

For my son, Michael:

Michael could have been anything he wanted to be…he was gifted with intelligence, kindness, and humor. He was athletic. He was caring. He had strong morals and believed in God. He loved his family and his friends. Michael had all the qualities that would enable him to easily succeed in this world.

Unfortunately, Michael also had a few qualities that would take him on a road no one saw coming: anxiety, depression and a predisposition to addiction that was ignited by pain management drugs for his many sports injuries.

Sadly, Michael became the "anything" he never wanted to be—he became an opioid addict.

By the grace of God, after years of abuse, what my son Michael accomplished is nothing short of a miracle. He fought his way back from a disease so insidious, so horrific, that many others succumb without hope. The fight against this disease required more courage,

more determination, and more dedication than most can fathom; however, he pushed forward bravely.

I am so thankful and proud that Michael is sharing his story in the hopes that it will clear the heavy burden in his mind and in his heart from all those years spent being someone not recognizable to himself or those who loved him so dearly. He is also sharing his story to help those currently struggling to get and stay clean. I pray that those in this fight will see that there is hope, that it can be done, and not to give up.

Today my son Michael is becoming that anything he wanted to be.

I am thankful and overjoyed.

I love you, Michael. I pray that God will keep you in the palm of his hand forever.

—*Mom*

From Logan Paul:

I met Mike when he was selling beanbags. As a social media kid trying to get free furniture, I had no idea that the "marketing manager" that I was texting would soon become my best friend, business partner, and roommate. See, most people fall in love with Mike's charisma and deceptive intelligence. But not me…I liked Mike because he was able to get me free beanbags.

However, as he continued to supply me with shredded memory foam stuffed inside a sack, I realized that the kid had real spunk. As a spunkster myself, I enjoyed every second chopping it up with Mike. Conversations were effortless. Jovial. Pragmatic. It was a blossoming love story akin to *Brokeback Mountain.* Without the gay sex.

Soon thereafter, I rescued Mike from his stable, secure, and lucrative corporate job in Connecticut and brought him permanently into my fucked-up life that is digital media. He quickly became the big brother I never had. And never wanted.

There are many things I like about Mike. His ability to navigate through the shit storm and come out victorious. His interpersonal communication skills. His humor. I've been lucky enough to experience the ripple effects of his unmatched energetic glow as he continues to make me the best version of myself. Mike is an invaluable and irreplaceable counterpart. But also, he's a pussy.

—*Logan Paul*

From FaZe Bank$:

Mike, whatever the fuck your last name is, let me start by saying congratulations on finally publishing your book. You've talked about this day for quite some time, and I know how much time/effort you've put into it. Seriously, good for you. I'm not sure I've connected to anyone in this Internet game the way I have with you. We're from the same place, grew up around the same shit, we're both dirtbags and not afraid to own it, and above all else, we're good people who at first glance might not seem like we could be/should be. If there's anyone who can relate to your come-up and who probably has the best idea of the journey from your perspective, it's me. So it goes without saying, I have a tremendous amount of respect for where you came from and how you got here. You're a smart motherfucker and a genius in your own right. I told you a long time ago that I believed you had "it" and, selfishly, I fkn love how right I was about that. It's been cool to see a fellow fuck-up shattering the expectations people

have of you…proving people wrong over and over and surprising everybody who's following your journey as well as, I'm sure, yourself. You're living proof that it's never really over, and that you can turn it around anytime. Excited to see where you take it from here. Mike, you're a fkn scumbag, but you're *our* scumbag.

<3 your friend,
Bank$

From Shawn Nelson, Founder and CEO of Lovesac:

Mike was a dog-walker when I put the ad on Craigslist looking for someone to help me part-time. I needed someone to help me post content and build up my followings to position me as an influencer in the entrepreneurial space as the founder and CEO of Lovesac. Despite his tiny personal following and experience, I knew Mike had "it" the minute we sat down for our first meeting at lunch…and as history has proven, I was right. So Mike, as I've always told you: Don't doubt my instincts. ☺

Mike and I worked out of the tool closet at Lovesac HQ one day a week to start, arguing over what to post and how often and all of that, in the early days of Instagram and vlogging. Anytime money came up I always promised him that if he'd just see it through, he would meet people and make connections through Lovesac that would be far more valuable than anything more I could pay him for his time. Fast-forward a few years and it is obvious that Mike put in the time and took advantage of the opportunity and ultimately forged his own path to becoming the real influencer among us. I am grateful to him for the years of his life he dedicated to building up me and my brand…and I couldn't be happier to see him go to even greater

heights on his own. Besides being a magnetic personality with impeccable taste and comedic timing, a lanky goofy body and ridiculous Northeastern accent and all that…Mike is a good person. He has a good heart, and he (most of the time) chooses to do the right thing. This is why, beyond being colleagues and co-workers, I've always considered Mike a good friend. I am proud of his boldness and transparency in putting his own story out there, and I expect to continue to learn from him—as I always have.

—*Shawn Nelson, Founder and CEO of Lovesac*

From Mike's childhood best friend, Jeff:

I can't put into words how proud I am of you. After twenty-five years of friendship, you continue to amaze me with your success and determination. However, you never forgot where you came from, and your humility is what makes you unique and special.

We have been through some tough times, but we always had each other. Addiction and mental health issues are debilitating and not spoken of enough. Yet, you share your life experience in the hopes of saving lives. You saved mine.

You've used your journey as a motivating factor. You've unselfishly shared your story, which has ultimately inspired millions of people, none more than myself. For that, I am forever grateful.

Congrats on this book and again, I am very fortunate to have you as a friend. You took me under your wing at the age of eleven, and I've been there ever since. Let's fly together, baby!! I love you. The best is yet to come, for both of us!

With love,
Duey

Connect with Mike Majlak:

Instagram: @HeyBigMike
YouTube: Mike Majlak Vlogs
Twitter: @MikeMajlak

hey man. just wanted to say congratulations on the success. you've came a long way. I understand the feeling of struggling with addiction and I relate to you a lot. just a guy in this big world wanted to make an impact somehow. you are doing it man and I gotta give props to you. I struggled with heroin addiction too for a while and I can say it was the worst time of my life. you motivate me to keep striving and "clocking in" everyday when I wake up. thank you man. also you should do a meet and greet. I've wanted to meet other youtubers but nobody has came up to my mind that I really want to meet other than you. you are hilarious and honestly a great dude man. keep it up.

Hey mike watching ur videos has really helped me mentally and given me motivation i left the college i was going to because i was struggling mentally there and didn't feel safe there alone listening what you say in the podcasts gives me hope because right now i feel stuck in like and don't know what to do

Aye bro can I share sum with you I jus wanna say you really inspire me cause I was going through a dark ass time fr and I be watching your impaulsive podcasts and it helps me realize that there's a light at the tunnel ya feel me you sayin you had addictions and anxiety and shi and I'm right there with you bro and it's jus real coo to see someone with your platform jus helping spread positivity

Love your shit bro, you MADE me grow so much AS a person and i cant thank you enough.. you got a serious big hart.. sorry For mye bad English , big UPS from Norway hope you and big man Logan will come visit sometime 💚 🤍

If you are having a bad day or bad thoughts, think about what you have achieved. I respect you bro ! I can't imagine what you've been through but i do can imagine feeling alone and addicted to something. Cut all the bs, love you bro !

Bro you are a fucking warrior, you are one of the strongest people I know and I'm so happy for your success, I'm sure you will change the life of thousands of people, keep up the good work.
Con todo Cariño te mando un abrazo

So I just became of a fan of yours recently and I watched a whole bunch of the podcasts and when u talk about mental health it really helps me to feel not so alone. What helped and continues to help you with your anxiety. Recently I've developed really bad anxiety and negative thought patterns and I'm wondering how to better deal with them

mike your statement about helping one person with addiction was so damn good! i myself struggle with heroin addiction (smoking) every day and it gives me a little bit of light seeing were you made it now because i dream of being in the entertainment industry myself but everyone around me keeps telling that it'll never happen so thanks for giving me a little bit of hope every day 🦋

Mike I heard what you said on the podcast about your 30 seconds or so about talking about your struggles and experiences, I just want to let you know that I fully back you because you have helped me with my struggles with anxiety from my stomach problems. Though they nowhere near as bad compared to your experience it has still helped me a lot so thank you. Also, I will be buying your book so can't wait for that one! 📖

U probably won't get this but i thought I'd send this I really respect what your doing you've changed a lot of people's opinions on there lives over u talking about your past and your stopping people going down the same road as you did I just want to say I love watching your content

Hey mike. I recently watched the podcast you did with Bradley Martyn where you talk deeper about anxiety. Made me realise a few things such as I have anger anxiety meaning my anxiety comes out in anger and I only feel anger. I don't really know what to do with it. It happens quite often and I was hoping If you see this what is something I can potentially do. You probably won't see this but you're fucking awesome and keep the great content up. I've been a day 1 ksi fan and never liked Logan but you brought out a fucking great side out of him which I fw sm. thank you for everything

Congrats bro, gonna cop it for sure. You help me and remind me to stay positive every day and I want to thank you for that. You deserve everything you have!

yo i really respect ur message and everything u went through to make it to where u are. ur a true inspiration and keep up spreading the positivity realness and sick content 🙏🙏

Hey man, I used to also be a junkie and was always fuoked up on dope or any other type of downers. Your guys podcast has really inspired me and driven me a lot, I was sober before I started watching but just listening to you talk, I can relate on a LOT of levels. You're a real, upfront, solid ass dude, and I can see that from the podcast. You're not a fake, you don't hide shit, you're like me and you feel better by dumping it all out and being real about shit, and I'll always support and respect you for that. Stay safe during these crazy and fucked times, much love man.

Hey mike I know you probably aren't gonna see this but listening to what you've been through has really changed my life for the better in so many ways and I see the world differently now and I know I'm just a dumb kid like everyone says but I really hope to accomplish great things and it will be because of you so mike thank you for being the voice for those who are too scared to speak up

Bro I just wanted to text you saying that you really are a role model and a really good down to earth human being I come from Ireland so I don't say this sloppy shit a lot to people but you have a background and the fact that you could come back from that and make your life into something big really sends me a message of that anything is possible which is what you made me believe in that anything is possible I know it's sloppy cringey shit but I love your content and your upbeat personality on your channel Logan's and the podcasts it really does spark up my day

Hey, it's mad but I feel like I'm reaching out just to say thanks. You don't understand how much I need to hear that it gets better or things will be okay and that last page of your book that you put on twitter about crawling until you can walk is my screensaver at the moment. It feels like it's all too much for me at the moment and I can't see what way I'm going or where to go to make things better but things like that really help, you really are reaching people who need it the most. Also you and Lana are the fucking cutest and I'm so here for it 🫶 anyways bye xx

Collage credit: Maclin Bilski

Connect with Riley J. Ford:

Riley J. Ford is a *NEW YORK TIMES* and *USA TODAY* bestselling author and UCLA graduate represented by Creative Artists Agency. She writes under multiple pen names and has sold more than one million copies of her novels worldwide. One of her books has been adapted into an upcoming movie for Netflix starring Julia Roberts. Riley loves hearing from readers, so drop her a line!

www.rileyjford.com

Instagram: @RileyJ.Ford

Facebook: Riley J. Ford

Twitter: @RileyJFord

Made in the USA
Middletown, DE
07 July 2020